*The Wheels Still Turn*

Today *Maid of Sker* rests in a park at Nerang.

# *The Wheels Still Turn*

## A History of

# AUSTRALIAN PADDLEBOATS

*Peter Plowman*

Kangaroo Press

Jacket designed by Darian Causby using a photograph of the
*Emmy Lou* (Emmy Lou Enterprises).

*First published in 1992 by Kangaroo Press Pty Ltd*
*3 Whitehall Road (P.O. Box 75) Kenthurst 2156*
*Typeset bt G.T. Setters Pty Limited*
*Printed in Hong Kong by Colorcraft Ltd*

ISBN 0 86417 428 4

# Contents

# Introduction

Paddleboats played a major role in the development of this country, yet they are almost totally overlooked today when Australian maritime history is discussed. This book is a brief attempt to set down the contribution made to Australia by the paddleboat.

I first became interested in paddleboats about 10 years ago, though initially it was the modern cruising vessels that attracted my attention. It was not until I purchased a small booklet detailing the paddleboats to be found along the Murray River that I realised the number of such vessels still in existence. When planning my next annual holidays, I decided to take my family on a driving trip along the Murray, starting at Albury and finishing at Goolwa and the mouth of the river. Over a two-week period, we visited all the major river towns: Albury, Echuca, Swan Hill, Mildura, Wentworth, Renmark, Berri, Morgan, Mannum, Murray Bridge and Goolwa. It was a journey of discovery and sheer delight for me, while my wife and three children voted it the best holiday we ever had.

Having had my appetite whetted, the thirst for knowledge about Australian paddleboats sent me delving for any available material, which I soon discovered was in short supply. A number of books contained various references to paddlers, but there were only a few books available that were entirely devoted to paddleboats, and those concentrated on the Murray River.

As the years went by, my collection of material grew steadily and I became aware of more and more of these fascinating craft that once plied local waters. When preparing to write this book, I first had to devise a format that would present the story of the paddleboat in Australia in a concise but logical manner. Eventually I came to the conclusion that, by dividing the country into regions, I could describe the various services and boats to best advantage. Paddleboats were often built for specific services and seldom strayed to other areas; hence it was relatively simple to categorise the various vessels I wished to describe.

For example, the paddleboats used on various ferry services on Sydney Harbour differed according to their route in the same way that non-paddle ferries do today. The magnificent excursion boats that plied Port Phillip Bay were totally different from the vessels that ran on coastal trades, not to mention the unique excursion boats that frequented Lake Wendouree at Ballarat.

In looking at the Murray River boats, it is surprising how many different designs there were to be seen, considering that all these boats operated on the same river system. Once again, boats were built for specific purposes, such as transporting cargo, towing barges, fishing or carrying passengers. Some 300 paddleboats were built over a 70-year period to cater for the Murray trade, but sadly most have now gone. When the river trade died, boats were simply abandoned on the bank and left to rot. Just north of the restored wharf at Echuca is a stretch of riverbank known as Rotten Row, from the number of boats abandoned there. Some years ago, the remains of these boats were blown up to clear the area for houseboats.

During the late 1980s, a number of new paddleboats were built. The building of the replica *William the Fourth* in 1988 focused attention on the ocean-going paddleboats, while around Australia half a dozen excusion paddleboats were built for commercial service and a handful of older boats were restored. In the early 1990s interest in Australian paddleboats is growing every year. The restoration of more old boats is proceeding, while several new boats are planned or under construction.

Today there are about 50 paddleboats still to be seen in various parts of the country, though the majority are to be found along the Murray River. One morning in October 1991, I stood on the Moama side of the river, looking towards the old Echuca Wharf, and could see no fewer than 11 paddleboats. Two were undergoing restoration, three had been restored, three were operating excursions, and the other three were privately owned. At Mildura, five paddlers were operating, but at most of the other river towns it is unusual to see more than one paddleboat. In Cairns, Brisbane, Newcastle, Sydney, Canberra, Ballarat, Launceston and Perth, paddleboats are operating excursions. There is a definite magic about the paddleboats, which I hope you will share with me in the following pages.

Peter Plowman
April 1992

# Acknowledgments

When I set out to write this book, I took as my starting point the notes I had been making over several years, from many sources. Having decided on the format of the book, it was necessary to locate further information, which required an extensive search of written material. Although paddleboats played a major role in the development of shipping services around the coast of Australia, and even more so on the rivers, very little has been written on the subject, and much that should have been recorded has been lost forever.

The bibliography contains those books that have given me the most assistance in preparing my manuscript. It will be noted that the only books devoted almost exclusively to paddlers, concentrate on the Murray River system. This is understandable, since this waterway is home to most of the surviving paddlers. However, the importance of vessels operating along the coast cannot be overlooked. I was fortunate to find useful information on these vessels in various periodicals. For example, much of the information on the building of the *Surprise* came from *The Dogwatch*, published annually by the Shiplovers' Society of Victoria. *Austraian Shipping Record*, published quarterly by Ronald Parsons, a noted authority on paddleboats, also provided much useful material.

When it came to illustrations, I had a small collection of older vessels. Since then I have photographed just about

every paddler to be seen in Australia today. In order to provide a suitable variety of pictures, I sought the aid of various friends and acquaintances, who were all more than generous in their support. In particular, I would like to thank Graeme Andrews, Robert Brookes and Frank Tucker for their enormous assistance in providing many of the older photographs. I am also most grateful to Barry Pemberton for the use of his maps, which had previously been published in his outstanding book, *Australian Coastal Shipping* (1979, Melbourne University Press).

To indicate the source of the various illustrations, the following code has been used:

GA    – Graeme Andrews collection
RWB – Robert Brookes collection
MRC – Murray River Cruises
IF     – Ian Farquhar collection
CDG – C.D. Gill
CJ     – Colin Jones
RM   – The late Richard McKenna
PN    – Peter Nicolson
BP    – Barry Pemberton
LR    – Lindsay Rex
FT     – Frank Tucker collection
LW    – Lionel Wood

All other photographs were supplied by the author.

# The Enduring Paddlewheel

The simplicity of the paddlewheel and its principle of operation may have something to do with its continuing appeal. Unlike the propeller, or the jet engine, the paddlewheel is visible, and can be understood by even the most casual observer. The speed of the boat is quite evidently proportional to the speed of the paddle blades as they rotate, and that speed depends on the wheel diameter and the rate at which it turns.

The first steamships ever built were propelled by paddlewheels, but the paddlewheel predates the steam-engine by centuries. It was first employed by the Romans, who powered their vessels with oxen walking around capstans geared to side-wheels. Later, in America, 'teamboat' ferries used horses walking either around capstans, like the Roman oxen, or on treadmills, geared to side-wheels or stern-wheels.

The first proper paddle-steamer was probably the *Pyroscaphe*, a 43-foot (13-m) experimental boat with side-wheels, built by the Marquis Claude de Jouffroy d'Abbans in 1783, which he tested on the Saône River, near Lyons. Jouffroy's experiments were interrupted by the Revolution. The first stern-wheeler was the 56-foot (17-m) *Charlotte Dundas*, built by William Symington in Scotland in 1802. This vessel was designed as a towboat, or tug, to operate on the Forth and Clyde Canal. The wheel was not like the later full-width paddle set right at the stern, but was the same width as a side-wheel and worked in a recess inside the hull. On trials the *Charlotte Dundas* proved highly successful, but she was not allowed to enter service as intended, for fear her wash would erode the banks of the canal.

In America, Robert Fulton was experimenting with steam propulsion, but the main difficulty he encountered was the weight and size of the early steam-engines. His first engine was so heavy that, when being lowered into his first boat, it went through the bottom. Fulton was able to construct an engine on a James Watt design that was smaller and lighter, which was placed in the *Clermont* in 1807. The side-wheels were 15 feet (4.58 m) in diameter and propelled the *Clermont* at 5 knots on its maiden voyage. The passengers taken along for the trip were not greatly impressed and doubted the value of steamships.

In 1809, the *Phoenix* made the first open-sea voyage by a paddle-steamer, from New York to Philadelphia. The voyage was not really a success, as it took 13 days, against two for a sailing ship. The problem was the fragile nature of the wheels, and the vessel had to be stopped when even a moderate sea was running.

Until the 1820s engine designers had no bank of experience from which to determine suitable sizes and powers for their engines. So unpredictable were the early engines that the first steamships also carried a full spread of sails in the event of a breakdown. The first steamship to cross the Atlantic was the *Savannah*, in 1819, but most of the voyage was made under sail. The first ship to steam right across the Atlantic was the paddler *Sirius*, in 1838, which took 18½ days. Only a few hours later, the *Great Western*, designed by Isambard Kingdom Brunell, arrived in New York, having crossed the Atlantic in 15 days.

From this slow, uncertain beginning, the steam-engine and the paddlewheel were developed, until eventually both were able to move quite large vessels across all the oceans of the world. The first Cunard liners were all paddlers, and many other major Atlantic shipping companies operated paddlers. The last paddler to be built for the Atlantic trade was the French *Napoleon III*, completed in 1866, while the last Atlantic crossing by a paddler was that of the Cunarder *Scotia* in 1876.

Paddle-steamers were not operated on many longer routes, though some did run beween Europe and South America. The first paddle-steamer to arrive in Australia was the *Sophia Jane*, which anchored in Sydney Harbour in May 1831, but she had made the voyage from Britain under sail. It was not until 1854 that a paddle-steamer, the *Pacific*, made the voyage to Australia entirely under steam, being one of the very few to do so. It was found that the paddles were too susceptible to damage to be really successful in open seas, but on rivers and sheltered waters the paddle was the equal of, and sometimes better than, the propeller.

The paddlewheel proved to be a simple yet efficient method of propulsion. Paddlewheels on the early vessels were fitted with fixed radial blades, called floats. To obtain a designed speed of the paddle blades, the choice lay between a large wheel turning slowly and a faster turning smaller wheel. That speed depends on the wheel diameter and the rate at which it turns, requiring only a correction for slip. Slip is due to the yielding of the water as the blades push against it, and amounts to about 25 per cent. The amount of slip varies between side-wheelers and stern-wheelers, because a side-wheel operates in water undisturbed by the boat, whereas the stern-wheel slides through the wake.

The basic paddlewheel, as shown in Figure 1, was known as the fixed-radial float design, but it was not necessarily the most efficient. The radial float engages the water at an oblique angle, so that the face of the blade slaps the surface of the water, causing the familiar thump-thump sound of a paddleboat. It requires effort to push the blade down into the water, an effort that does not contribute to driving the boat forward and represents lost energy. As the float approaches full immersion its attitude becomes more favourable, with the flat face more nearly at right angles to the direction of travel. As the float leaves the water at an oblique angle it carries water with it, some of which drains off while the rest is thrown into the air, creating the familiar spray. However, pushing the water up takes energy too, which is also wasted and cuts down the efficiency of the paddlewheel.

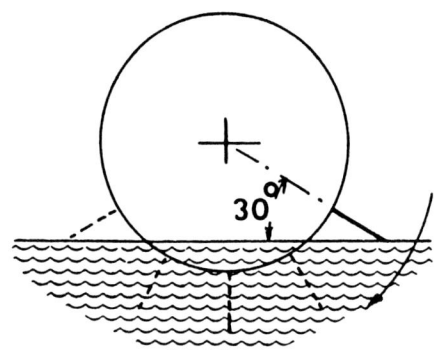

*Figure 1*

In order to improve the smoothness of the paddle blades' entry into and exit from the water, it was necessary to increase the diameter of the wheel in relation to the immersion of the floats. Figure 2 shows a wheel twice the diameter of Figure 1, but with the same immersion. On the

smaller wheel, the angle between the blade face and the water surface at entering and leaving is about 30 degrees, but on the larger wheel it is closer to 50 degrees. As the angle grows closer to 90 degrees, so the wheel's efficiency increases. This was a direct cause of American riverboat designers using the stern-wheel so extensively.

The fixed-radial float design was simple and sturdy, and it could be easily repaired in the event of the floats being damaged. No dry-docking was necessary because the structure of the wheel was above the water and in plain view. The floats themselves were made of wood, and replacements could be fashioned from spare timber carried on board. Fixed-radial floats were used extensively by paddleboats working on the Murray River, and were also fitted to the largest paddlewheeler ever built, the *Great Eastern* of 1858. Her 58-foot (17.7-m) diameter wheels turned over at a mere 11 revolutions per minute, and transmitted 3,400 horsepower. *Great Eastern* also had a single propeller to assist the paddles.

Boats operating on services needing a good turn of speed required lightweight machinery of high horsepower. That meant a faster running engine in association with a relatively smaller paddlewheel, but also a good depth of float immersion. To mitigate the undesirable negative effects of a small wheel, inventors came up with a variety of designs, from which one survived to become standard throughout the world. This design is called the 'feathering' paddlewheel, because it adjust the blade angle while in operation, in similar fashion to the skilled oarsman who feathers his blade between strokes.

Several inventors were associated with the development of the feathering paddlewheel, but it was patented in 1829 by Elijah Galloway. The following year Galloway's patent was purchased by William Morgan, who made further improvements to the design in the early 1830s. Since then, this type of paddlewheel has been generally known as a Morgan wheel.

The working of the feathering paddlewheel is illustrated in Figure 3. It is based on a mechanism known as the 'drag-link', which has three moving links turning about two fixed axis. One of the links, AB, is a spoke of the wheel which revolves about its axis, A. Another is the short link or lever, BC, to which the float is attached and which pivots about a pin, B, secured to the spoke. The third moving link is a connecting rod, DC, which rotates about a fixed bearing, D, in line with but eccentric to the wheel centre. As the wheel revolves, the link DC causes the float unit BC to assume different angles with respect to the float, giving the desired feathering effect.

The mechanism for a nine-float wheel is shown in Figure 4. It will be noted that the float faces at entry into and exit from the water are not radial to the wheel, as in the fixed-float design, but are at less oblique angles for smoother engagement with the surface of the water.

If the float faces of the immersed floats in Figures 3 and 4 are extended upward by imaginary lines, it will be seen that these lines meet at a point considerably above the centre of the wheel. This indicates that the feathering paddlewheel action is equivalent to that of a fixed-float wheel of much

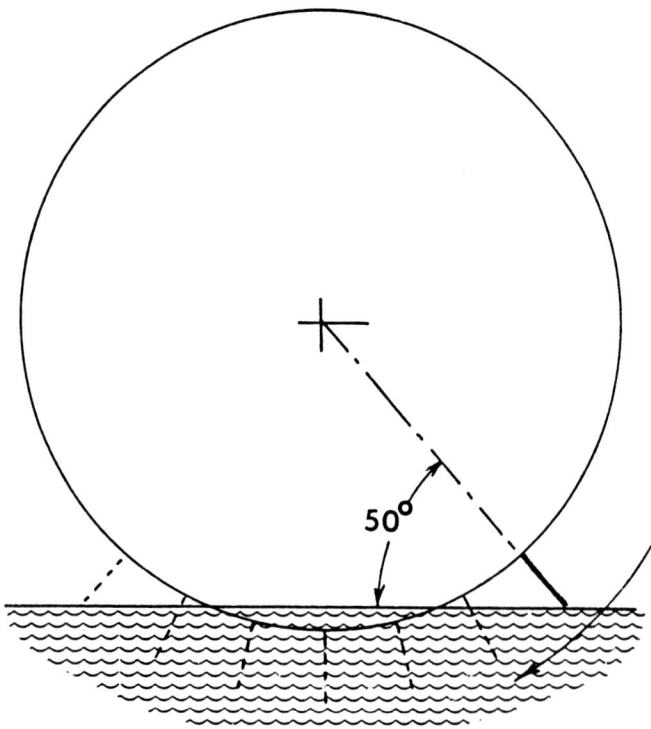

*Figure 2*

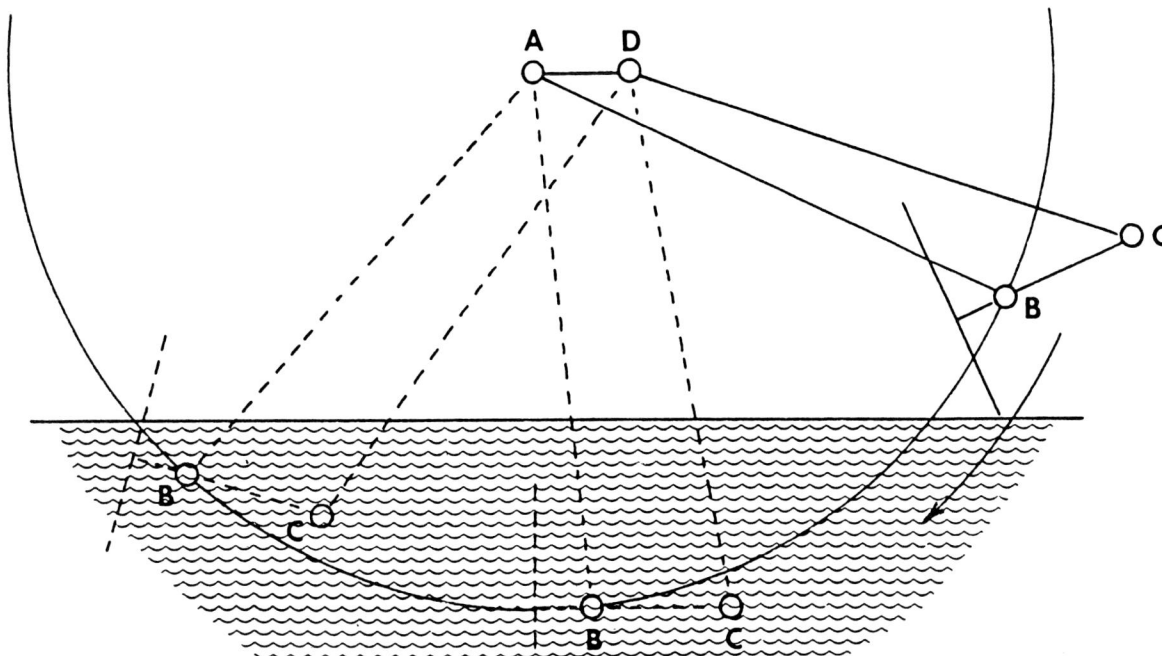

*Figure 3*

larger diameter. Sometimes this equivalent diameter was as much as three times the actual wheel diameter.

A major drawback with the feathering paddlewheel was a vulnerability to damage from hitting floating objects. At least some of the structure was metal, and broken or bent parts were difficult to repair at sea. The first boat to appear in Australian waters with feathering paddlewheels was the *Collaroy*, built in 1853. Most of the later coastal vessels were also fitted with these wheels.

The paddlewheel was gradually superseded by the propeller, yet in some areas the paddle still reigned supreme. On Lake Erie in North America, two companies built a succession of increasingly larger paddlers, all designed by Frank E. Kirby, which reached their zenith in the early years of this century. The Detroit & Cleveland Navigation Co. built the *City of Cleveland III* in 1907, followed by the *City of Detroit III* in 1912, which topped 6,000 gross tons, and were 455 feet (138.7 m) long. To counter these boats, the Cleveland & Buffalo Transit Co. built the *Seeandbee* in 1913, which was 6,381 gross tons and 485 feet (147.8 m) long. *Seeandbee* was the most impressive paddlewheeler ever built, having four funnels, and 1,500 berths. In 1924, the Detroit & Cleveland Navigation Co. took delivery of two new paddlers, *Greater Buffalo* and *Greater Detroit*, which were the largest pure paddlers ever built. With three funnels and four decks, including an additional line of outside cabins which side-wheels allowed, this pair were 519 feet (158.2 m) long, and topped 7,700 gross tons. They provided more than 1,500 berths, and were among the most notable American steamboats ever built. They were also something of an anachronism and were the last large side-wheelers built in America.

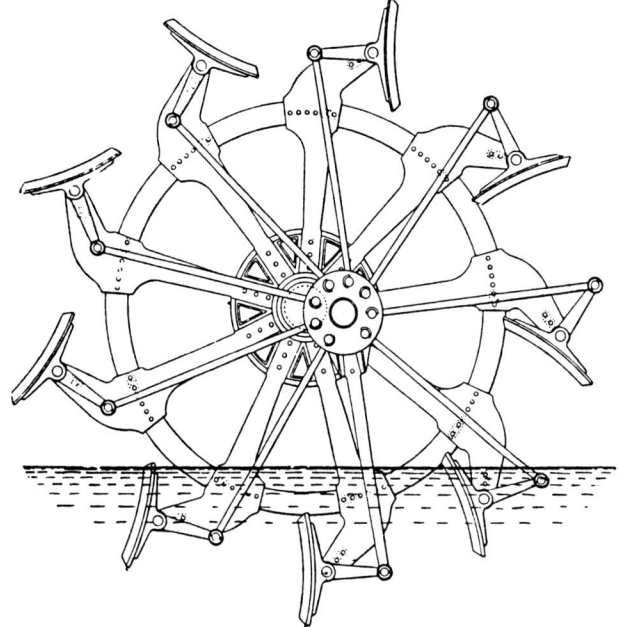

*Figure 4*

In Australia, the paddlewheel era passed quite quickly in most areas, but the Murray River remained faithful to the paddler until the 1920s. In recent years there has been a resurgence of interest in paddleboats, which has resulted in the restoration of several older boats, while a number of new boats have been built for cruising and excursion work. So, happily, the wheels still turn, and long may they continue.

# Steam-Engines

The earliest successful steam-engine arrangement comprised a vertical cylinder with its piston rod leading to an overhead walking beam. The other end of the beam was connected by a linkage to whatever was being driven, such as a suction pump, or later a paddlewheel. In 1712 Thomas Newcomen erected the first successful steam-engine for which records still exist. In 1782 James Watt introduced a modification which produced a rotary motion with a connecting rod from the end of the beam opposite to the piston driving a shaft and flywheel. Later developments by pioneering marine engineers replaced the single walking beam high in the air with two levers, one on either side of the cylinder.

Early engine-rooms had no electric light, and tending the machinery was a hot and dangerous occupation. In the days before safety legislation, machinery was not railed off and there was always the danger of being thrown under a side lever or connecting rod in rough weather. The only light was supplied by slush lamps, and the engine-room crew were forced to slide about on greasy floorboards in near darkness while surrounded by hot, moving machinery. On the river steamers, the engine was usually placed in the open, so the problem was not as serious, but still an occasional accident occurred.

Over the years, numerous types of steam-engines were installed in paddlewheel vessels, which varied considerably in design and construction. Although generally described as either horizontal or vertical engines, the machinery fell into several distinct categories within two main groups. The first used an indirect method such as a beam to transfer piston movement to the crank, that is, the side-lever or the grasshopper engine. The second group used a more direct connection between piston and crankshaft, these comprising the steeple engine, the oscillating engine and the diagonal engine. Several variants of all these types were installed in Australian paddleboats.

Unfortunately, records do not indicate the exact type of machinery installed in most of the older vessels. The following examples are typical of machinery that was used in paddle-steamers, both in Australia and overseas.

## The Side-Lever Engine

The most popular of the early paddle engines, the side-lever engine took the beam of James Watt's rotative beam engine and placed it low in the bilge instead of above the cylinder and crank. This produced an engine in which all moving

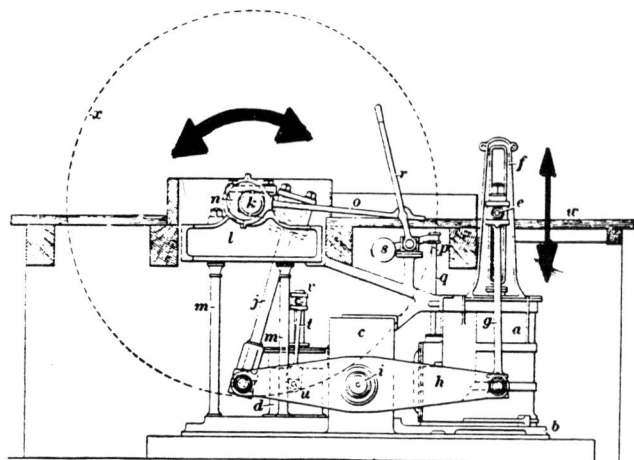

*Figure 5*

elements were concentrated in the engine-room, with a low centre of gravity to improve stability, good power and excellent reliability. However, it required extensive foundations of cast-iron girders, heavy posts and forged iron rods to keep all machinery elements in alignment.

In Figure 5, the side lever or beam is marked 'h' and pivots about its fulcrum 'i'. Lever 'r' is the manual valve gear control by which the engine is started. The loose eccentric valve gear would then follow and be coupled up.

The side-lever engine reached its peak of popularity in the 1850s and 1860s, when it was used to power the Atlantic record-breakers. The Cunard liner *Scotia*, built in 1862, had side-lever engines rated at 975 horsepower. Two giant 100-inch (2.5-m) bore cylinders with a stroke of 12 feet (3.7 m) pushed this liner along at speeds of more than 16 knots.

The first steamer to arrive in Australia from Britain, the *Sophia Jane*, was fitted with this type of machinery. Side-lever engines were installed in some of the Australian coastal and river steamers, both imported and built locally.

## The Grasshopper Engine

The half-lever, or grasshopper, engine was a variant of the side-lever engine, in that the side lever pivoted at the end instead of in the middle. The grasshopper engine was more compact than the side lever, being practically self-contained. Grasshopper engines were also very popular, and as late as 1914 paddle tugs with these engines were being built in Scotland.

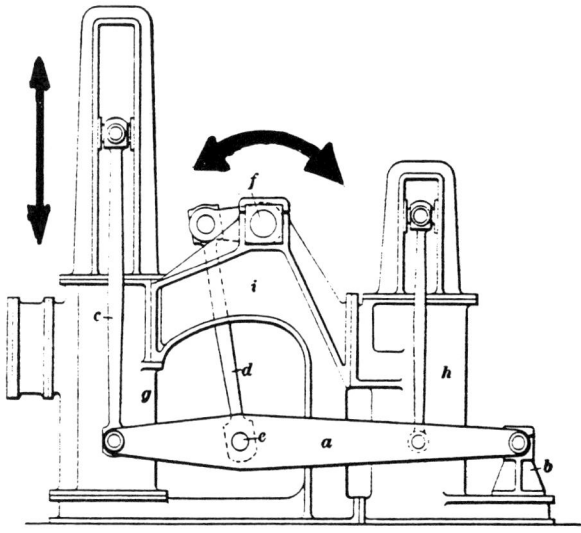

*Figure 6*

The side-lever and the grasshopper engines were both very cumbersome to start. Boiler pressures were very low and the engines relied on condenser vacuum to produce full power from the piston. To start, the engine would first be flooded with steam. The drive to the slide valve could be disconnected, and the slide valve operated by hand until the crankshaft picked up the eccentric which drove the valve gear. The drive to the slide valve could then be reconnected, and the engine could run in that direction. To go astern, the engine would be manually started in that direction until the crankshaft picked up the loose eccentric in the astern position.

A notable Australian vessel to be fitted with a pair of grasshopper engines was the *Mystery*, which spent many years in Melbourne and Sydney.

## The Steeple Engine

This type of engine attempted to maximise the length of the connecting rod by splitting the piston rods and carrying them around the crankshaft to an overhead crosshead. A long connecting rod then took motion down to the crankshaft which drove the paddles.

The steeple engine first appeared in 1834 and became popular for river craft, but as it was a tall engine, it was not widely used in ocean-going craft where steam was an auxiliary to sail. Shipowners probably felt they were paying for a lot of machinery for the power developed, and all for the benefit of a slightly longer connecting rod. The Manly ferry *Breadalbane* was fitted with an 80-horsepower steeple engine.

## The Oscillating Engine

This type of engine became popular in the 1870s and could still be found in paddle-steamers operating in the 1930s. It was light, powerful and compact, but for large ships the

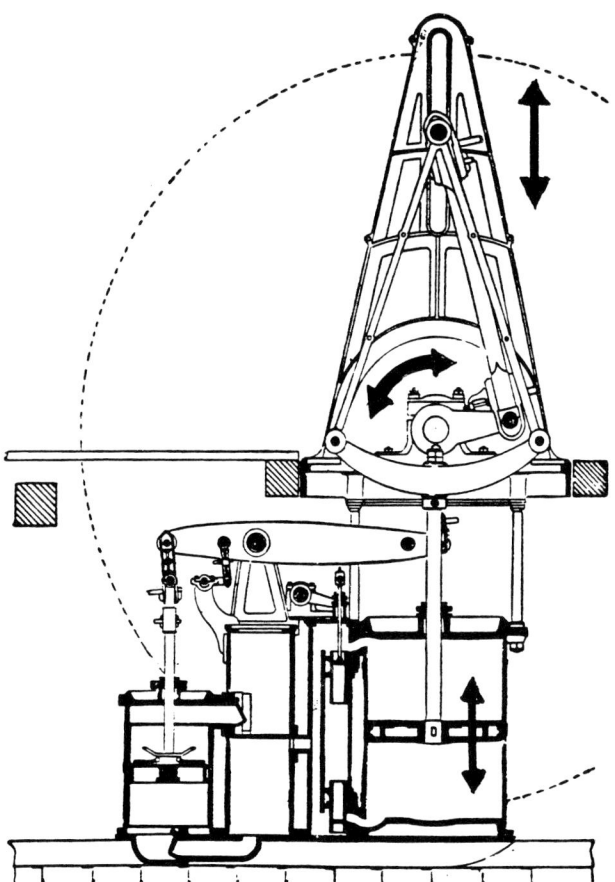

*Figure 7*

cylinders were uncomfortably wide for the narrow hulls of the day.

The oscillating engine did away with the connecting rod, instead connecting the piston rod directly to the crankshaft and paddleshaft. The cylinders rocked, or oscillated, on trunnions to accommodate the crank motion.

An early oscillating engine built by John Penn in 1866 was fitted into the 370-foot (113-m) paddle yacht built for the Khedive of Egypt. This remarkable engine had pistons of over 8-foot (2.4-m) diameter and produced 6,000 horsepower to give a speed of 19 knots. The single eccentric valve gear required 20 men in the engine room during manoeuvring to handle the engine.

The paddle engine installed in the *Great Eastern*, built in 1858, was of the oscillating type with four cylinders. The

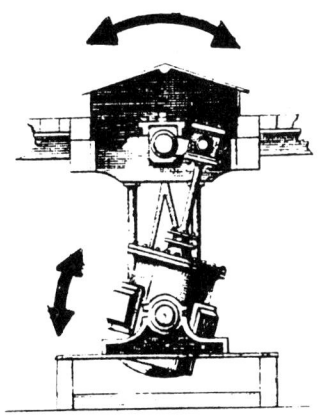

*Figure 8*

bore was 74 inches (1.88 m) and stroke 14 feet (4.28 m). Each cylinder weighed 30 tonnes, and the whole engine stood some 52 feet (15.8 m) high.

Among the Australian paddlers to be fitted with oscillating engines were the coastal traders *City of Grafton, Namoi, Newcastle, City of Newcastle, Collaroy* and *Coonanbara,* the Manly ferry *Brighton* and the *Golden Crown* (built in New Zealand in 1870 and later used on Port Phillip Bay).

# The Diagonal Engine

The diagonal engine was probably the most successful of all the machinery used in paddleboats. The engine was narrow, especially when fitted with slide valves over the cylinders, and much lighter than other contemporary machinery. Double-eccentric (Stephenson) or radial (Joy) valve gear meant that one man only was required to manoeuvre the engines. Boiler pressures were much higher, while fuel efficiency reached new standards.

It will be seen in Figure 9 that the cylinders are mounted low in the bilge, with piston and connecting rods inclined up towards the crankshaft. Among Australian boats to use this machinery was the *Decoy*, while the Manly ferry *Fairlight* and the Port Phillip Bay excursion boats *Lonsdale* and *Ozone* each had a pair of diagonal engines.

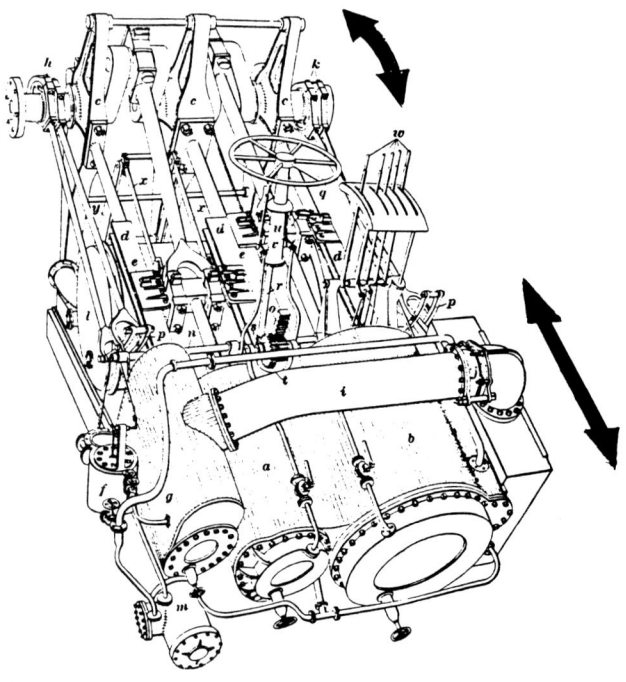

*Figure 9*

# The Walking-Beam Engine

The Americans were the only ones to retain and develop the walking-beam engine. This machinery was found to be particularly successful when installed in paddleboats operating coastal and river routes. Though most of the paddle-steamers built in America for ocean trading were fitted with side-lever machinery, from 1830 to 1850 the walking-beam engine was also used on 17 vessels. This machinery was quite distinctive, as the moving beam was located on top of the engine and protruded above the upper deck of the ship.

The walking-beam engine enjoyed two major advantages, the first being that the machinery could withstand a large amount of misalignment if the hull hogged, sagged or twisted out of shape. The second was the amount of ironwork required for foundations was almost nil. Timber could be used to support the walking beam, the paddleshaft bearings, the cylinder and other working parts. Only a series of iron tie rods were needed to lace the various wood elements together.

The single-cylinder walking-beam engine was the cheapest American type that could be built, since it had the minimum of mechanical parts, was lighter than the side-lever type, and was easy to erect in a ship because of the lack of heavy bed plates. However, they had to be started and stopped by hand, to avoid the 'dead centre' position which would prevent the engine from starting under steam. Beam engines were especially satisfactory, although more costly, if two cylinders and beams were used.

Only a few vessels fitted with walking-beam engines visited Australia, the first being the *Golden Age*, which was built in 1853 and made a voyage from Britain the same year. This type of engine was also fitted in the *General Urbistando*, which crossed the Pacific in 1854, and when sold to Australian owners was renamed *Ben Bolt*. In the 1870s a trio of American paddlers fitted with beam engines, the *Dakota, Nebraska* and *Nevada*, operated a regular trans-Pacific service for a short time.

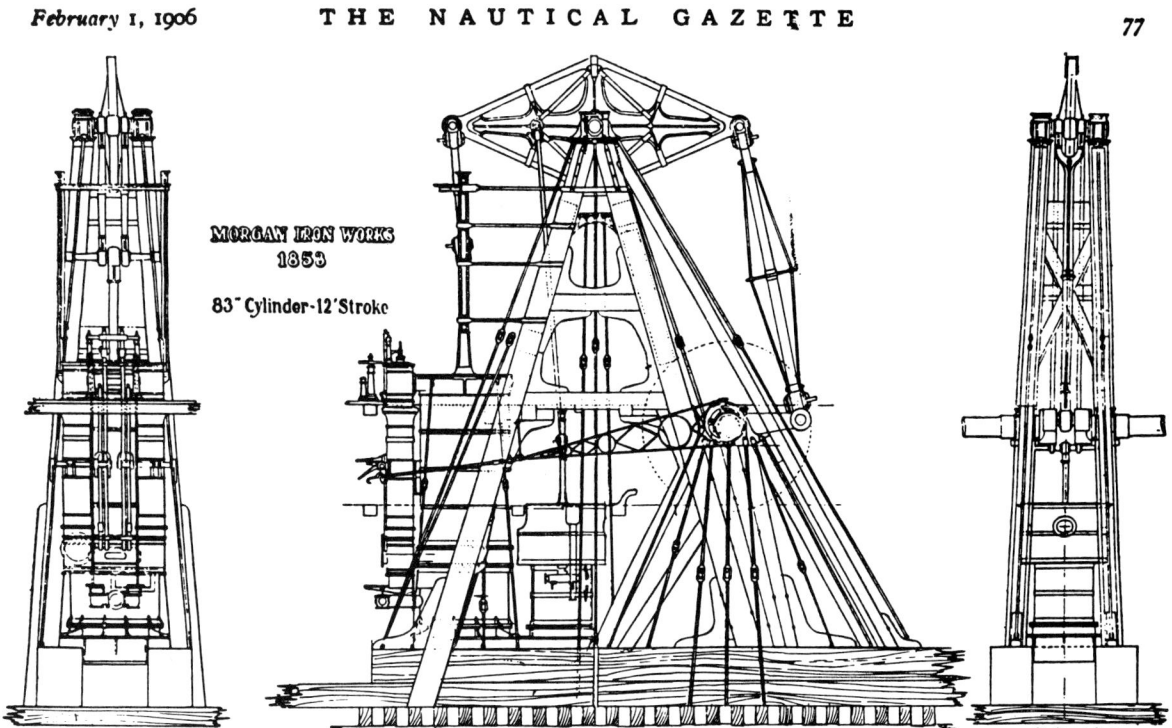

MORGAN IRON WORKS
1853

83˝ Cylinder-12´ Stroke

ENGINE OF THE AMERICAN STEAMSHIP GOLDEN AGE, FROM THE ORIGINAL PLANS MADE BY THE MORGAN IRON WORKS, N. Y.

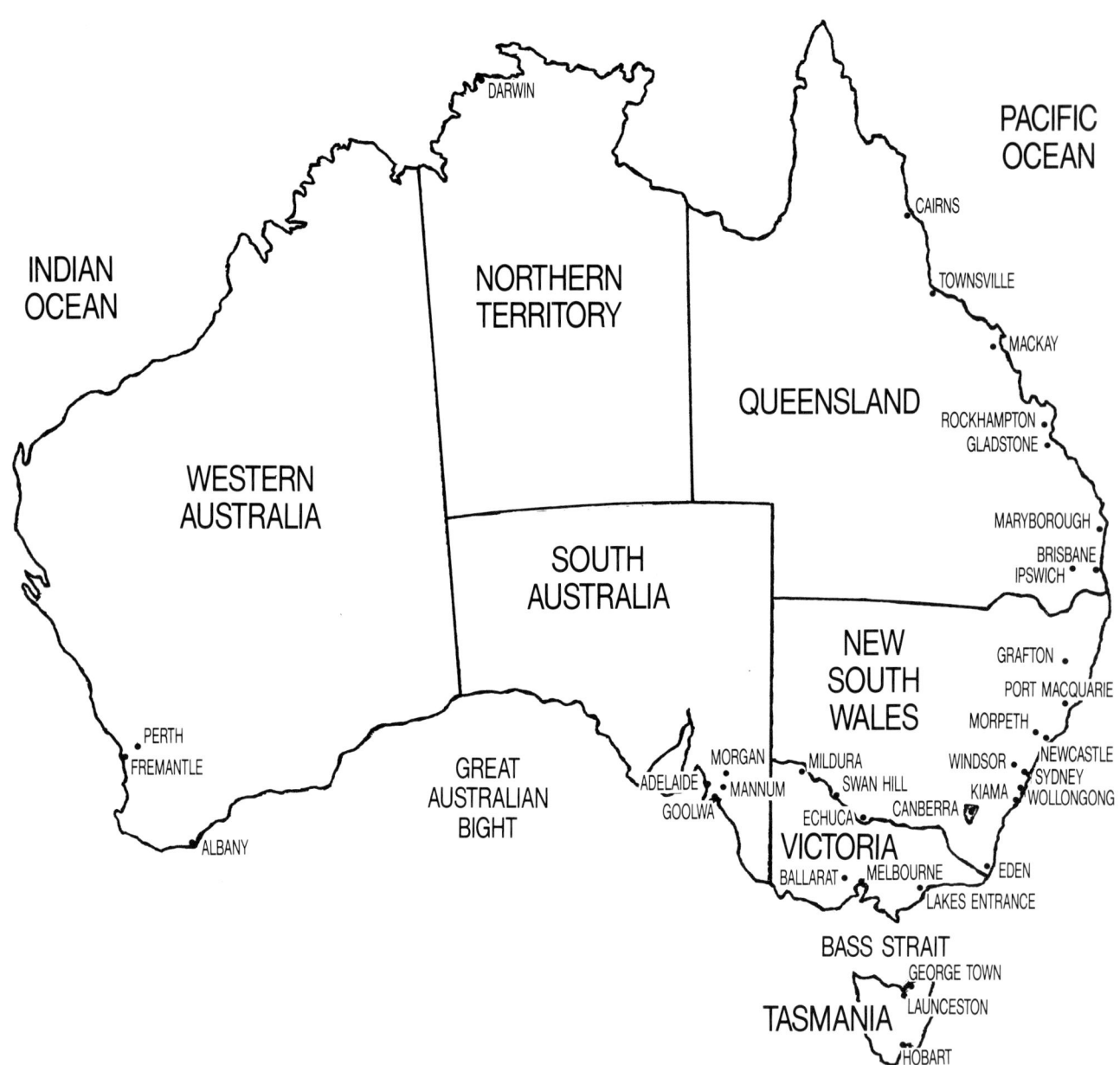

# Part One: Ocean and Harbour Boats

# 1 The Pioneers

In 1830 the population of Australia numbered just 70,000. The majority of the populace were criminals transported from Britain, and their families, with only a few free settlers, who had been lured to the country by the promise of huge tracts of land. At that time the country was divided into three colonies, Western Australia, New South Wales and Van Diemen's Land. In 1836 South Australia was extracted from New South Wales, Victoria in 1851, and Queensland in 1859, at about which time Van Diemen's Land was renamed Tasmania.

In the 1830s Sydney was the main town for the colony of New South Wales, while Hobart Town was the major centre in Van Diemen's Land, and the Swan River and Albany were the only settled areas in Western Australia. Numerous small townships had begun to develop in New South Wales and Van Diemen's Land. Some were penal settlements, others centred in agricultural development areas. All had one thing in common: they were situated on the sea or a river, or in some cases, both. Apart from the Parramatta and Derwent rivers, settled areas were being developed along the banks of the Hawkesbury and Hunter rivers, and also the Tamar and Esk in Van Diemen's Land. The people did not travel much from their homes, but there was a need to transport produce and other goods to the main centres. This was being done in sailing craft, which provided an erratic and unreliable service.

Despite the fact that no steamship had ever visited Australia, several local men gave consideration to the construction of such craft, to be paddle-driven and operate along the coast and rivers. So it was that during 1830 a Sydney merchant, Joseph H. Grose, ordered the construction of a steamship on the banks of the Williams River, near Newcastle. This vessel was to be used on a regular service between Sydney and the Hunter River. Messrs H.G. Smith & Brothers, a Sydney firm, also placed an order for a steamship, which was to be built at Neutral Bay, in Sydney Harbour, to operate a ferry service to Parramatta. Dr Alexander Thomson, of Hobart, ordered a small steam vessel from a British shipyard, to be transported in sections to Hobart, where it would be assembled and placed in service.

On 31 March 1831, the paddle-steamer *Surprise* was launched at the shipyard of Mr Millard in Neutral Bay. The event was reported by the *Australian* newspaper in glowing terms:

> Yesterday the first steam vessel that ever appeared in this country was launched (amidst colours flying and the acclamations of some hundreds of spectators in boats whom the novelty of the scene drew to the spot) at the top of high water; and soon she floated gracefully in her natural element. This specimen of naval architecture does infinite credit to Mr Millard; she is a beautiful model, and appears to be well constructed for a clipper for light draft of water.

The report went on to state that the vessel was to be fitted with a 10-horsepower high-pressure engine, would ply with goods and passengers and be ready to start in the trade in about four weeks. *Surprise*, built entirely of wood, was 58 feet (17.6 m) long with a beam of 9.8 feet (2.8 m).

On 16 May 1831 the *Sydney Herald*, under 'Shipping Intelligence, Arrivals', noted: 'On Saturday last, from London, Plymouth, Pernambuco and the Cape, the *Sophia Jane*, steam vessel, 256 tons'. The reference to her as a steam vessel was slightly premature, as the Sydney papers of 19 May carried the following notice:

> Captain Biddulph begs to inform his friends and the public that in consequence of the engineer and crew of *Sophia Jane* being engaged with the fitting of the engine and putting the vessel in order after the voyage, he cannot at present admit visitors, but as soon as these objects are accomplished, he will be glad to see on board, such Gentlemen and Ladies as will favour him with their company.

The *Sophia Jane* had not made her long journey under steam, but in sail. The paddlewheels had been removed and stowed on board, and apparently the engine had also been disassembled for the voyage.

The *Sydney Herald* of Monday, 30 May 1831, carried a report of the first steaming of the *Surprise*, which was 'tried on Wednesday last in the Cove and around Pinchgut Island, and from the manner in which she worked, there is no doubt of her success after undergoing some necessary alterations'. Thus the *Surprise* was the first vessel to operate under steam in Australian waters. The *Sophia Jane* did not make her first trip under steam until the morning of 11 June, carrying the governor and invited guests. In the afternoon she steamed outside the heads with a large party of prominent citizens aboard. On 12 June it was recorded that

> the public were highly gratified in witnessing the *Sophia Jane* towing the *Lady Harewood* (for London direct) down the Harbour; the ease and rapidity with which she drew the *Harewood* excited the greatest admiration and applause. This is the first application of steam power to the purpose abovementioned that Australia can boast of; and from the important benefit that must issue to the Colony by the

general introduction of this valuable discovery, we think the Proprietors of such vessels deserve every support that the Government of the Colony and the community at large can give them.

Her first commercial voyage, departing Sydney on 13 June 1831, was to the Hunter River.

The *Sophia Jane* was not a new ship, having been built in London in 1826 for the British coastal trades. She was built of wood, 120.3 feet (36.5 m) long, 20 feet (6.1 m) wide, and powered by a side-lever jet-condensing 50-horsepower steam-engine. When her owners, who included Captain Biddulph, decided to take the ship overseas for sale, their first destination was Cape Town. Here the paddles were fitted and the ship steamed, but no sale was finalised. The *Sophia Jane* then continued on to Sydney, where the owners hoped that a sale could be arranged at a suitable profit to them. On the voyage the ship carried only the crew and the family of Captain Biddulph, but *Sophia Jane* had been designed to carry passengers, for whom there were three cabins, one for ladies, with 11 beds, while that for gentlemen had 16 beds, and 20 in steerage.

The vessel being built by Marshall & Lowe on the Williams River for Mr Grose was launched on 14 November 1831 and named *William the Fourth*. She was taken to Sydney under sail to have an 18-horsepower jet-condensing steam-engine fitted, entering service on 2 February 1832, with a voyage from Sydney to Newcastle, becoming the first ocean-going steamship to be built in Australia. *William the Fourth* was 74 feet (22.5 m) long, with a beam of 15.6 feet (4.7 m).

*Surprise* had been placed in service as a ferry on the Parramatta River, but was not a success. She made the journey in about three and a half hours, but rolled uncomfortably and had other problems. The Smith brothers were able to dispose of the vessel to Dr Thomson of Hobart, and the *Surprise* left Sydney, under sail, in January 1832. On her arrival in Hobart, the paddlewheels were fitted again and she became the first vessel to steam on the Derwent River. *Surprise* was mainly used on the ferry service from Hobart to Kangaroo Point, but also went up the river as far as New Norfolk.

Dr Thomson had previously placed an order with a British shipyard for a paddle-steamer to be delivered to Hobart in sections, which duly arrived on the barque *Platina* early in 1832. The vessel was assembled on the banks of the Derwent, being named *Governor Arthur*, in honour of the King's representative in the colony. *Governor Arthur* was quite small, just 63 feet (19.2 m) long, and powered by a 14-horsepower steam-engine. She joined the *Surprise* in ferry services on the Derwent, but in October 1833 she made a voyage to Launceston, becoming the first steam vessel to voyage along the coast of Tasmania.

Naturally, all these paddle-steamers created a great many firsts for steamships in Australia. Their advent created considerable interest, and soon they were joined by other paddle-steamers. Some were built locally, others imported, and they met with varying degrees of success.

# 2 The Sydney Region

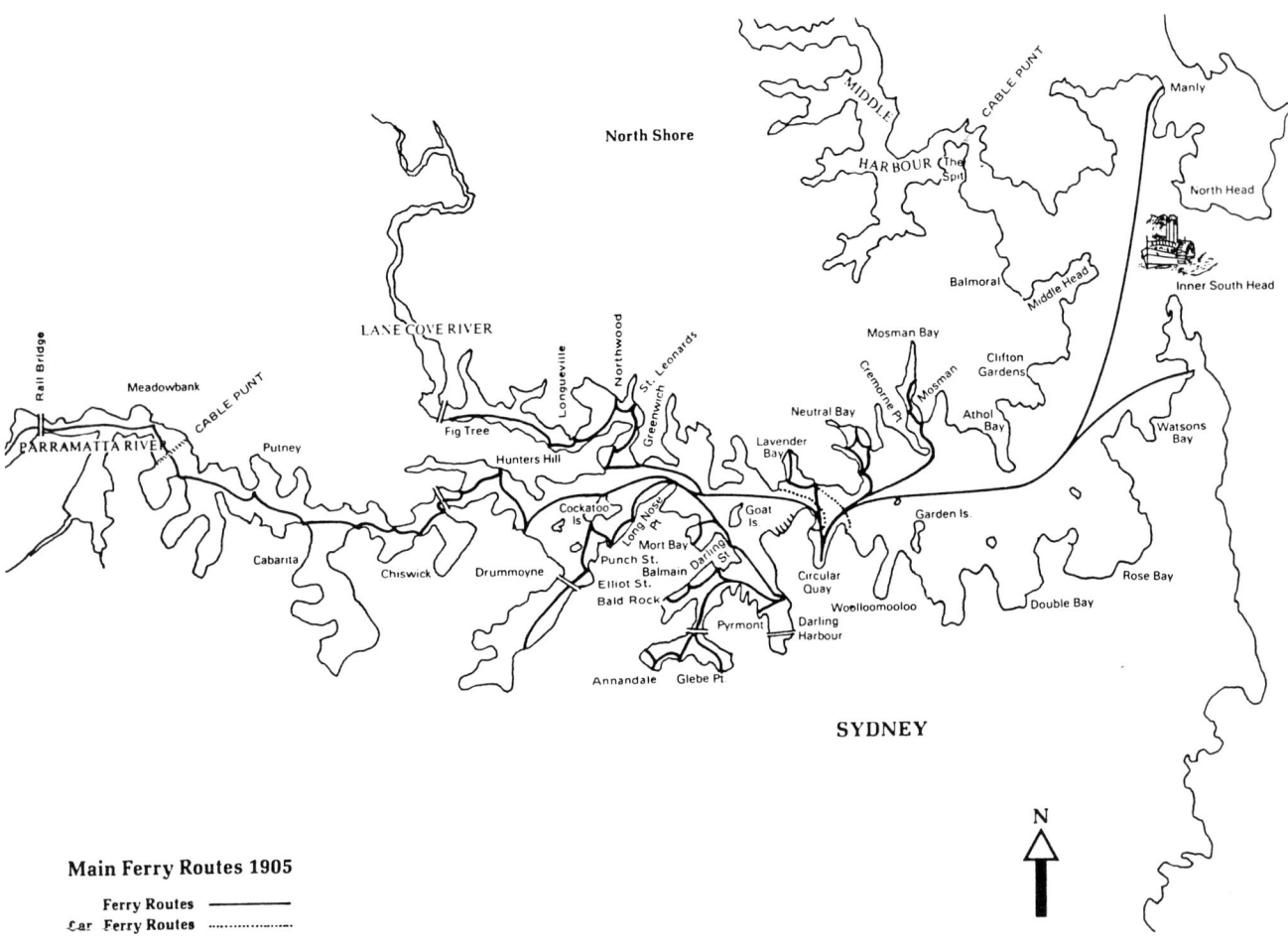

**Main Ferry Routes 1905**

Ferry Routes ————
Car Ferry Routes ··············

Map of Sydney Harbour (GA)

Sydney Harbour was not only the cradle of white settlement in Australia, its waters were the first to be disturbed by mechanically powered vessels. The first of these to be built in Australia, the paddler *Surprise*, was launched into Sydney Harbour in 1831, and it was also in Sydney Harbour, during the same year, that the first steamship from overseas arrived, also a paddler.

It is not surprising that the first steamer to be built in Australia should have been designed for the ferry service between Sydney and Parramatta, as this is the most historic route in the country. Subsequently, Sydney Harbour was host to a diverse fleet of paddle-steamers, operating a network of ferry services, both within the harbour and along the Parramatta River, requiring a diverse fleet of paddlers. These ferries served the growing population of Sydney for

many years, until they were replaced by propeller-driven vessels in the early years of this century. Further north, along the Hawkesbury River, a different type of vessel was required to serve the needs of those residents, but these boats were fewer in number. Undoubtedly the finest of the paddle ferries were built for the 11-kilometre run from Sydney to Manly, but sadly these boats are all but forgotten today.

## Parramatta River Ferries

Having established an initial settlement on the shores of Sydney Harbour, Arthur Phillip, the first governor of New South Wales, set out to explore the river that emptied into the harbour. On 23 April 1788 he found an area some 25 kilometres upstream from Sydney where crops could be grown, which he named Rose Hill. By the following year the first crop had been harvested and settlers were being attracted to the area in growing numbers. A town was laid out in 1790 and the following year the name was changed to the Aboriginal Parramatta. At that time, the only land connection between Sydney and Parramatta was by a twisting bush track, the first road not being completed until 1794.

In May 1789 work commenced in Sydney on the first vessel, apart from very small boats, to be built in the new colony. Very little is known about this sailing boat, though she was only about 40 feet (12 m) long and took five months to build. The vessel was named the *Rose Hill Packet*, though she was popularly known as 'The Lump', which at that time was how a stout and heavy lighter used to carry stores was known. The purpose for which this vessel was built was to carry supplies between Sydney and Parramatta, returning with produce. From the few reports that have survived, the *Rose Hill Packet* was no flyer, sometimes taking a week to complete one round trip.

Over the next half century, numerous sailing vessels were built for the Parramatta River run, but they operated at the whim of wind and tide. Overseas, the steam-engine was being put to use in vessels, but Australia remained totally reliant on sailing ships. In 1830 Sydney businessman Henry Smith placed an order with Mr Millard's shipyard at Neutral Bay, on the north shore of the harbour, to construct the hull of a paddle vessel, for which a steam-engine would be imported from Britain. The purpose of the new vessel would be to run between Sydney and Parramatta.

It was in 1827 that the brothers Henry Gilbert Smith and Charles Smith came to Australia from England to seek their fortune. Charles was not enamoured with Sydney, and soon returned home, but Henry found himself lodgings in George Street, went into business and soon prospered. Fortunately some of the letters he wrote home during his time in Sydney have survived and provide an interesting insight into the construction of the first Australian steamboat. Henry must have enjoyed the summer weather, as he wrote that 'every morning by five o'clock I am out of bed and am promenading in the Domain or bathing in Woolloomooloo Bay'. In April 1829 Henry Smith left Sydney to return to England, to improve his business contacts, particularly for the exporting of wool from Australia, returning to Sydney in September 1830. During his time in England he arranged for a steam-engine to be built and sent to him in Sydney. Either on his arrival, or by mail before his return, he had arranged for the hull to be built in Sydney.

In December 1830 another brother, Thomas Smith, arrived in Sydney with his wife and went into partnership with Henry. Possibly on the same ship came the steam-engine, as in a letter dated 19 December 1830 Henry Smith wrote that 'the steam engine has arrived safe, the bright parts are much rusted'. Henry went on to describe progress on the new boat, stating:

the new boat is building and I hope to get it afloat in two months. It will carry 25 tons besides engine and passengers; a small half deck cabin will be made for the latter. The

boat will run between this and Parramatta every day; as the distance is but 18 miles she will not be more than two hours. I am told by everyone, men of business and gentlemen, that it is sure to answer well, so much so that it is to pay for itself in a year; many are more sanguine than this. It should pay well, for you can hardly imagine the uneasiness it is to me and will be until it is afloat; there is so much to do and arrange.

Obviously the construction of the steamboat was being widely followed in Sydney, and many were sure the venture would be an outstanding success. Among those who supported Smith was the governor, who, Henry wrote,

has promised me every assistance; he is to give me a waterside allotment at Parramatta and he has lent me a carpenter. The people here are looking forward to the period of its starting with great anxiety; the newspapers frequently have paragraphs about it. It is our intention to have a receiving or booking office at Parramatta. I shall, I can assure you, look after it myself. I must give my whole attention to the boat for the first three or four months.

In February 1831, Henry wrote to his parents that

my time is now fully taken up superintending the building of the steamboat; every morning at sunrise I leave Sydney in a boat to go to the builder's yard, distant two miles, stop there till half past eight and return; in the afternoon I go over again and stay until sunset. In a fortnight I hope to have the boat afloat and in a month or five weeks completed.

Referring to his other business interests, Henry wrote that they were 'loading a big ship with oil and wool, she will leave on 1st April. There will be exported this year two million pounds of wool.'

Thomas Smith also wrote letters at this time that have been preserved. It was he who mentioned the manner in which an engineer was found for the new boat, writing:

his name is John Smith; he is a very large man and was formerly in the Army. He came here free. Soon after he arrived, finding we wanted a man to put the engines together, he offered himself, and having learned we were Northamptonshire people thought the best recommendation he could bring us was to tell us he came from the same county.

The launching of the boat, which must have been a momentous occasion for Henry Smith, did not mean as much to his brother, who wrote on 1 April 1831:

I have but little to add since my last letter was despatched about three weeks back, and nothing has happened in the interim, except that yesterday the steamboat was launched. She was built on the opposite shore, but is now lying over here, and tomorrow the first part of the engine will go on board.

Later in the same letter Thomas said that Henry Smith had 'exerted himself a great deal and is very anxious indeed to get her completed, as also to receive the credit he expects will be given him for his undertaking... The interest about the vessel is very great, and a very kind feeling prevails in her favour.'

The local press gave the launch of the new boat considerable coverage. The *Australian* reported that:

> yesterday the first steam vessel that ever appeared in this country was launched, amidst colours flying and the acclamations of some hundreds of spectators on boats, from Mr Millard's slip at Neutral Harbour, North Shore, at the top of high water, and soon she floated gracefully in her native element. This specimen of naval architecture does infinite credit to Mr Millard; she is a beautiful model, and appears to be well constructed for a clipper for light draft of water.

The article went on to describe the vessel, stating:

> her fastenings are copper and her rudder is peculiarly fitted so as to work in a groove and not with pintles standing out from the stern post. She is to ply with goods and passengers and we wish the owners, Messrs. Smith Brothers, every success which their enterprise deserves. In about four weeks the *Surprise*, as she is christened, will be ready to start the trade.

Just why the new vessel was named *Surprise* is not known, as its construction was widely known. No doubt Henry Smith was surprised, and disappointed, when he heard of the arrival of the *Sophia Jane* in Sydney Harbour just six weeks later. However, that vessel arrived under sail and her engines and paddlewheels had to be assembled before she could steam.

Apparently fitting the engine into the *Surprise*, and other work, did not go as quickly as planned. On 24 April Thomas wrote that: 'we have had some tremendous rains during the last week, and this has greatly hindered the steamboat, but if it clears up, as there seems a very good prospect of, in three weeks more we hope to see the *Surprise* surprising the natives'. The next day, Henry was writing that:

> the workmen, carpenters, joiners and engineers are getting on with their work and have the greater part of the engine on board. On the 10th May we expect we shall begin to run; it is generally thought that the speculation will be a good one and we shall make a fortune... I have almost become engineer and shipbuilder, so diligently have I watched its progress.

On completion, the *Surprise* was 18 tons burthen, 58 feet (17.6 m) long, with a beam of 9.8 feet (3 m) and a depth of 4.9 feet (1.5 m). The only detail known about the steam-engine is that it was 10 horsepower.

On 25 May 1831, *Surprise* operated under steam for the first time. The *Sydney Gazette* of 2 June described her trip, giving the speed as 4½ mph, while the time taken from Sydney Cove to Ball's Head was said to be 20 minutes. The *Sydney Herald* also covered the first trip, but mentioned the need for 'some necessary alterations'. A few days later the *Surprise* made her first voyage up the Parramatta River, going aground at Red Point en route. The return trip was made the following day, departing Parramatta at 1 p.m. to arrive back in Sydney at 4.30 p.m. The *Herald* also

mentioned uncomfortable rolling when the vessel was in the wider reaches of Sydney Harbour.

On 6 June, Thomas Smith wrote:

> Henry and I went to the Governor today to ask for a grant of land as a reward for introducing the first navigation by Steam into the Colony. In due course we shall have an answer, and from his manner I expect a favourable one, but great bodies move slowly. The Boat has made one trip to Parramatta, but being crank, as sailors say, or topheavy and unsteady as you country folks would call it, she is obliged to be altered and will not ply for two or three weeks more. Henry has encountered a great deal of anxiety in superintending her building.

Being the first steamboat built in Australia, it should not have been unexpected that there would be problems. On 23 July Thomas Smith was writing that 'the Steamboat has been running this month and Henry has had a good deal of trouble with it, but now it goes reasonably well, and as the summer is coming on there seems every possibility of his reaping ample reward for his pains'.

Unfortunately for Henry Smith, the hoped-for success did not come. *Surprise* remained a problem for him, and by the end of 1831 he had decided to rid himself of the boat. On 6 January 1832 Thomas wrote: 'Henry is going to Van Diemen's Land in the course of a few days, and sends before him his Steamboat, which he intends, if he can, to sell there, as they have been long anxious for one at Hobart Town'. Hobart really offered the only alternative place of employment for the *Surprise*, so the first attempt to operate a ferry service using steamboats in Sydney came to a sudden and unfortunate end. *Surprise* made the voyage to Hobart under sail. In March 1832 Thomas Smith wrote to his brother John:

> Henry has returned from Van Diemen's Land, having sold the Steamboat, though at a sad loss. I am glad for his sake it is gone, for it is a great weight of care and anxiety off his mind, the relief from which is very apparent. It is a truly unfortunate business for all concerned... I can, however, assure them that Henry laboured day and night to make it answer, but the further it went the worse luck seemed to attend it, and I am persuaded that the best thing that could be done was to part with it.

In May 1832 Thomas and Henry Smith dissolved their partnership and developed their own business careers.

The desire to have a paddleboat operating between Sydney and Parramatta was still strong, despite the lack of success enjoyed by the *Surprise*. Early in 1832 Benjamin Singleton placed an order with a shipyard on the Williams River near Raymond Terrace, to build a vessel for service on the Parramatta River. On completion, the vessel was named *Experiment* and voyaged to Sydney under sail to be prepared for service. The name was very apt, as the vessel was to introduce a novel form of propulsion. At that time, steam-engines and engineers to work them were almost unknown in Australia, so the *Experiment* was provided with horsepower, two to be exact. A treadmill was placed in the centre of the vessel, on which the two horses would plod along, providing sufficient power to turn the paddle wheels.

The *Experiment* was 80 feet (24.3 m) long, with a 12½-foot (3.8 m) beam. She departed Sydney on her first voyage to Parramatta on 5 October 1832. The horses caused a few problems, but eventually they settled down to their task and the vessel duly arrived after a voyage lasting six hours. Next day, the return trip to Sydney took only three hours, and as skills in operating the horses improved, this time was further reduced. However, the experiment was not a great success. Passengers found the sight, and even more so the smell of the horses not to their liking. Two months after starting his service Benjamin Singleton had lost £1,000, so he advertised the *Experiment* for sale, adding that the installation of a 12-horsepower steam-engine would greatly improve matters. Just why Singleton did not install machinery himself is unclear, but probably he lacked the necessary financial resources.

In March 1833, the *Experiment* was purchased by Captain Edward Biddulph, who had brought the *Sophia Jane* to Australia and was a part-owner of that vessel. The following year a steam-engine was installed and the *Experiment* began operating regularly along the Parramatta River. This time she enjoyed great success, and remained on the run for the next five years.

During 1834 the *Experiment* was joined in the Parramatta trade by the *Australia*, also built on the Williams River. Her owners were the Australian Steam Conveyance Co., whose backers included Messrs James Thomas Wilson, John Lord and H.H. Macarthur. *Australia* was slightly larger than the *Experiment*, and proved very successful at first. At the end of its first year's trading, the Australian Steam Conveyance Co. was able to declare a 35 per cent dividend. Unfortunately, Wilson, whose name is associated with several failed business enterprises of this period, brought the fledgling company undone by causing them to lose a lawsuit, and the company had to be wound up. *Australia* passed through several owners in subsequent years, but remained on the Parramatta trade until about 1842, when she began operating the short route from Balmain to Sydney.

John Lord ordered a new ferry for the Parramatta trade, which was shipped out to Sydney in sections and assembled there in 1838. It is believed that this was the first iron-hulled ferry to be built for Sydney service, though some sources claim the hull was of wood. Of almost identical size to the *Australia*, the new vessel was named *Rapid*, but proved to be spectacularly unsuccessful and saw little active service. Sold in 1842 to Edye Manning, the *Rapid* was eventually hulked in 1853, when run ashore on Glebe Island, and used as a home by a waterman for many years.

Edye Manning took a great interest in the development of steam services in Australia, and he was responsible for the next two vessels to be added to the Parramatta trade. The first was built locally, by John Korff at Raymond Terrace in 1840, and named *Kangaroo*. She had a wooden hull and was 82 gross tons, with a length of just over 88 feet (26.9 m). *Kangaroo* was sold to the Tasmanian government in 1847. The second vessel was the iron-hulled *Emu*, built by Ditchburn & Mare at Blackwall on the River Thames and imported in sections in the sailing ship *Standerlings*. Assembled by John Struth, the *Emu* was completed in November 1841, being powered by a jet-condensing 32-horsepower steam-engine. It was also in 1841 that Manning purchased the *Australia*.

In March 1843 H.H. Macarthur, acting as trustee for an unincorporated company in which Edye Manning appears to have had an interest, took delivery of yet another paddle-steamer for the Parramatta service, the *Comet*. Built on the Williams River by W. Lowe, the *Comet* had a wooden hull, and was 83 gross tons. In 1844 the smaller *Native* was completed in Sydney for J. & W. Byrnes and provided competition to the *Comet* and *Emu* for a brief time. In 1845 Edye Manning bought the *Native*, which was then used mainly as a relief steamer. It is reported that this vessel had problems with its non-condensing steam engine, in which salt water used to accumulate, despite frequent blowing off. In 1850 the boiler of the *Native* exploded, causing some fatalities.

It was not until 1854 that further new tonnage was added

*Emu* spent 30 years operating as a ferry on the Parramatta River. (GA)

to the Parramatta ferry service, when two vessels were imported in sections for W. Byrnes & Partners, one of whom was Edye Manning. The two vessels were built at Blackwall on the River Thames and sent out to Australia in sections on the barque *Daniel Wheeler*, which arrived in Sydney in April 1854. The sections were then assembled by Young & Mather in Sydney and launched in August 1854 as the *Black Swan* and the *Pelican*. Though not much larger than their predecessors, this pair were a great improvement and spent many years on the Parramatta service. The railway line between Sydney and Parramatta was completed in 1855, but did not run parallel to the river, which still left ample scope for the river trade. In 1858 Edye Manning bought three further paddle-steamers, *Nautilus, Pearl* and *Peri*, all built in 1856 as harbour ferries for Mr S. Crook, but they were initially used on inner-harbour services only.

On 6 June 1855 a collision occurred between the *Pelican* and the *Emu* as they were making their first trips of the day. The *Pelican*, coming downriver from Parramatta, was rounding Pulpit Point when the *Emu* suddenly appeared, headed upriver. Both vessels decided to steer towards the point and *Pelican* stopped engines, but *Emu* kept going and the two hit with their paddle boxes. The wheels of both were crippled and a small deckhouse on the *Emu* was carried away. One passenger standing by the rail was thrown overboard, but managed to swim to the shore. The vessels continued on their way and were repaired overnight.

In the mid-1860s the Parramatta River ferry service suddenly became the centre of a bitter fight between two operators. It all began in 1865, when entrepreneur Charles Edward Jeanneret, in partnership with Jules Joubert and others, suddenly entered the river trade. They formed the Parramatta River Steam Co. and commenced service with a chartered propeller-driven vessel, the *Ysobel*. At that time the Manning group were running three services a day to Parramatta from the Erskine Street wharf in Sydney, calling at Hunters Hill, Gladesville and Ryde en route. A rate war erupted, with the fare to Parramatta coming down to 1*s*. 6*d*. in cabin class and 1*s*. steerage.

To improve his fleet, Manning arranged for two of his boats, the *Peri* and the *Pearl*, to be lengthened. As built they were 55 feet (16.7 m) long, but an extra 42 feet (12.8 m) was inserted at the shipyard of Mr Mather, in Bathurst Street. At the same time, new machinery was installed, raising their speed to 14 knots. Meanwhile, the Parramatta River Steam Co. chartered the veteran paddle-steamer *Brothers* and also ordered a new vessel. The *Sydney Morning Herald* of 23 August 1866 reported that 'within three weeks an extraordinary fast craft will be in active service'. Built by J. Stewart on the Macleay River, the new wooden-hulled vessel was described as being

> built entirely of hardwood, copper fastened throughout; the sponsons run from end to end, and have 29 feet amidships, giving splendid deck room, independent of saloons at either end which will be formed principally of glass panelling. The designs for these compartments are very elegant and commodious, a portion being exclusively for the accommodation of ladies.

The new vessel was named *Adelaide* and proved to be larger than the boats owned by Edye Manning.

The arrival of the *Adelaide* intensified the competition between the two companies, and also resulted in unofficial races between their boats, which sometimes resulted in accidents, and also further rate cutting. There were also fights among the crews of the rival boats and at the end of

*Adelaide* was a wooden ferry built on the Macleay River. (GA)

1866 Mr Jeanneret and the crew of the chartered *Brothers* were charged at Parramatta with assaulting members of the Manning's crews. Jeanneret claimed that evidence had been falsified, and even hinted that the Parramatta magistrate was in league with Edye Manning.

Despite this unpleasantness, amalgamation talks between the two rivals began early in 1867, and in May an acceptable conclusion had been reached. The Parramatta River Steam Co. purchased two of Manning's boats. Manning sold several other of his boats at the same time and subsequently concentrated on other trades. Once again, things settled down on the Parramatta River.

Up to this time, all the vessels operating to Parramatta had been paddle-steamers, with the exception of the chartered *Ysobel*. In 1871 the Parramatta Co. added the paddler *Platypus* to its fleet, which was joined by the *Alchymist* in 1871. However, in 1873 three new propeller-driven vessels joined the trade, and all subsequent vessels were of this type. One problem was the greater depth required by these steamers, which prevented them operating all the way to Parramatta, and a tramway had to be built from a new wharf near the Duck River to the business area of Parramatta. The paddle-steamers continued to operate to Parramatta until the final years of the century. A passenger service between Parramatta and Sydney continued in operation until 1928, and a cargo service survived until 1941.

# Inner-Harbour Ferries

The early settlement of Sydney was concentrated on the land bordering the south side of the harbour. In some cases these areas were separated from the centre of Sydney by water, such as Balmain across Darling Harbour, but the distances were quite short and rowboats operated by watermen sufficed to provide the necessary connections. The north shore of the harbour only gradually became inhabited. Connections across the harbour were supplied by watermen, one of the most famous being Billy Blue, after whom Blues Point was named. Blue was said to have been an early immigrant to Australia, supposedly from Jamaica, and died in 1834. One of his daughters married a hulk attendant, George Lavender, after whom Lavender Bay is named, while another daughter married a man named French, who gave his name to Frenchs Forest.

In 1838 a meeting was convened with the object of forming the North and South Shore Steam Bridge Co. A notice was published indicating that it was proposed to build a 'Steam Bridge or Punt for the constant conveyance of passengers, horses, carriages, cattle etc. to and from Dawe's Battery to the opposite point'. The object of the service would be to 'throw open so large a portion of the country adjacent to Sydney, at present of comparatively little value, being cut off by the harbour, but which by this means, will become united with Sydney'. Unfortunately nothing came of this venture.

In March 1841 a passenger and vehicular paddle-driven punt named *Princess* was built for the North Shore Ferry Co.,

though the imported engine did not arrive until 1842. In August 1842 the *Princess* commenced operations, running numerous trips daily from Windmill Street to the North Shore, the passenger fare being 3*d.*, while carriages cost 2*s. 6d.* This service soon failed and on 11 June 1844 the hull, which had cost £1,300 to build, was sold for £60. The engine, bought for £1,800, was sold for just £275 and was subsequently used to drive a steam mill at Maitland.

This old painting is reputed to show two of the earliest Sydney Harbour ferries. In the middle is *Ferry Queeen*, with *Waterman* at the far right. (GA)

It is widely accepted that the first regular steam ferry to operate across Sydney Harbour was the *Ferry Queen*, built at Pyrmont in 1844 by Thomas Chowne for the brothers Thomas and Joseph Gerrard. Thomas Gerrard had established a reputation as a good engineer when working on the *Victoria* on the Hunter River trade. Very little is known of this paddle vessel, which was very small, and powered by a 41-horsepower steam-engine. The *Ferry Queen* carried passengers only from Millers Point to Blues Point, though there are reports that punts were tied on either side for the transportation of vehicles and livestock. The Gerrard brothers enjoyed great success with their ferry service, as in 1847 they took delivery of another, larger vessel. Also built by Thomas Chowne, it was named *Brothers*, of 23 gross tons, and was 67 feet (20.4 m) long. In 1850 the Gerrards added a third paddle-steamer to the ferry service, the *Agenoria*, of similar size to the *Brothers*.

The Gerrard brothers enjoyed a monopoly in the North Shore ferry service until 1854, when a group of North Shore residents formed the North Shore Steam Ferry Co. Amongst the prime movers in this firm were members of the Blue family and Alexander Berry, after whom Berrys Bay was named, who owned a large estate on which he had his mansion, Crow's Nest. An iron-hulled paddle-steamer was ordered from England, which was imported in sections and assembled at Darling Harbour, being launched in May 1855 and named *Herald*. She was 41 gross tons and 74 feet (22.7 m) long, and commenced a service from Pottinger Street to Blues Point. At first the company prospered, but in 1859 the North Shore Steam Ferry Co. was wound up and the *Herald* sold. The vessel then operated a service from Circular Quay to Milsons Point, with Captain Hall in charge. He is said to have remained in command of the *Herald* for 23 years, at one time even owning the boat, though after 1861 she was mainly used as a tug. The *Herald* survived until 1 April 1884, when she sank off Sydney Heads, the result of the bottom of her boiler being blown out.

The first part of Sydney to be settled was in the area now known as The Rocks, between Sydney Cove and Darling Harbour. The Tank Stream, which emptied into Sydney Cove, was very shallow at its mouth, which was then known as Semi-Circular Quay. When the tide was out, it was possible to walk from one side of Sydney Cove to the other across the sand; otherwise there was a crooked wooden structure, the Bon Accord Bridge, for which a penny toll was paid. Further up the Tank Stream there was another bridge, at present-day Bridge Street. Gradually the land surrounding Sydney Cove was reclaimed and filled in, resulting in the construction of numerous new buildings, which would become the heart of the City of Sydney, while the name of the wharf was amended to Circular Quay. In 1860 a new North Shore Ferry Co. was formed, which operated ferry services out of Circular Quay, where all future services would be based.

The North Shore Ferry Co. was originally formed in 1860 as J. Milson & Partners, but its name was changed in 1861. Milson was a wealthy resident of North Sydney, and his partners included Charles Firth, Francis Lord, William Tucker and Thomas Laurie. Their first vessel was the *Kirribilli*, a wooden-hulled paddler built in 1860 by John Cuthbert at Darling Harbour. The *Kirribilli* was placed in service to Milsons Point, and from April 1863 her Sydney terminal was Circular Quay. She could carry 60 passengers and operated daily between 7 a.m. and 7 p.m. The company prospered and in 1864 added the *Alexandra*, followed by the vehicular ferry *Transit* in 1866.

In 1869 the North Shore Ferry Co. took delivery of another paddle-steamer, the *Warrah*, which had a wooden hull 73 feet (22.3 m) long and was powered by a 14-horsepower high-pressure steam-engine. An interesting description of travelling conditions of that time has been preserved. The writer stated that:

> there was at this time no waiting room at the Circular Quay wharf. Passengers in bad weather had to avail themselves of the shelter of a large fig tree at the end of Phillip Street, near Mort's store. During heavy southerly winds at Milson's Point it was with much difficulty that the steamer could be made fast. The steamer went alongside a floating pontoon regulated according to the tide by weights suspended from posts at either side.

The writer went on to describe how 'on many occasions it was necessary to trim the steamers if more than an even number sat on one side. For this purpose the engineer kept two 56-pound weights, which he moved to one side or the other as circumstances demanded.'

As for the *Warrah*,

> there was no protection whatever from wind and rain, being very similar to the earlier *Herald*, except an awning overhead, and a small cabin below. If a storm arose during transit, the steamer often had arrived at its destination before the deckhand had rigged the awning. The Captain at the tiller had no shelter and had to face all weathers. The ladies cabin was downstairs aft, where the stoking was also attended to. When the furnace door was opened, ladies put up umbrellas for protection from the heat. Ashes were carried in buckets and placed on the deck, and when opportunity offered, they were dumped overboard. In the centre of the deck, not far from the funnel, was a controlling upright bar in connection with the machinery, which worked backwards and forwards, and kept time with the paddle wheels, which one had to keep clear of. Later on improvements were made, and the bar was removed after the starting of the engine, and inserted again as the steamer approached the wharf.

> The Captain steered with a large iron tiller, and on some of the steamers a plank was arranged upon which he could sit down.

The reference to the tiller is interesting, as this was the accepted form of steering on all the early Sydney ferries. The tiller was slung over the stern, and the captain had to stand there and steer, his view forward often being obstructed by passengers or deckhouses. The first North Shore ferry to have a wheelhouse was the *Coombra*, built in 1872.

In 1878 the North Shore Ferry Co. was incorporated into a limited liability company and renamed the North Shore Steam Ferry Co. Ltd. It took over the existing fleet of the old company, which comprised both paddlers and propeller vessels, and also continued to build both types of vessels for the next 12 years. The size of these vessels gradually increased, the *St Leonards* of 1881 being 110 gross tons, while the double-enders *Cammaray* and *Waratah* of 1884/85 were 197 gross tons. Also in 1885, another double-ended paddle ferry was built by David Drake at Pyrmont, the *Bunya Bunya*, which was 202 gross tons and could carry 671 passengers.

Vehicular ferries grew in importance as the population of the North Shore increased. As recorded previously, the first attempt to establish a service had been with a vehicular ferry, the *Princess*, in 1842. The North Shore Ferry Co. added the *Transit* in 1866, joined by the *Bungaree* in 1873. In 1883 the North Shore Steam Ferry Co. Ltd placed the *Warrane* in service. This 109-gross-ton vessel had a central wheelhouse and space for horse and carriages on each side. She survived until 1921. Another notable vessel of this period was the *Benelon*, built as a vehicular ferry by Drake in 1885. The last paddlewheel ferry to be built for service on Sydney Harbour was the vehicular ferry *Barangaroo*, completed in November 1889 by Drake at Pyrmont. These wooden-hulled vessels could carry about 28 vehicles and 80 passengers, and operated from Milsons Point to Bennelong Point, where the Sydney Opera House now stands.

In 1900 Sydney Ferries Ltd was formed and took over the 16 vessels then owned by the North Shore Steam Ferry Co. Ltd. The only paddlers then in service were the *St Leonards*, *Victoria*, *Cammaray*, *Waratah* and *Bunya Bunya*, along

*Benelon* was built in 1885 to carry vehicles across the harbour. (GA)

*Warrane* served on the harbour from 1883 to 1921. (GA)

with the vehicular ferries *Warrane, Benelon* and *Barangaroo*. By 1910, all the passenger ferries had been disposed of, but the vehicular ferries carried on. *Benelon* was rebuilt in 1916, and sunk in a collision in May 1923, but soon raised and returned to service. Both remaining vessels continued to operate across the harbour until 1932, when the Sydney Harbour Bridge was opened and they were sold.

The other main inner-harbour service to utilise paddle-steamers extensively was the short route across Darling Harbour to Balmain and Pyrmont. There were numerous watermen offering passages in their rowing boats across this stretch of water but in 1844 a small paddle-steamer, just 49 feet (14.9 m) long, was built by J. Robertson at Millers Point for the Waterman's Co. Named *Waterman*, this vessel began operating from the Gas Company's Wharf at the foot of King Street to Balmain, but suffered intially from numerous engine problems. In fact the little vessel broke down quite frequently, the stops being referred to by passengers as 'catching her breath'. On 29 October 1844 an advertisement in the *Sydney Morning Herald* advised: 'The Balmain steam boat *Waterman*, having undergone a thorough repair, with new paddle shafts and wheels, will again resume plying on Wednesday, the 30th instant, from the Gas Company's Wharf to Balmain Ferry, every quarter of an hour, from light until dark, for the accommodation of the public'. *Waterman* remained on this route until 1874, when it was broken up.

In 1845 a second small ferry entered the Balmain trade, the *Gipsey Queen*, of which very little is known. It was built at Pyrmont by Thomas Chowne for J. Entwhistle, who also bought the *Waterman* in 1846. However, in 1847 *Waterman* was sold to H. Perdriau & Partners, who would become the major operators of ferries to Balmain, though they did not add any further vessels until 1855, when the *Alma*, of 28 gross tons, was built. The following year the slightly larger *Premier* was added.

Up to this time the steam ferries had concentrated on providing a service to Balmain only, but in the *Sydney Morning Herald* of 22 December 1855 it was reported that:

> the residents at Pyrmont will not be much longer dependent upon watermen's boats to cross over, in all weathers, from Market Wharf. A new ferry steamer about 50 feet long, 12 feet beam, and 18 inches draught of water, will soon be plying. She is built by Mr Holdsworth, of Pyrmont, and will be propelled by engines of eight nominal horse power, and, from the description of her build, will doubtless be a most serviceable boat. She is owned by Messrs Byrnes and Richards. The engines, which are direct acting, diagonal high pressure, are being constructed by Messrs. Halliday, Laing & Co., formerly of the Sydney Engineers Company.

The vessel in question was the *Pyrmont*, which entered service in January 1856 and was the first of a fleet to be operated by Byrnes and Partners up to 1897.

In 1855 Mr S. Crook, in a bold move, ordered three paddle ferries from Britain for a service to Balmain. On 29 December 1855 the *Sydney Morning Herald* reported:

> yesterday forenoon a small steamboat was launched from Crook's Wharf, Johnson's Bay, Balmain, the first of three boats in every respect similar in appearance and construction, intended to facilitate the communication between the city and the populous suburb of Balmain. By means of these new steamers, the inhabitants of Sydney

Built at Balmain in 1877, *Nellie* is shown here in Mosman's Bay. (GA)

*Victoria* ran to the North Shore between 1883 and 1910. (GA)

will have direct, and consequently speedier transit than heretofore to and from the more distant parts of Balmain, a circumstance which will enhance the advantages of the latter as a place of residence to many whose business compels them to spend a great portion of their time in the city. At the hour appointed for the launch, several ladies and gentlemen from Sydney, and a considerable number of the inhabitants of Balmain were assembled to witness the ceremony, who with hearty cheers and other demonstrations of pleasure, hailed its successful termination.

The vessel was named *Nautilus*, and the report noted that:

the other vessels will follow as soon as possible, Mr Crooks calculating upon having the three plying between Sydney and Balmain in the course of two months. The *Nautilus* will commence running in about ten days between the Phoenix Wharf and Crook's Wharf, Johnson's Bay. The vessel is 60 feet long, breadth of deck 11 feet; the steering wheel is placed amidships, and not at either end as in other ferry boats; she has two cabins below, fore and aft, neat and roomy. The engine is constructed upon the oscillating principle, having two cylinders, 14 inch diameter; the engine is of 12 nominal horse power, but is capable of being worked up to 20. The boiler is of the vertical tubular construction, strong enough to carry 20 pounds of steam in ordinary working. She is also supplied with a donkey engine for feeding the boiler. The boats are of iron, and were manufactured expressly as ferry boats, by Randolph Elder & Co., of Glasgow.

The *Nautilus* entered service in January 1856, it being noted that the one-way fare was 3*d.* She was joined shortly after by the other two, *Pearl* and *Peri*, and this enabled Crook to extend his operation to include Pyrmont too. However, just two years later, Crook sold all three of his boats to Edye Manning, who maintained them for some years on inner-harbour routes. In 1865 the *Peri* was purchased by H. Perdriau & Partners, the first addition to their fleet since the *Premier* was built in 1856.

As the population of Balmain and surrounding areas grew, so the number of ferries required increased. The Perdriau fleet was increased by the purchase of paddlers that had been built for other routes, including the *Kirribilli* in 1868 and the *Warrah* in 1870, and more vessels in the next few years. In 1873 J. Watson & Partners commenced operations, purchasing three paddlers, *Alma, Courier* and *Atlanta*, then building several new vessels. Another rival, Byrnes, purchased the *Alexandra* in 1874 and the *Fawn* in 1881.

In 1882 H. Perdriau & Partners was reconstituted as the Balmain Steam Ferry Co. Ltd, which commenced operations with seven paddle-steamers. In 1883 they took delivery of a new vessel, the *Balmain*, of 177 gross tons, built by Mort's Dock & Engineering Co. in Sydney. In 1884 she was joined by the slightly smaller *Waterview*, then in 1888 came the 174-gross-ton *Me Mel*. To counter this, Watson built the *Bald Rock* in 1884 and the *Lincoln* in 1886, but in 1887 the fleet of J. Watson & Partners was absorbed into the Balmain Steam Ferry Co. Ltd.

The Balmain New Ferry Co. Ltd came into being in 1892 and initially operated two propeller-powered vessels. M. Byrnes & Partners went out of the ferry business in 1897 and in 1900 the fleet of the Balmain Steam Ferry Co. Ltd was absorbed into the Balmain New Ferry Co. Ltd. They introduced more propeller-powered ferries into the service, and gradually the paddlers were withdrawn. The last paddler running to Balmain was the *Me Mel*, whose career came to an unfortunate end when she was involved in a collision on 31 January 1914 and subsequently broken up.

# The Manly Service

The largest and finest paddle-steamers to operate on Sydney Harbour were undoubtedly those used on the 11-kilometre service from Sydney to Manly. One of the most popular holiday spots for Sydneysiders for many years, with superb surfing beaches stretching for miles, Manly eventually became a popular residential area as well.

Located just inside North Head, Manly was the first site inspected by Governor Phillip in January 1788, when seeking a better location for a settlement than Botany Bay. Phillip was impressed by the appearance of the Aboriginal men who met him on the shore when he landed, and he named the place Manly Cove. In September 1790 Phillip again went to Manly Cove, but while talking to the Aborigines, one took fright and speared him through the shoulder. As a result, the Manly area was ignored by white settlers for 20 years, but in 1810 the first land grants were made, including 30 acres (12 ha) given to Gilbert Baker. By the 1830s the population still numbered only 50, mostly engaged in agriculture. Their access to Sydney was very difficult, requiring a lengthy overland trek, crossing several rivers, just to reach the ferry wharf at Milsons Point.

The greatest problem faced by vessels operating to Manly was crossing the Sydney Heads. The Pacific Ocean swells would come through the Heads, and especially in bad weather, the vessels would encounter huge waves coming on them broadside. Passengers frequently became seasick on this portion of the trip and it deterred many from even attempting the voyage.

The first boat to operate to Manly, though providing only one or two trips a week, was the paddler *Brothers*, owned by Thomas and Joseph Gerrard. Built in 1847 for a service from Sydney to the North Shore, the tiny *Brothers* began running to Manly in 1848. She could carry just 50 passengers and the fare was 3*d.* each way. On Sundays and public holidays a number of steamers would operate excursions from Sydney to Manly which proved very popular.

The man who is largely credited with opening up the Manly region is Henry Gilbert Smith, the same man who built the first steamboat in Australia, the *Surprise*, in 1831. Smith bought most of the land granted to Gilbert Baker and began to improve it. This land now forms the centre of the Manly business district. In 1853 he began subdividing his land holdings and offering them for sale. To improve communications with Sydney, Smith arranged to charter the *Brothers* from the Gerrards and ran the boat to Manly. In 1855 Smith chartered another paddler, the *Huntress*, of 86 gross tons, which ran regular Sunday services to Manly for a short time.

Henry Smith built the first pier on the harbour side of Manly in 1855, and the adjoining Italian-style Pier Hotel. He then came to an arrangement with Edye Manning, who operated several of his paddle-steamers to Manly between 1855 and 1860, including *Black Swan, Pelican, Emu* and *Victoria*. These vessels all departed from Manning's Phoenix Wharf, in Darling Harbour. As the number of visitors to the area grew, Smith cleared a swampy area between the harbour and the ocean, which he named The Corso, after a Roman street, and also the areas that now front the beach as the East and West Esplanades. Several guesthouses were built, followed by a funfair and then a public bathhouse.

It was reported that the *Emu* was operating two trips a day to Manly in 1855, while *Black Swan* made her first trip to Manly on 25 July 1855. *Pelican* did not join the Manly trade until 6 December 1855. These vessels, which had been built for the Parramatta River trade, were all quite small, being about 40 gross tons, and had great difficulty coping with the crossing of Sydney Heads. In March 1856 they were replaced by the much larger *Victoria*, of 107 gross tons and built in 1851 for service in Port Phillip Bay. In many ways, *Victoria* can be considered the first regular Manly ferry, as she remained on the route until 1860. However, Manning's boats also called at Watsons Bay, on the southern side of Sydney Heads, which led Henry Smith to organise a permanent service exclusive to Manly.

Smith tried to form a new company, but failed to attract sufficient capital, so in 1859 he went into partnership with S.B. Skinner, who owned the iron-hulled paddle-steamer *Phantom*. Built in 1858 in Melbourne from sections imported from Britain, the 63-gross-ton *Phantom* originally operated on Port Phillip Bay, but in May 1859 the vessel was sent to Sydney, passing through the Heads on 19 May.

Shortly after, the *Phantom* entered the Manly trade, where she soon became known as 'Puffing Billy' from the sound her engine made. She took as long as two hours to make the voyage at times, and was painted in what became the standard Manly ferry colours, green hull with white band, white superstructure, white funnel with black top. *Phantom* was not a good sea boat, being 120 feet (67 m) long, but having a narrow beam of just 13 feet (3.9 m). Several times while crossing the Heads in heavy weather, huge seas caused the fires to be extinguished and a jury mast had to be rigged to finish the journey. To counter the rolling, the crew of the *Phantom* used to hang weights on poles slung over the windward side. Despite these problems, the *Phantom* operated to Manly for 10 years. In 1860 Edye Manning retired from the Manly route, and in the same year Henry Smith sold his interest in the vessel back to Skinner, who then sold out to Captain Thomas Heselton and T.J. Parker. As Henry Smith owned the only pier at Manly, as well as the waterfront land around it, he was able to control the ferry service without actually owning the vessels. However, in 1864 Smith sold the pier to Heselton and Parker.

The next vessels added to the Manly service were all second-hand purchases. The first, *Breadalbane* of 144 gross tons, built in 1853, made her initial trip to Manly on 30 November 1862. In January 1868 Heselton and Parker formed the Brighton & Manly Steam Ferry Co. and added

*Goolwa* was used as both a tug and a ferry on Sydney Harbour. (GA)

their *Goolwa*, built in 1864, to the route, followed by the *Cobre* in 1869. In 1874 they added another similar vessel to the fleet, the *Mystery*, which had previously been operating on Port Phillip Bay.

*Breadalbane, Goolwa, Cobre* and *Mystery* were basically tugs fitted with some passenger accommodation, though the *Breadalbane* was altered for the route and was described in the *Sydney Morning Herald* as a fast, roomy boat, admirably adapted for passenger traffic. *Goolwa* and *Cobre* were used as both tugs and ferries, and provided more basic passenger facilities. Sometimes one of these vessels would sight a sailing ship coming in through the Heads and, regardless of passengers being aboard, would race out to sea to secure the tow ahead of a rival tug and bring the sailing ship into port.

It was not until 1873 that the first large passenger ferry was placed on the Manly run. This was the *Royal Alfred*, of 141 gross tons, built in 1868 in Auckland, New Zealand. *Royal Alfred* operated on the Thames River trade out of Auckland, but in October 1873 was purchased by Thomas Heselton and placed on the Manly trade. *Royal Alfred* and *Breadalbane* formed the basis of the Manly ferry service for the next 10 years. In 1874 the first vessel built specifically for the Manly route, the propeller-powered *Manly*, entered service, but only served five years and was frequently used as a tug.

On 23 January 1877 the Brighton & Manly Steam Ferry Co. was reorganised and became the Port Jackson Steam Boat Co. Ltd, the first limited liability ferry company to be formed in Sydney. Its initial fleet consisted of the paddlers *Phantom, Breadalbane, Goolwa, Cobre* and *Royal Alfred*, as well as the screw steamer *Manly*, but this was immediately increased by the purchase from Brisbane of the *Emu*. Imported in sections from Britain in 1865, the 270-gross-ton *Emu* was owned by the Queensland Steam Navigation Co., running mainly on the Brisbane River, but was sold

*Brightside*, formerly named *Emu*, is shown here as a cargo boat. (GA)

when the railway line to Ipswich was completed. *Emu* was similar to the earlier vessels on the run, having a small central structure with limited covered accommodation, but could carry up to 800 passengers. In September 1887, after 10 years as *Emu*, she was renamed *Brightside* and is best remembered as such.

In 1878 the *Phantom* and the *Goolwa* were sold, and two new vessels were added to the Port Jackson Co. fleet. The first was a tug, the *Commodore*, which was sometimes used on weekends and public holidays as a ferry. The second

*Brighton* was the finest of all the Manly service paddle ferries.

vessel was quite different, a 314-gross-ton passenger ferry named *Fairlight*. Built in Scotland, *Fairlight* made the long haul to Australia under steam and sail, departing Glasgow on 14 August 1878 and voyaging via Suez to arrive safely in Sydney on 2 November, having come through several storms unscathed. *Fairlight* was a welcome addition to the Manly service, being 171 feet (52 m) long and capable of carrying 950 passengers. The vessel introduced a new standard of comfort to the service, with cushioned seats in pleasant, carpeted saloons instead of the wooden benches and open decks of her predecessors, and remained a popular ferry on the route for the next 30 years.

The Manly passenger service was now being maintained by the *Fairlight* and *Emu*, supported by the *Royal Alfred*, and the *Commodore* in peak periods. In the early 1880s six return trips were being operated daily from Circular Quay, with a stop at Woolloomooloo. At weekends and on public holidays, a more frequent service was provided. For night arrivals at Manly, a watchman had to stand at the end of the pier with a red light, to guide the ferries in. In 1881 the Port Jackson Steam Boat Co. Ltd was reconstituted as the Port Jackson Steamship Co. Ltd.

More and more people were settling in the Manly area, and its popularity as an excursion and holiday destination was booming. As a result, a lucrative cargo trade had been established, as this was the only way in which goods could be supplied to the area. The Port Jackson Co. used their older vessels in this capacity, though their passenger boats also carried cargo as well. At the time there were complaints from passengers that the cargo seemed more important than they were. The *Breadalbane* had been reduced to the cargo trade in 1871, and was sold for breaking-up in 1882.

The passenger business was growing so quickly that another, larger ferry was needed to cater for demand. An order was placed with T.B. Seath & Co., of Rutherglen in Scotland, for the construction of an iron-hulled paddle-steamer, 220 feet (67 m) long, which was launched on 14 December 1882 and named the *Brighton*. Fitted with a

160-horsepower two-cylinder compound diagonal oscillating surface-condensing steam-engine, with four horizontal coal-fired boilers, she achieved over 15 knots on trials. Although designed to have no masts, for the delivery voyage to Australia *Brighton* was fitted with two temporary masts, schooner rigged, though the voyage was to be made under steam.

The delivery voyage of the *Brighton* went anything but smoothly. Leaving Glasgow on 2 June 1883, she went first to Malta, where, for reasons unknown, Captain Roderick left the ship and the chief officer, Thomas Japp, took over command. Her next coaling stop was Aden, but crossing the Indian Ocean *Brighton* was besieged by wild monsoonal weather for eight days. Huge seas crashed onto the vessel, smashing part of a deckhouse, ripping away protective planking to break nearly all the windows on one side and causing internal damage to furniture and fittings. Eventually *Brighton* staggered into Colombo, where she stayed two days, coaling and repairing. After further coaling stops at Singapore and Sourabaya, which she departed on 4 August, *Brighton* again encountered monsoonal storms hitting her head-on. Huge seas rolled down the decks, flooding all the accommodation and even getting into the stokehold. The strong headwinds further impeded her progress and coal supplies began to run very low. Unable to raise her sails in the bad weather, the crew resorted to burning cabin doors, protective planking and even the ship's woodwork to keep going, managing to reach Thursday Island on 16 August. With a full load of coal, *Brighton* set off again but did not take on a Torres Strait pilot. The seas were much calmer now and the vessel pushed on at top speed, but early in the morning of 20 August there was a bump and a jolt and she came to a sudden stop. *Brighton* had run aground on a sandbar, and fortunately was able to get off quite quickly and resume her voyage. After stopping at Townsville for more coal, *Brighton* continued her voyage, but two days later ran aground a second time on a sandbar, again refloating herself with no damage. Passing Cape Bustard

*Sophia Jane*, the first steamer to arrive in Australia from overseas. (GA)

*William the Fourth*, the first ocean going steamer to be built in Australia.

*Commodore* is shown here as originally built, with twin funnels. (GA)

*Fairlight* introduced new standards of comfort on the Manly service. (GA)

on 28 August, a hidden reef was suddenly sighted right ahead and only an emergency stop saved the vessel from running aground yet again. Finally, early in the morning of Saturday, 1 September 1883, *Brighton* steamed through Sydney Heads, her 89-day voyage over.

The *Brighton* was a magnificent vessel of 417 gross tons, being similar in size to the modern Freshwater-class ferries employed on the route today. She was double-ended, which greatly enhanced her manoeuvrability, and had an iron hull with a wooden superstructure, and two funnels. The bridge amidships was originally open, with only a canvas awning for protection, but this was later enclosed. The top deck was also open, and also had canvas awnings. Below was the main deck, which comprised three saloons, including one for ladies, and a smoking room amidships, all furnished with plush velvet-upholstered lounges. The outside seating still comprised wooden benches. *Brighton* could carry a maximum of 1,137 passengers in summer, reduced to 885 in winter, and at weekends was often packed to capacity. She was an outstanding vessel, by far the favourite ship on the Manly route, in much the same way as the *South Steyne* would be over half a century later.

The addition of the *Brighton* seemed to bring another increase in passenger demand. The *Royal Alfred* was sold in 1885 and the existing fleet could not cope with the demand, so another new vessel was ordered. Instead of going overseas, the order was placed with Mort's Dock Co. at Balmain, who built the smaller, iron-hulled *Narrabeen*, of 239 gross tons. Entering service in August 1886, she proved to be an excellent seaboat, but was really too small for the Manly service. *Narrabeen* was the last paddlewheel vessel to be built for the Manly service.

*Narrabeen* operated with the *Brighton*, the *Fairlight* and the *Emu*, which was renamed *Brightside* in 1887. The accommodation on these vessels was divided into two classes, saloon and second. During the 1880s the fares began to rise, the saloon-class fare being 2s. return, while second-class was 1s. 6d. Passengers complained bitterly about the high fares

being charged, and the second-class fare was reduced to 1s., but in May 1892 it rose again to the previous level.

In 1893 a rival firm was formed, the Manly Co-operative Steam Ferry Co., which chartered two propeller ferries and placed them on the Manly route. The fare charged was 6d. return, which was immediately matched by the Port Jackson Co. A period of intense rivalry followed, with races between ferries, and even missiles being thrown at the opposition. Passengers flocked to the ferries to take advantage of the low fares, so many at weekends that timetables were abandoned as ferries departed as soon as they were full. Neither firm was making any money out of the battle, and on 15 May 1896 they amalgamated to form the Port Jackson Co-operative Steamship Co.

The *Brighton* was still the pride of the Manly fleet, assisted by the *Brightside, Fairlight* and *Narrabeen*, but in 1896 the propeller-driven *Manly* joined the trade. She proved to be a real flyer, making the voyage to Manly in just 22 minutes, while the paddlers took over half an hour.

The career of the *Brighton* almost came to a sensational end in 1900. On 7 August she left Circular Quay at 10.30 p.m. on her last run to Manly for the day, with only 40 passengers aboard. After rounding Bradleys Head, the lights of an inbound steamer were sighted in the western channel and the captain of the *Brighton* prepared for a port to port pass. However, he then realised that he had insufficient room to perform this manoeuvre and ordered his engines reversed. The steamer carried on and crashed into the *Brighton*, forward of the sponson on the port side. As the ships lay locked together, some passengers scrambled onto the deck of the steamer, while *Brighton* lowered her lifeboats with more passengers.

When the ships separated, the *Brighton* was in a bad way, taking on a huge amount of water. Aware his vessel was sinking, Captain Sutterfield called for full speed ahead and managed to run the *Brighton* ashore in Chowder Bay, where the stern eventually sank, though the bow was held firm above the water. The steamer with which *Brighton* collided,

*Narrabeen*, the last paddle ferry built for the Manly service. (GA)

the collier *Brunner* inbound from Newcastle, suffered a crumpled bow but was in no danger. She took on board all the survivors from the *Brighton* and transferred them to the *Narrabeen*, which took them to Manly. The *Brighton* was refloated, repaired, and soon returned to service. In 1901 the *Brighton* came to the rescue when the *Manly* broke down near North Head in heavy seas and was in danger of being wrecked on the rocks. The *Brighton*, on a regular run from Sydney, managed to send a towrope across and pull the other vessel to safety.

The Port Jackson Co. had purchased considerable land holdings in the Manly area, and in the early years of this century offered it for sale. As an inducement, buyers were offered a free pass on the ferries for five years if they built a house worth more than £1,000. Fares were reduced to their lowest ever level, 4*d.* for adults, 2*d.* for children, and the ferries were full, especially at weekends. In 1908 the master of the *Brighton* was fined for overcrowding his ferry.

In 1901 the Port Jackson Co. embarked on the construction of a series of new, propeller-powered ferries for the Manly service, which gradually displaced the paddlers. In 1902 the *Brightside* was reduced to a cargo ship, then disposed of in 1908. To replace her, the *Fairlight* had her accommodation removed in 1908 and served as a cargo ship only until 1912, when she too was sold. The *Narrabeen* was rebuilt as a cargo carrier in 1911 and continued on the trade until 1917, by which time she was the last paddler operating between Sydney and Manly. The magnificent *Brighton*, still the largest vessel on the route, remained a passenger carrier throughout her career on Sydney Harbour, but in 1916 she was withdrawn from service and reduced to a hulk. In this capacity she was moved to Port Stephens, and her remains can still be seen in Salamander Bay.

# The Hawkesbury River

A short distance north of the entrance to Sydney Harbour lies another large inlet, which was named Broken Bay in 1770 by Captain Cook. However, Cook did not enter the bay and it was not until March 1788 that the first white man, Governor Arthur Phillip, seeking suitable land for agriculture to support the first residents of Sydney, entered the bay. During the course of this expedition he entered the lower reaches of a river that emptied into Broken Bay. The following year, Phillip returned, followed the river upstream for a considerable distance, and named it after Charles Jenkinson, first Earl of Liverpool and the first Baron Hawkesbury. Phillip found a site with good soil in a region he named Green Hills, which developed into the present-day towns of Richmond and Windsor. A settlement was established in the area to supply food to the struggling penal colony on the shores of Sydney Harbour. Phillip described the Hawkesbury as 'this noble river, three hundred to eight hundred feet in breadth, was from soundings taken navigable for the largest ships to the foot of Richmond Hill'.

The Hawkesbury River below Windsor flowed through rugged country and the settlement's sole contact with Sydney for many years was by water. Foodstuffs grown along the river were transported to Sydney by sailing ship, but the river was prone to major floods and silting.

By June 1795 there were 400 people settled along the Hawkesbury. Green Hills and Parramatta were connected by a rough bush track, which was impassable in wet weather, so the settlers remained dependent on water transport for their livelihood. For the next 40 years this was carried out solely by sailing vessels, but in 1832 the first steamer entered the Hawkesbury River. This was the paddle-steamer *William the Fourth*, the first ocean-going steamship built in Australia. Although intended to operate between Sydney and the Hunter River, Joseph Grose, who owned the vessel, was always on the lookout for other profitable destinations. On 24 July 1832 the *William the Fourth* made a voyage up the Hawkesbury to Green Hills, but this was not the start of a regular service—the vessel did return occasionally over the next few years, but the sailing ships still dominated the Hawkesbury trade.

It was not until February 1855 that a second steamer went up the Hawkesbury to Windsor. The *Huntress* was an 86-gross-ton wooden vessel built in 1853 for ferry service on Sydney Harbour. She left Sydney on a Thursday afternoon, but was only under steam for 13½ hours, relying on sail for most of the voyage. Her arrival in Windsor was described in the *Sydney Morning Herald* in the following way:

> Last Friday afternoon several gunshots were heard fired in quick succession from the neighbourhood of Thompson Square, and numbers of men, women and children, were seen hurrying towards the river. What was the cause of the consternation? Nothing more or less than the anxiously looked for steamer, the arrival of the *Huntress*, walking the water of our noble Hawkesbury, like a thing of life.

The paper went on to comment that it was 'amusing to see the excitement amongst the inhabitants, many of whom had never beheld such a sight before'.

The voyage of the *Huntress* excited interest in the use of steamers on the Hawkesbury River on a regular basis, and on 9 May 1856 a meeting was called at the Fitzroy Hotel in Windsor for the purpose of 'taking into consideration the desirableness of establishing a company for navigating the Hawkesbury by steam'. The convenor of the meeting, Mr R.S. Ross, already had a steamer under construction, which could be in service within three months. Despite an enthusiastic response to the meeting, sufficient capital was not raised to form a company, and the steamer did not enter the river trade.

In 1857 William Marshall attempted to establish a regular service between Sydney and Windsor, using the paddle-steamer *Star*. This was another Sydney ferry, built in 1852. The *Sydney Morning Herald* of 8 August 1857 carried a report that:

> taking advantage of the increased volume of water upon the Hawkesbury, occasioned by the recent flood, the paddle steamer *Star* made a trip upwards on Sunday afternoon last as far as North Richmond. There was a considerable number of passengers on board, who enjoyed the novelty of the excursion amazingly, as we believe it is the first time that ever the Hawkesbury was navigated by steam past Windsor.

The venture was short-lived, as when the *Star* was returning to Sydney it ran aground in Broken Bay after mistaking its bearings, and was wrecked, with the loss of one life.

In 1858 William Marshall built another paddle-steamer, the *New Moon*, specifically for the Hawkesbury trade. The vessel was fitted out to carry passengers as well as cargo and was advertised in September 1858 to depart Sydney every Tuesday for Windsor, leaving there every Friday on the return trip. Unfortunately the trade did not come up to expectations, and two months later the service was terminated.

Another paddle-steamer to ply the Hawkesbury was named *The Brothers*. Built on the Colo River by John and William Jones, she was owned by the Hall family and traded between Wisemans Ferry and Windsor prior to the 1867 flood. Over the next 20 years a variety of paddle-steamers, mostly former Sydney Harbour ferries, were used on services to the Hawkesbury. Among such vessels used were the *Phantom*, *Alma*, *Sir John Young*, *Wonga* and *Pelican*.

A succession of floods caused major silting problems along the upper reaches of the Hawkesbury, which adversely affected the river trade, so that by 1886 very few ships were able to reach Windsor, and those that did were of such a small size their arrival was no longer reported in the papers. By this time most of the steamers still operating on the river were propeller-driven and only ran from Windsor to Broken Bay, where cargo and passengers were transhipped to larger vessels for the coastal passage to Sydney.

One steamer running on the Hawkesbury at this time was the *Young Charlie*, owned by John Barden, of Windsor.

The vessel would make two or three trips a week and excursions at weekends. Although a popular boat, the *Young Charlie* was not large enough to cater for demand, but had difficulty navigating the river due to the numerous sandbars. Barden realised that he needed a larger steamer, but with a shallower draught, if he was to maintain a viable service. He ordered a paddle-steamer to be built by W.S. Lockhart on the banks of South Creek, just below Windsor. Launched on 15 January 1886, the vessel was named *St Albans*, being 52 gross tons, 76 feet (23.1 m) long with a beam of 16 feet (4.8 m) and drawing just 2.8 feet (0.84 m). The boiler and 18-horsepower steam-engine installed in the *St Albans* came out of the old *Alma*, which had been a much smaller vessel, built in Sydney in 1855 and broken up in 1891.

While the *St Albans* was larger than the *Young Charlie*, she was severely underpowered and could not match the older vessel for speed. The hull was squared off, without rounded bilges, which would have given extra strength, and the vessel was rather unflatteringly described as being 'simply a square box'.

Barden had hoped that, by building a larger vessel, he would retain the business of the farmers and orchardists along the river, but later in 1886 the newly formed Hawkesbury Steam Navigation Co. built a fine propeller steamer, the *Hawkesbury*, which was shallow enough to run from Windsor to Sydney. The new boat quickly claimed the majority of the fruit and produce business, at the expense of the *St Albans*. The paddle-steamer struggled on for several more years, but then was abandoned on the river bank near Windsor. The Hawkesbury River trade was subsequently

Sternwheeler *General Gordon*, built to an American design. (GA)

dominated by propeller-powered vessels until it died out in the 1930s.

During the 1880s the railway connection between Sydney and Newcastle, 160 kilometres to the north, was under construction, and by 1886 it had almost been completed. The only gap was the crossing of the Hawkesbury River, which would require the construction of a long bridge in a major feat of engineering. To enable a railway service to be operated, it would be necessary in the interim to operate a ferry between the two ends of the railway line. In 1886 Tom Davis of Terrigal, near Gosford, began constructing a large stern-wheel steamer for this purpose on behalf of Captain Sinclair Murray, who would be both owner and master of the vessel.

Named *General Gordon*, the vessel was quite imposing, being 117 feet (35.66 m) long, with a beam of 25.6 feet (9.14 m) and a draught of 5.4 feet (2.54 m), measured 164 gross tons, and was powered by a 56-horsepower steam-engine located at the stern, while the boiler was positioned a little forward of midships. There were two decks to carry several hundred passengers, but no cabins or other facilities, as the run was done in daylight.

On 15 August 1887 the *General Gordon* made its first run across the Hawkesbury. At that time the northern end of the railway line terminated at Gosford, from where the steamer carried the passengers to the southern bank of the Hawkesbury River, near present-day Brooklyn. This was quite a long trip, lasting several hours, but during the next year the Woy Woy tunnel was completed and the railway line extended south from Gosford to Mullet Creek. This greatly shortened the distance *General Gordon* had to operate, as the trip took less than an hour. The rail bridge was opened on 1 May 1889, which eliminated the necessity for a water connection.

The *General Gordon* was subsequently used for excursion work along the Hawkesbury River and on Broken Bay. These trips were run in conjunction with the railway service from Sydney, passengers detraining at the Hawkesbury River station in Brooklyn, from where it was a short walk to the wharf. *General Gordon* would then carry them upriver to Wisemans Ferry and back, or downriver and across Broken Bay to Newport.

Occasionally one-way excursions up the river to Windsor were also run, advertised like this one in 1890: 'Sat. 1/11/90 passengers will depart Sydney on a train for the Hawkesbury River at 8.20 a.m. On arrival the ship will take passengers to Windsor connecting with the 8.07 p.m. train for Sydney. On Tues 4/11/90 10.48 a.m. from Windsor to connect with the 7.45 p.m. train to Sydney'. The *General Gordon* made three excursions of this nature in 1890.

For almost 20 years the *General Gordon* continued to operate between 30 and 40 excursions each year, the last being in April 1907, following which the vessel was laid up. In 1909 it was sold to Edward C. Windybank, who lived on Cowan Creek and hired out boats, as well as running a ferry service from Bobbin Head to Newport. Windybank was a shrewd businessman who saw that Cowan had a potential for holidaymakers and fishermen. He cut the *General Gordon* in half, to form two houseboats. He later cut the two halves in two and based the sections in a part of Cowan Creek that is known today as Houseboat Bay. The skeletal remains of one of these houseboats can still be seen in Waratah Bay, where it was abandoned many years ago.

# 3 New South Wales Coastal Trades

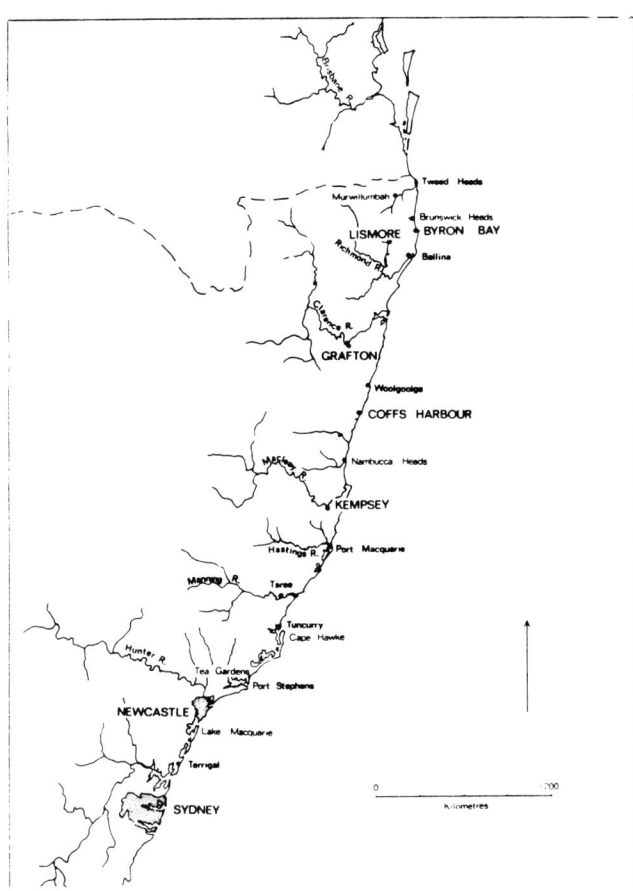

Map of NSW North Coast (BP)

The first coastal steamship services to be established in Australia were those from Sydney to the north and south of New South Wales. These can be divided into three distinct routes—to the Hunter River, the North Coast and the South Coast. All these routes were pioneered by paddle-steamers, in particular *William the Fourth*, and were instrumental in the opening up and development of New South Wales.

The most historic coastal route in Australia was established in 1831, linking Sydney with the Hunter River, 160 kilometres to the north, where large deposits of coal had been discovered. The main settlement on the Hunter was Newcastle, at the mouth of the river, but major settlements also sprang up further upriver, particularly at Green Hills, later known as Morpeth. To serve this route, a special type of vessel was required—one capable of operating in the open

ocean, but small enough to negotiate the bends of the Hunter River. For many years the Hunter River route was the most important in New South Wales, but with the construction of a railway connection between Sydney and Newcastle, the sea trade died away. However, this was the last major trade route in Australia to utilise paddle-steamers, the last being withdrawn in 1928. Further north, the penal settlement of Port Macquarie began accepting free settlers in 1830, and five years later the first steamer services were established. As further settlements became established on other northern rivers, so the necessity to provide connections with Sydney grew, and a flourishing trade developed. Paddle-steamers played an important part in the North Coast trade, but were eventually superseded by propeller-driven vessels.

The South Coast of New South Wales was particularly difficult for shipping, there being few rivers and a lack of safe anchorages. The first services were to the Illawarra region in the mid-1830s, but they never developed to the extent of those to the north. Again, it was paddle-steamers that provided the link for many years, but they were almost all gone by the turn of the century. With the development of rail and road links, the shipping services along the New South Wales coast declined, and today there are none. The once-bustling little harbours and wharves are either gone, or only used by fishing boats and pleasure craft.

## The Hunter River Trade

At 7.13 a.m. on 13 June 1831, the paddle-steamer *Sophia Jane* departed her Sydney wharf, bound for the Hunter River, arriving at King's Wharf, Newcastle at 3.13 p.m. The vessel then proceeded further up the Hunter River to Green Hills (now Morpeth) in three and a half hours. This was the first commercial voyage performed by a steam vessel in Australian waters. The *Sydney Gazette*, reporting on the voyage, stated:

> the steam boat *Sophia Jane*, which sailed for Hunter's River early on Sunday morning, arrived at Newcastle in the short space of eight hours, to the astonishment of the good folks in that neighbourhood, who crowded on board her, examining every part with the greatest minuteness. Many of them accompanied her on a trip which she made to Green Hills. She sailed again from Hunter's River on

Wednesday afternoon at one o'clock, and was moored along side Campbell's wharf at eight bells.

The return trip had taken just 7 hours and 40 minutes.

The route between Sydney and the Hunter River was the only one that offered sufficient trade to support a regular steamship service, as the area was developing rapidly as an agricultural and industrial centre. The discovery of coal had resulted in the establishment of several villages, such as Waratah, Lambton and Merewether. In 1811 the population of the region had numbered just 124, but by 1817 it had risen to 1,817, and over the next decade many new settlers had arrived. In 1830 a Sydney merchant, Joseph Grose, ordered the construction of a paddle-steamer for the trade by Marshall & Lowe on the Williams River, a tributary of the Hunter.

The hull of the new steamer was built of flooded gum, considered to be the best timber available in Australia for shipbuilding. Launched on 14 November 1831, the vessel was named *William the Fourth*, in honour of the reigning monarch. The vessel was then schooner-rigged, and sailed to Sydney, where her machinery was installed. An 18-horsepower single-cylinder, jet-condensing low-pressure type engine, built by W. Fawcett of Liverpool, was installed by A.L. Patterson of the Phoenix Foundry. The engine was 14 feet (4.2 m) long, 7 feet (2.1 m) wide and 6 feet (1.8 m) high, while each paddlewheel contained 10 paddle boards. Trials were run on Sydney Harbour during the third week of January 1832. Internally, the vessel had been fitted up in 'the most comfortable manner'. Her accommodation consisted of a large cabin forward with bunks for 18 men, and a smaller cabin aft with bunks for 12 women. There was a single, rather small cargo hold, but deck cargo could also be carried.

On 27 January 1832, at 7.30 p.m., *William the Fourth*, described in the *Sydney Gazette* as 'that beautiful specimen of colonial enterprise', left Barker's wharf in Darling Harbour on her maiden voyage to the Hunter, passing through the Heads in 44 minutes and arriving in Newcastle at 6.a.m. the next day. *Sophia Jane* and *William the Fourth* shared the Hunter trade, making one return trip per week. *Sophia Jane* generally left Sydney on Fridays, and made the return journey on Wednesday, while *William the Fourth* departed Sydney on Monday, and Newcastle on Friday. The vessels used to visit several ports along the river, the *Sophia Jane* being the first to go as far as Maitland.

An unexpected effect of the introduction of steamships on this route was a decline in the state of the road between Sydney and Newcastle, it being reported that 'the road between Wiseman's Ferry and the Chain of Ponds is at present in a shocking bad state, the steam navigation of the Hunter having almost superseded the use of the road, which has therefore been allowed to fall into decay'.

The regularity of the sailings by the two steamers was occasionally upset by mechanical problems or bad weather conditions, it being recorded that 'the steamer *Sophia Jane* was compelled to bring up in Watson's Bay, when outward bound, on Friday night, owing to a heavy sea running between the Heads. She started on Saturday morning for

her destination', and 'the delay of the *Sophia Jane*, last week, was occasioned by heavy gales from the southward, with a head sea, which forced her to put into Broken Bay'. During 1832 the *Sophia Jane* increased her schedule to two return trips per week, and the papers commented: 'we hope the present competition in steam will have the effect of reducing the fares. At present they are too high.' In fact, no sooner had the steamers entered service than there were complaints about the fares being charged, despite the convenience of a reliable schedule. Sometimes public meetings were held to discuss the subject, which on occasion resulted in calls to form a new company to provide cheaper competition. Usually such organisations foundered without trace within a short time, but in May 1833 the Hunter River Packet Association was formed, with a capital of £10,000. They placed an order with Marshall & Lowe for the construction of a new paddle-steamer, to operate between the Hunter and Sydney.

Before the new steamer was completed, a third steamer was placed on the route in 1834. This was the *Tamar*, which had been built in Britain to the order of the Tamar Steam Navigation Co., of Launceston. The *Tamar* was the first paddle-steamer ordered from Britain to actually undertake the voyage to Australia, though she did it under sail, arriving in Launceston in September 1834. It was soon apparent that the vessel could not succeed in operations along the Tamar River, so on 5 December 1834 she arrived in Sydney, where she was offered for sale.

The purchaser of *Tamar* was one J.T.S. Wilson, who immediately placed her in the Hunter trade, in competition with *William the Fourth* and *Sophia Jane*. On 13 January 1835 *Tamar* and *Sophia Jane* came into collision, which resulted in a lengthy court battle. The arrival of the *Tamar* had a marked effect on the operation of both the pioneer steamers on the route. The *Sophia Jane* made several voyages to ports south of Sydney during 1834, while the *William the Fourth* was withdrawn altogether from the Hunter trade. She became the first steamship to visit Port Macquarie, but spent most of the remaining years of her career in Australia running to ports south of Sydney.

The vessel being built for the Hunter River Packet Association was launched late in 1835, and named *Ceres*. As with the *William the Fourth*, the engines had been ordered from England, so *Ceres* also had to sail to Sydney for their installation. The vessel arrived there before the machinery, which was brought out on the *Mary Sharp* early in 1836. *Ceres* made her first trial trip on Sydney Harbour on 21 February, and soon after joined the Hunter trade. Unlike other vessels of her day, the boxes which enclosed the paddlewheels did not extend over the side, but were enclosed by the decks. Accommodation comprised one large cabin for gentlemen, with 20 berths, a ladies cabin with 12 berths, steerage quarters forward for 20 passengers, and an unusual feature, six cabins for families.

*Ceres* was well received by the residents of the Hunter region, and proved to be a major competitor for the *Sophia Jane* and the *Tamar*. Whether the three ships could have survived in the trade for any length of time was never known, as the *Ceres* was wrecked after a mere six months in service. The steamer had left Newcastle on the afternoon of Monday, 29 August 1836, but soon after she struck a rock called Bullee Noglen, near Bird Island. With her bow badly damaged, the captain ordered the vessel run ashore, but the fast rising water extinguished the fires in her boilers. The ship's boat could only hold about a quarter of the 50 persons on board, and it had to make four trips to the shore. The final group of survivors were rescued from the rigging, as the *Ceres* settled in four fathoms, with only her masts showing. The loss of the *Ceres* also brought about the collapse of the Hunter River Packet Association.

From 1835 to 1837, the Hunter service was maintained by just two steamers, the *Sophia Jane* and the *Tamar*. The *James Watt*, second steamer to arrive in Australia from Britain, reached Sydney on 18 February 1837 and was placed on the Hunter service, but proved highly unsuccessful. This vessel was then tried on intercolonial trades, becoming the first steamer to enter Port Phillip Bay, and later the first steamship to visit Moreton Bay. She was used occasionally on the Hunter service, but overall was a complete failure on the Australian coast, being broken up in 1847.

Some confusion was caused in Sydney by the arrival from Britain, on 20 January 1838, of another paddle-steamer named *William the Fourth*. This vessel had been built in 1830 in London for work on English rivers, and made the long voyage to Australia under sail, seeking a buyer. She was bought by Joseph Grose, who already owned the Australian-built *William the Fourth*. Under the regulations of the day, it was not permissible to rename a ship, so the newcomer was referred to as the *King William the Fourth*. She was slightly larger than her Australian counterpart, and was placed in the Hunter River trade, but not with any great measure of success.

These three ships were then joined in 1838 by the second ocean-going steamer to be built in Australia, the *Maitland*. Owned by the noted shipping identity of the time, Edye Manning, who also had large landholdings south of Sydney, the *Maitland* was built in Darling Harbour, Sydney, by William Bourne, and was 103 feet (31.4 m) long. The *Maitland* had been intended to operate only to the Hunter, but on completion began making alternate trips to Morpeth and Wollongong.

With four ships on the route, the Hunter region was very well served, especially as each ship made two return trips per week. The *Tamar* and the *Sophia Jane* ran in direct competition, both leaving Sydney at 8 p.m. on Mondays and Thursdays. The *King William the Fourth* departed on Tuesdays and Fridays, while the *Maitland* took the Wednesday and Saturday sailings. The latter two vessels took it in turns to wait at Morpeth over the weekend, to run a service back to Sydney on Sunday nights. This type of schedule proved so successful it was followed by succeeding companies for the next half century.

In May 1839, when the Illawarra Steam Packet Co. was formed, in which Manning held a substantial interest, the *Maitland* was used almost exclusively on south coast services. Also in 1839, the *King William the Fourth* became the first steamer to enter the Clarence River, but in July the vessel

was wrecked on the notorious Oyster Bank, at the mouth of the Hunter River.

Edye Manning maintained his interest in the Hunter trade when, in 1840, he placed the new *Victoria* on the route. Following the wreck of the *Ceres*, her boilers and engine had been salvaged by Mr John Korff, though the boilers broke away in a heavy sea and were lost. Using the salvaged engine, Korff then built the *Victoria* at Raymond Terrace, and she was described in the *Sydney Morning Herald* as 'a splendid looking sea boat, length 157 feet, 24 feet between paddle boxes', with 'two watertight bulkheads carried from keel to deck'. The main cabin for gentlemen had 33 berths, the ladies' cabin 12, and there was also a six-berth family cabin. *Victoria* left Sydney on her maiden voyage to the Hunter on 20 May 1840, and was very well received, being the fastest vessel yet used on the service. Korff had claimed the vessel would be able to do 13 miles per hour, but she never did achieve this speed.

There continued to be great dissatisfaction with the service being provided between Sydney and the Hunter region. The historian Henry Stuart Russell wrote of a passage he took on the *Tamar*, which he described as 'a steam craft remarkable neither for size, symmetry nor civility'. He was much affected by 'the smell and presence of enormous cockroaches', and on arrival in Newcastle 'disembarked in front of a public house, called, I think, Alanby's, at a filthy kind of platform', though he was 'glad indeed to escape from the cockroaches'. On 1 August 1839 a meeting was convened in Sydney by John Eales to

> take into consideration a proposition for establishing a Steam Navigation company between Sydney and the Hunter River, with a view to obviating the great inconvenience and expense incurred from the present line of conveyance. It is requested that those gentlemen who feel interested in promoting this object will give their attendance.

The meeting resulted in the establishment of the Hunter's River Steam Navigation Co. They immediately ordered three iron-hulled paddle-steamers to be built in England, designed for the Hunter trade. In September 1839 the Illawarra Steam Packet Co. and the Brisbane Waters Steam Packet Co. merged to form the General Steam Navigation Co. Their initial fleet consisted of four ships, *Maitland*, *Sophia Jane*, *Tamar* and *William the Fourth*, which maintained services from Sydney to various destinations, the *Tamar* running to the Hunter.

The first two new vessels, named *Rose* and *Thistle*, were built at Poplar, on the Thames, by W. Fairburn & Co., and fitted with 100-horsepower side-lever jet-condensing steam engines. On trials, the *Rose* attained a speed of 12 miles per hour, and she left London on 31 October 1840 on her delivery voyage. Heavy weather in the Bay of Biscay forced her to divert to Lisbon, from where she continued under sail to Cape Town. The remainder of the voyage was made under sail and steam, arriving in Newcastle on 7 April 1841 after a passage lasting 158 days. There was much speculation as to which ship would prove to be the faster, the imported *Rose* or the locally built *Victoria*, and it was

*Rose*, pioneer steamship of the Hunter's River S.N. Co.

not long before the pair were racing between Sydney and Newcastle.

The first time the pair faced each other, on a trip from Newcastle, the *Victoria* won by 50 minutes. The *Sydney Morning Herald* of 21 April 1841 reported: 'leaving Newcastle the *Victoria* was two miles ahead, and kept so for several miles, when a northeaster sprang up and she set square sails; the *Rose* had none. The *Victoria* gradually gained three miles'. The *Rose* was reported to still have a dirty bottom from her delivery voyage, but once she had been scraped and painted the paper reported on 6 May 1841 that 'the *Rose* arrived before the *Victoria*'. In effect, there was very little difference in their speed, as both regularly made the trip in about eight hours.

The second of the new iron-hulled steamers, the *Thistle*, was completed in November 1840 and arrived in Sydney on 22 April 1841, after a voyage lasting 130 days. The engineers on the *Thistle* had heard about the competition between their sister ship and the *Victoria*, so they prepared well for their tilt at the opposition. They took three weeks to thoroughly overhaul the *Thistle* before she entered service, and increased the boiler pressure by three pounds per inch. On their first encounter with the *Victoria*, southbound for Newcastle, the *Thistle* was let go full out, and with a bone in her teeth came home an easy winner in the record time of 6 hours and 20 minutes. The *Rose* was then given a similar overhaul and increased boiler pressure, and was soon matching her sister's times.

The third of the new steamers for the Hunter's River Steam Navigation Co. was the *Shamrock*, built at Bristol. She was the same length, but slightly wider than the other pair, and arrived in Sydney after a 123-day voyage on 18 October 1841. She went into the Hunter River trade initially, but at the end of 1842 was transferred to a new route, from Sydney to Brisbane.

A fourth new steamer introduced to the Hunter trade at this time was the wooden-hulled *Sovereign*. Built for Joseph Grose by Chowne & Thompson at Pyrmont in Sydney, the vessel was fitted with the engine salvaged from the wrecked *King William the Fourth*.

With their three iron-hulled steamers, the Hunter's River Steam Navigation Co. completely dominated the Hunter trade. They were the finest vessels on the coast. The General Steam Navigation Co. found itself unable to compete, and

went out of business in November 1841. *Victoria*, so recently the pride of the colony, was also forced out of the trade, and in July 1842 she was dispatched to India looking for a buyer. This was the first instance of an Australian-built steamer going overseas. The brand-new *Sovereign* also could not maintain her place on the Hunter service, and was transferred to other routes. In 1842 Grose sold both the *Sovereign* and the *James Watt* to the Hunter's River Steam Navigation Co., and later they also purchased the *Tamar*, but mostly they were used on trades other than that to the Hunter.

The first decade of steam navigation in Australian waters had seen constant changes in the local shipping scene, as new vessels were placed in service at a regular rate. The Hunter trade had proved the most lucrative in Australia, along with Sydney Harbour ferry routes, and most of the vessels built locally or brought from overseas were placed in one of these trades. The depression that lasted from 1841 to 1843 affected the whole country, including shipping. In April 1843 the *Sydney Morning Herald* reported that nine steamships were laid up in Sydney, but by the end of the year conditions were beginning to improve.

The dominance of the vessels operated by the Hunter's River Steam Navigation Co. proved so great that by the end of 1843 they were in complete control of the services from Sydney to the Hunter, Brisbane and Melbourne. However, in 1844 Edye Manning bought the veteran *Sophia Jane* and placed her back on the Hunter River trade. Although her machinery was still sound, the hull, built of Baltic pine, was waterlogged. In 1845 Manning arranged for the *Sophia Jane* to be broken up and her engines placed in a new ship built in Sydney, the *Phoenix*. When this vessel entered service in 1846, it was to the northern rivers of New South Wales, not the Hunter.

Despite the success enjoyed by the Hunter's River Navigation Co., there were those who were dissatisfied with the service they were providing the Hunter. Eventually the shareholders split into two camps. One group, no doubt comprising residents of the Hunter region, claimed that the company, having been founded to serve the Hunter, should limit itself to only that, while the other group felt the company should trade wherever a profit could be made. The matter eventually ended up in the courts, where the 'expansionist' second group were victorious. On 30 June 1851 the affairs of the Hunter's River Steam Navigation Co. were wound up, and the following day the Australasian Steam Navigation Co. took over the business as a going concern.

In 1852, the service being provided to the Hunter region was very poor, with only two ships operating, the *Rose* and the *Thistle*. Once again the residents felt compelled to take matters into their own hands, and mass meetings were convened. These resulted in the formation at Maitland on 16 June 1852 of the Hunter River New Steam Navigation Co., familiarly known as the New Co., whose intention was to provide a service between Sydney and the Hunter only. They followed the lead of the group who formed the earlier company, and ordered three new paddle-steamers to be built at Greenock in Scotland for the Hunter trade.

The first of the iron-hulled steamers ordered by the New Co., the *Hunter*, was launched in January 1854 and made the voyage to Australia under sail. Having been fitted out with paddles in Sydney, the *Hunter* ran trials in April 1854, then began operating to the Hunter. In December 1854 the other two vessels being built for the New Co., the *Williams* and the *Paterson*, were also completed, and joined the Hunter trade in 1855. The new trio were slightly larger and faster than the *Rose* and *Thistle*, now operated by the ASN Co., and proved very popular with travellers. This threat to their dominance brought a swift response from the ASN Co., which obtained two new vessels for the trade.

The first vessel to be added to the Hunter service by the ASN Co. was the iron-hulled *Collaroy*, which was bought while on its delivery voyage to Australia. The story of the construction of the *Collaroy* actually goes back to 1851, when J. Thacker & Partners took delivery of a paddle-steamer named *Clarence*, which they intended to operate to the northern rivers of New South Wales. However, when the *Clarence* arrived in Sydney, the owners received an offer for the ship, reported to be twice the amount she had cost to build, from Tasmanian interests, which was accepted with alacrity. The enormous financial gain induced Thacker and his partners to order another paddle-steamer from Britain, which they also hoped to sell as advantageously as possible. *Collaroy* was completed late in 1853 and was on her delivery voyage to Australia when the ASN Co. made an offer of £20,000, which was accepted. On arrival in Sydney, *Collaroy* was immediately placed in the Hunter trade, where she was the largest vessel yet to be employed on the route.

To partner *Collaroy*, the ASN Co. took delivery of a paddle-steamer built to their order, the *Illalong*, which was the native name for the Morpeth area. She was longer than the *Collaroy* and soon became a great favourite on the Hunter trade.

With the ASN Co. operating four ships, the New Co. decided to add a fourth vessel to their fleet. They obtained the *Fenella*, which had been built in Britain in 1846 but sent to Australia in 1855 seeking a buyer. Initially she was placed in service between Melbourne and Launceston, but in June 1856 the *Fenella* was purchased by the New Co., being of similar size to the trio built for the company.

The establishment of the Hunter River New Steam Navigation Co. resulted in a fierce fare war with the ASN Co. As one company reduced its rates, so the other would undercut them, until both were operating at absurdly uneconomic levels. In October 1855, the New Co. reduced the Sydney–Morpeth first saloon fare to 10*s.*. The ASN complained bitterly, but followed suit, then six weeks later reduced their first saloon fare to just 7*s.* The fore-cabin fare was also reduced, from 5*s.* to a mere 3*s.* 6*d.* from 1 January 1856.

During 1856 the companies agreed on a truce. Instead of vessels running in direct competition against each other, leaving Sydney at night and Morpeth in the morning, it was agreed that there would be a morning and evening departure from both ports, each company taking a month in turn in roster. Fares were also restored to a more economically realistic level, and while this may not have

pleased the passengers, it resulted in prosperity for both companies.

With eight ships in service, the Hunter region enjoyed what was really a surplus of tonnage on the route to Sydney, a situation that could not last for long. The changes began in 1858, when the ASN Co. withdrew the *Rose*, and later the *Thistle*, from the Hunter trade. The *Thistle* had made over 1,300 trips between Sydney and the Hunter by the time she was withdrawn in July 1859, but only five months later she was wrecked on the Victorian coast. The New Co. also disposed of one of their ships, the *Hunter*, which was sold and began trading to the south coast of New South Wales. However, the New Co. also placed an order for a new vessel, to be the largest and fastest paddle-steamer yet placed in service to the Hunter. The ordering of this vessel was the cause of some dispute between the directors and shareholders, as there were many who thought there was no need for such a large ship.

Built in Scotland, the new ship was named *City of Newcastle* and she left the Clyde on 2 May 1859 on her delivery voyage, which was made under steam and sail. Arriving in Sydney on 24 September, *City of Newcastle* entered the Hunter trade the following month, at which time the *Fenella* was withdrawn by the New Co., and sold. The *City of Newcastle* soon proved to be the fastest steamer in the colony, and enjoyed a successful career on the Hunter trade. Unfortunately, the operations of the New Co. were thrown into disarray when the *Williams* and *Paterson* collided near Raymond Terrace. Both vessels were quite badly damaged, and out of service for several months undergoing repair.

The New Co. soon ordered another vessel to be built in Britain, which was named *Morpeth*. Delivered to Australia in 1861, she was even larger than the *City of Newcastle*, being 527 gross tons and having a length of 213 feet (64.9 m). Once the *Morpeth* was settled into service, the *Williams* was sold to the rival ASN Co., who used her mainly on the Queensland coast.

The Hunter River New Steam Navigation Co. was now the dominant operator on the Hunter trade, with their magnificent large steamers *City of Newcastle* and *Morpeth*, assisted by the *Paterson*, while the ASN Co. was running the *Illalong* and *Collaroy*. As new ships were added to the ASN fleet, they were being placed on inter-colonial trades, and the Hunter service was relegated to secondary importance. In 1863 a small paddle-steamer, the 109-gross-ton *Bolwarra*, built at Pyrmont, was placed on the Hunter route, but only carried cargo. However, in 1864 a new passenger vessel was built for the trade by the ASN Co., the *Cawarra*.

Of similar size to the *Morpeth*, the *Cawarra* did not really increase the ASN representation on the Hunter route, as she replaced the *Illalong*, which was sold to the Illawarra Steam Navigation Co. in June 1864. Unfortunately, the *Cawarra* was destined to enjoy a very brief career. On 12 July 1866, on a voyage from Sydney, *Cawarra* encountered a severe gale, and ran aground on the notorious Oyster Bank while trying to enter Newcastle. The vessel was completely wrecked, and only one of the 61 persons on board survived. It was the worst wreck ever recorded in the Newcastle area.

*Morpeth* served the Hunter trade from 1861 to 1888. (GA)

To replace the *Cawarra*, the ASN added the *Coonanbara* to the Hunter service in 1867. The pace of change in the coastal shipping trades was so fast that, while *Coonanbara* had been the crack ship on the inter-colonial trades when brought out in 1862, just five years later she had been totally outclassed by newer tonnage. There was also an increasing number of propeller-driven vessels appearing on the coastal trades, which were proving more suited to maintaining regular schedules in all weathers. *Coonanbara* was much larger than the New Co. ships, being 900 gross tons, and 223 feet (68 m) long.

In a bid to match the *Coonanbara*, the New Co. placed an order in Britain for yet another new paddle steamer. Built by McCulloch Patterson & Co. at Port Glasgow, the vessel was completed in December 1870 and named *Maitland*. She was 880 gross tons, and 232 feet (70.7 m) long, and soon became the most popular ship on the Hunter service. Once she was settled in service, the New Co. disposed of the last of the inaugural trio of steamers, the *Paterson*, though she remained at Newcastle, serving as a tug. In 1872 the *Paterson* was sold to New Zealand owners, only to be wrecked in July 1874.

The ASN responded to the arrival of *Maitland* by transferring another of their older inter-colonial traders to the Hunter run. The 633-gross-ton *City of Brisbane* dated from 1863, and had spent the first years of her career operating along the east coast of Australia between Melbourne and Queensland ports. She was destined to be the last steamer the ASN Co. would place on the Hunter trade.

In the early 1870s, the Hunter region was being served by a fleet of fine, large paddle-steamers. The New Co. employed *City of Newcastle*, *Morpeth* and *Maitland*, while the ASN was represented by *Collaroy*, *Coonanbara* and *City of Brisbane*. It was one of the few trades still maintained exclusively by paddlers, which were best suited to going up the shallow and twisty Hunter River to Morpeth. A major problem was a bend known as the Devil's Elbow, between Raymond Terrace and Morpeth, which for many years had restricted the length of Hunter ships to below 165 feet (50 m), though in later years much longer paddlers were able to negotiate the bend successfully.

In 1873 the Australasian Steam Navigation Co. was running a ship to the Hunter almost daily, sometimes twice a day. During January 1873 the ASN provided 36 departures from Sydney to the Hunter. The timetable for the Hunter River New Steam Ship Co. showed the following departures from Sydney: 6 a.m. on Mondays and Thursdays to Morpeth, 11 p.m. on Tuesdays and Fridays to Maitland. The vessels carried passengers and mixed cargo, and the following list for the *Morpeth* in the *Sydney Morning Herald* of 17 January 1873 is typical of the cargoes carried: 'wool, skins, hay, potatoes, onions, bonedust, pears, maize, tin ore, coke, hides, eggs, poultry, soap, wine, oysters, tobacco, horns and bones, copper, tallow, and 200 live sheep'.

The situation on the Hunter trade was changing in the 1870s, with Newcastle developing as a major port, rivalling Morpeth. While the latter port was still a major destination for cargo, the majority of passengers were using Newcastle. With the expanding rail network, passengers could now travel to Newcastle to board a steamer, rather than endure the long, slow trip down the Hunter River.

In February 1874 a new competitor appeared, when C.J. Stevens bought the *Kembla* from the Illawarra Steam Navigation Co. and placed her on the Hunter trade. Built in Britain in 1860 for the Illawarra company, *Kembla* had originally been offered for sale in 1861, when it was found there was insufficient business on the Merimbula trade to support her. Unable to sell the vessel, the Illawarra company had chartered her to the ASN Co., and later operated her on their own route to Eden. At 449 gross tons, she was smaller than the ships operating to the Hunter for the New Co. and the ASN Co., but instead of going up the river to Morpeth, she terminated her voyages at Newcastle.

*Kembla* was scheduled to operate return trips daily except Sunday, departing Sydney at 10 a.m. and Newcastle at 11 p.m., the fare being 12*s.* 6*d.* saloon and 7*s.* 6*d.* fore cabin. It proved to be a profitable venture for the owner, as the ship earned some £20,000 in her first 15 months of operation. The enormous success of the *Kembla* caused considerable concern to the established companies, which was further aggravated when, in February 1876, a new company was formed, the Newcastle Steam Ship Co., who purchased the *Kembla* from Stevens as their first steamer.

In January 1877 the three companies were able to offer a total of 88 departures from Sydney to Newcastle. The New Co. steamers departed on Tuesday, Wednesday, Friday and Sunday, while the ANS offered a service on the Monday, Thursday and Saturday, all going up the river to Raymond Terrace and Morpeth, while the Newcastle Co. departed Newcastle each weekday at 11 p.m., returning the next day at 11 a.m. from Sydney. It was at this time that a fourth competitor entered the trade, William Howard Smith. The owner of a small but rapidly growing fleet of propeller-driven vessels, Howard Smith had established himself along the east coast of Australia, though based in Melbourne.

The operations of the New Co. were adversely affected at this time, due to the loss of one of their vessels. On 12 September 1878, near the end of a voyage from Sydney to Newcastle, the *City of Newcastle* ran into thick fog, which caused her to run ashore near Nobbys. The bow of the steamer ran into a fissure between some rocks and was held fast, but the passengers were able to walk ashore on a plank. Unfortunately, the vessel was beyond saving and became a total loss.

The ASN was becoming more disenchanted with the Hunter trade and in April 1879 it sold the *Collaroy* to the Newcastle Steam Ship Co., reducing its interest in the Hunter trade to just two ships, the same as the New Co.

The Newcastle Co. spent a considerable amount overhauling the vessel, which had a new superheater, sponsons, paddle-boxes, funnel and donkey engine fitted, while all the hull plates were sounded for decay. *Collaroy* then joined the *Kembla* on the route between Sydney and Newcastle.

Going into 1880, there were 16 return services a week being operated by four companies between Sydney and the Hunter. The ASN Co. and the New Co. still avoided direct competition, with the ASN steamers departing Sydney on Monday, Thursday and Saturday at 11 p.m., and on Wednesday at 9 a.m., while the New Co. had sailings on Tuesday, Wednesday, Friday and Sunday nights. The Newcastle Steam Ship Co. offered a sailing every night except Sunday, while Howard Smith had one ship on the route, leaving Sydney on Monday and Friday nights.

An advertisement from the period for the Newcastle Steam Ship Co. stated:

> The steamers *Kembla* and *Collaroy* leave Sydney and Newcastle every Monday, Tuesday, Wednesday, Thursday and Friday at 11.00 p.m., and on Saturdays from Sydney and Sundays from Newcastle at 12.00 p.m., and make daylight trips from Newcastle Tuesday, Thursday and Saturday mornings and from Sydney Monday, Tuesday and Thursday mornings. Saloon 10/–, steerage 4/–, 2/6 extra in *Kembla*'s deck state rooms. Cargo received for Tea Gardens, Myall, Booral wharf, Stroud and Barrington daily to be forwarded on by the *Agnes* from Newcastle, leaving Tuesday morning.

On 30 September 1880 the Australasian Steam Navigation Co. sold its entire interest in the Hunter trade, which it had been founded to operate, to the Newcastle Steam Ship Co. Included in the sale were all their wharves and the three ships they had been operating, *Coonanbara*, *City of Brisbane* and *Bolwarra*. The sale price was reported to be £52,500. Soon after, Howard Smith also dropped out of the Newcastle passenger trade.

In one fell swoop, the Newcastle Steam Ship Co. had

*Maitland* is best remembered for the tragic circumstances of her loss. (GA)

*Collaroy* aground on the beach that now bears her name. (GA)

become the dominant company on the Hunter trade, a mere four years after it was established. However, just four months later their progress was interrupted by the sudden loss of the *Collaroy*. The vessel departed Newcastle on the evening of 20 January 1881, under the command of Captain Thompson, but failed to arrive as expected in Sydney. It was only later that day that a message was received by the Sydney office, advising that the *Collaroy* had run hard aground on the southern end of Narrabeen beach, near Long Reef, and was lying with a list to port. Fortunately, the seas had been calm at the time of the grounding, 4.15 a.m. on 21 January, and the tide at its peak, so the 40 passengers were able to walk down a gangway onto the beach as the tide fell. To prevent the vessel being pushed further onto the beach, an anchor was run out, but could not find a purchase on the sandy bottom.

During the afternoon, 40 pigs and 30 sheep were also landed from the stranded ship and driven into a nearby paddock. The rest of the cargo consisted of 7 bales of wool, 170 bags of potatoes, 200 hides, 40 casks of tallow and sundry smaller items. Two tugs and a diver were dispatched to the scene, but little could be done to refloat the *Collaroy*, which had been proceeding at full speed when she fetched up on the beach. Eventually salvage attempts were abandoned and the wreck was sold at auction in March 1881 for £515. Salvage attempts continued for the next two and a half years, but despite the vessel being severely battered at times by storms, she did not break up. On 9 September 1884 the *Collaroy* was refloated, with surprisingly little damage showing. Converted into a sailing ship, she made

two trips to California, being wrecked off the American west coast in June 1889. The area in which the *Collaroy* stranded is known today as Collaroy Beach.

Rather than immediately purchase a replacement for the *Collaroy*, the Newcastle Co. refitted the *Coonanbara*, which returned to service in July 1882 to enjoy many more years on the Hunter trade. It was also in 1882 that the New Co. purchased the *Lady Bowen* from the Australasian Steam Navigation Co. Built in 1864, this 702-gross-ton steamer had operated on the coastal trades from Sydney and Brisbane to northern Queensland ports, being lengthened in 1875. On 7 May 1881 *Lady Bowen* had been holed when striking a rock in the Brisbane River, and run ashore to prevent her sinking. Following repairs she was offered for sale, and spent seven years on the Hunter trade before being converted into a sailing ship.

The Hunter service was now the only coastal route still operated by paddle-steamers. Competition between the Hunter River New Steam Ship Co. and the Newcastle Steam Ship Co. was intense, and each offered a sailing from Sydney every day except Sunday, the New Co. using *Morpeth, Maitland* and *Lady Bowen*, while the Newcastle Co. had *Coonanbara, Kembla* and *City of Brisbane*. Not satisfied with these fleets, each company ordered one new vessel in 1882, both being built by the same yard, J. Key & Son of Kinghorn, but to different designs. They would be the largest, and last, ocean-going paddle steamers to be built for service in Australian waters.

The first to be completed, at the end of 1883, was the vessel for the Hunter River New Steam Ship Co., which

*Namoi* was considered the finest paddle steamer on the Australian coast.

*Newcastle* was built with three funnels.

was named *Namoi*. When she arrived in Sydney in April 1884, she was hailed as a 'wonder ship' by the press. Of 1,416 gross tons, her steel hull was 245 feet (74.7 m) long, with a beam of 31 feet (9.4 m). The interior had electric light, and comfortable cabins with running water, even some bathrooms. The cabin panels were polished teak, and there were brass fittings. This was a vast improvement on previous ships to the Hunter, which had offered oil lighting, hard bunks, inadequate ventilation and primitive sanitation.

*Namoi* was fitted out to carry 150 first-class and 90 second-class passengers, and looked very smart with her gracefully raked twin funnels and masts. There was little doubt that her two 350-horsepower compound oscillating steam engines would drive her along at a comfortable 12 knots, making her the fastest ship ever on the route. Unfortunately, her maiden voyage from Sydney was marred by atrocious weather and heavy seas, so it took her four and a half hours to reach Newcastle, but in better conditions she could make the journey in three and a half hours. As with other New Co. ships, *Namoi* proceeded up the Hunter as far as

Morpeth, managing the tight Devil's Elbow with little trouble.

Towards the end of 1884, the new paddler for the Newcastle Co. arrived in Australia, suitably named *Newcastle*. Smaller than the *Namoi* at 1,251 gross tons, the *Newcastle* was longer, 264 feet (80.4 m), and could carry more passengers—about 300 in two classes. *Newcastle* also proved to be faster than the *Namoi*, achieving a top speed of 16½ knots. However, her appearance gave cause for comment, as she had three funnels, two forward of the paddleboxes close together, while the third was isolated further aft. The fore mast had yards, most unusual for a steamer of this era. Appearance aside, the *Newcastle* was a fine addition to the coastal trade, but both these vessels were obsolete before they entered service, as the age of the large paddle-steamer was over. In fact, just why the Newcastle Co. chose to build another paddler is something of a mystery, as it did not have to concern itself with the vagaries of the Hunter River, as did the New Co.

The Newcastle Co. scheduled the *Newcastle* to depart

In 1890, one funnel and two boilers were removed from *Newcastle*. (GA)

Sydney every Sunday, Tuesday and Thursday, returning from Newcastle on Monday, Wednesday and Friday, with sailings on other days taken by older vessels. The New Co. provided a service daily except Sunday as well, with the *Namoi* and the *Maitland*. The *Namoi* had a rather unfortunate start to her career, when on 16 September 1884 she collided with the Sydney Harbour ferry *Agenoria*, which was sunk, fortunately without loss of life. On 21 May 1885, *Namoi* was involved in another collision, this time in Newcastle Harbour. The paddler struck the schooner *Grace Lynn*, which sank very quickly, but again there was no loss of life. *Namoi* was not damaged in either incident.

In 1884 the Newcastle Co. had withdrawn *City of Brisbane* from service for an extensive refit. This included an extensive overhaul of the engines and the installation of new boilers. On her return to service the vessel was renamed *Sydney* and became the major partner for *Newcastle* on the Hunter trade. Meanwhile, the New Co. had decided to try operating a propeller-driven vessel on their route, and took delivery of the *Gwydir* in 1886, though the paddlers remained the prime passenger carriers.

At the time *Namoi* and *Newcastle* were placed in service, a railway line was being constructed to link Sydney and Newcastle, and it was completed in 1887, except for a bridge across the Hawkesbury River, where train passengers had to board the sternwheeler *General Gordon* for the crossing. The railway took custom away from the steamers immediately, but when the railway bridge over the Hawkesbury was completed in 1889, the decline in patronage for the steamers was even more marked. In 1888 the Newcastle Co. had disposed of the *Morpeth*, which was converted into a collier and remained in service between Sydney and Newcastle. The New Co. also disposed of one of their older ships, *Lady Bowen*, which was converted into a sailing ship. Despite the inroads made by the railway into the shipping company patronage, it would be another 50 years before the sea link between the two cities was finally severed.

The opening of the railway connection caused considerable upheavals for the steamer companies. In October 1889 the *Newcastle* was chartered to Huddart Parker to operate their newly opened service across Bass Strait from Melbourne to Launceston. The charter was organised with an option to purchase, but *Newcastle* proved too expensive to operate, and when Huddart Parker had one of its own ships available for the Bass Strait trade in April 1890, *Newcastle* was returned to her owners. The main problem with *Newcastle* was an unhealthy appetite for coal, so the vessel was given a major refit on her return to Newcastle. The after funnel and the two boilers it serviced were removed, reducing her maximum speed to 12 knots, but increasing cargo capacity and also improving her appearance.

In September 1890 the fleet of the Newcastle Co. was further reduced when *Kembla* was sold and converted to a cargo carrier. This left the Newcastle Steam Ship Co. with just three ships, *Newcastle* and *Sydney* operating regularly, while *Coonanbara* was in reserve as a spare ship. The Hunter River New Steam Ship Co. operated two paddlers, *Namoi* and *Maitland*, along with the *Gwydir*. The two companies realised they could not remain viable in opposition, so during 1891 they held talks which resulted in an amalgamation, effective 1 January 1892. The new organisation was named the Newcastle & Hunter River Steamship Co., which continued to operate the vessels as before, some to Newcastle and others up the Hunter to Morpeth.

The amalgamated companies were better placed to compete against the railway for patronage. In June 1894 the *Coonanbara* was sold, being reduced to a hulk in Sydney. Then two major disasters within a few years caused considerable distress to the new company. On 29 November 1894 the *Gwydir* was wrecked on the coast near Norah Head, but a worse fate befell the *Maitland* four years later. The vessel left Sydney as usual at 11 p.m. on the night of 5 May 1898, with 30 passengers and 33 crew aboard, but on leaving the shelter of the Heads, a fierce storm was encountered, with gale-force winds and huge seas. One huge sea swept in from the starboard quarter, carrying away the rail and demolishing the sponsonhouse. Some heavy items of cargo broke loose, sliding around the deck and smashing holes in the hull.

Crew members, working in water up to their waists, tried to block up the holes with wood, but water poured in, sweeping them off their feet. In a desperate attempt to prevent the water reaching the fires in the boilers, all cargo was jettisoned, while the captain attempted to turn his stricken vessel around and head back to Sydney. The inrush of water could not be stopped, and at about 3 a.m. the engine-room flooded, extinguishing the fires. Now totally helpless, at the mercy of wind and sea, *Maitland* began drifting towards the Barranjoey lighthouse, near the entrance to Broken Bay. The captain advised everyone to stay on board as long as possible once the vessel went aground. At 5 a.m. the *Maitland* was caught by a bombora and was swept ashore just off the headland near Cape Three Points.

According to a survivor, *Maitland* struck first almost stern-on and the ship broke in half between the two funnels as huge waves crashed over her. The forward section, in which the steerage passengers were travelling, settled in the water and most who had sought shelter there were drowned. The stern section was swung round and flung onto rocks, causing more casualties. Those flung into the sea were either dashed against rocks, or managed to reach a sandy beach nearby, but there were some who remained on the wreck. Five women refused to leave the forward section, which broke up quickly, and all were lost. The captain and 18 others remained on the stern section, awaiting rescue.

Many attempts were made to rig a line to the wreck before one was finally secured, but it snapped after 10 people had been brought to safety. As the tide dropped in the afternoon, another line was rigged, and the remaining survivors brought to the shore. In all, 21 persons lost their lives, and the storm was known afterwards as the 'Maitland Gale'. The boilers of the *Maitland* were washed onto rocks at Bouddi Head, near Kilcare, where their rusted remains can still be seen today at low tide.

The loss of the *Maitland* caused enormous problems for the Newcastle & Hunter River Co. Not only did it deprive them of a ship, albeit one 28 years old, but the circumstances of the disaster turned more passengers away from the steamers to the railway. There were now just three ships left in the fleet, *Newcastle*, *Namoi* and *Sydney*, all paddlers, but the level of trade did not warrant any further tonnage. One profitable venture for both *Namoi* and *Newcastle* during this period was the operation of day excursions on Sundays and public holidays. These would be from Sydney to Broken Bay, or from Newcastle to Port Stephens, and were always well patronised, the decks being crammed with hundreds of trippers.

The service up the Hunter River to Morpeth became more difficult for the *Namoi* as the years passed. The cutting out of vast areas of timber in the headwaters of the Hunter and its tributaries resulted in millions of tons of silt being swept down the river. As it was not being dredged, the river became less and less navigable each year, until it finally reached the point where *Namoi* was having great difficulty reaching Morpeth. Once, when the river was in flood, *Namoi*

attempted to turn at her Morpeth dock, only to have her bow become embedded in the opposite bank while the stern lines held her to the wharf. Debris being swept down the river jammed the paddleboxes, rendering her engines useless, and the vessel began to heel over under the pressure of water. For several minutes there was great anxiety on board, but then the stern lines broke, and the *Namoi* was able to swing round and settle in midstream. The *Namoi* began experiencing difficulties in rounding some of the bends in the river, as the channel became increasingly tight, and eventually it was decided she would have to be replaced. In 1906 the Newcastle & Hunter River Steamship Co. ordered a new vessel from Scotland, but she was to be propeller-driven.

The new vessel arrived in Sydney in June 1907, having been named *Hunter*. Although larger than *Namoi*, she had twin propellers, which made her more manoeuvrable in the Hunter River. Once the *Hunter* was settled in service, the *Namoi* was relegated to being a reserve ship. The *Sydney* was withdrawn from service altogether, and eventually broken up in 1909.

*Newcastle* continued to operate regularly between Newcastle and Sydney, while *Namoi* only operated as required. This situation continued until 1922, when another propeller vessel was added to the fleet, the second *Gwydir*. Built in 1911 as *Morialta* for the Adelaide Steam Ship Co., the *Gwydir* was slightly smaller than the *Hunter*. With the arrival of *Gwydir*, *Namoi* was surplus to requirements and in 1923 she was taken out of service and sold. *Newcastle* was then relegated to being reserve ship, leaving the two propeller vessels, *Hunter* and *Gwydir*, to maintain the Hunter trade. This was the first time since its inception that the Hunter River trade was not served on a regular basis by paddle-steamers. *Newcastle* became the last ocean-going paddler to operate commercially in Australian waters, but in August 1928 she too was withdrawn from service.

Both *Namoi* and *Newcastle* were laid up for some years after being withdrawn from service. In the early 1930s they were sold to Sydney shipbreakers and reduced to bare hulls. In June 1933 the remains of both boats were towed out to sea off Sydney and scuttled.

For 60 years the waters of the Hunter River were not disturbed by the turning of paddlewheels, but in 1988 a new vessel was built, a replica of the pioneer *William the Fourth*, as a Bicentennial project. Constructed at Raymond Terrace, near the site where the original vessel was built, the replica was launched on 26 September 1987 and completed in January 1988. Following a series of visits to Sydney and other east coast ports, the replica *William the Fourth* returned to Newcastle, where it began operating excursions. It is fitting that the river that spawned the first paddle-steamer operations in this country should still be home to one of these stately vessels.

## North Coast Services

The first steamer to visit the north coast of New South Wales was the *William the Fourth*, which made several trips in 1835 to Port Macquarie, at the mouth of the Hastings River, but no regular service developed. Further north, on the Clarence River, settlements were being established rapidly, and the imported steamer *King William the Fourth* made an experimental voyage there in August 1839. The first steamer to enter the Clarence, *King William the Fourth* travelled 135 kilometres up the river before running aground on 30 August, near rapids. It took three days to refloat the vessel, but the voyage had proved the suitability of the area to development. A hill near where she stopped was named King William's Mount. Whether or not this would have developed into a regular trade is unknown, as the following month the *King William the Fourth* was wrecked off Newcastle.

In the 1840s, the trade to the north coast still did not warrant regular services, but vessels operating to Brisbane would call in as required. The entrances to the various rivers were all protected by dangerous bars, over which the ships would bounce when entering and leaving. Those towns that were established along the coast had no natural harbours, so trading to the north coast presented many difficulties. In 1842 the *Maitland*, a wooden-hulled steamer built in Sydney in 1837, began a regular service between Sydney and Port Macquarie, but in 1847 she was sold, and joined the Hunter River trade. The first vessel to be actually built for a north coast service was the *Phoenix*. She was launched on 24 June 1846 from the yard of Thomas Chowne, at Pyrmont in Sydney, and was fitted with the steam-engines removed from the pioneer steamer, *Sophia Jane*, when she was broken up.

The *Phoenix* began trading from Sydney to the Clarence River, under the command of Captain Wiseman. The only steamer operating regularly to the area, she became the main lifeline for the local residents. On 27 February 1850 the *Phoenix* left Grafton for Sydney, but on reaching the mouth of the Clarence found a strong southerly gale blowing at sea. The vessel remained inside the bar until the morning of 3 March, when she crossed it and headed for Sydney. Unfortunately, another southerly gale struck, causing the *Phoenix* to lose power, and she began to drift towards the shore. Both anchors were dropped, but the cables parted, and the *Phoenix* finally grounded in a bay, 15 kilometres south of the entrance to the Clarence. Pushed high on the

beach by the violent seas, the *Phoenix* was declared a wreck and offered for auction. Being uninsured, the owners faced financial ruin when no buyers came forward, so they decided to salvage the ship. The machinery was removed, and the hull returned to the water, and taken to Sydney for repairs and to have the engine put back.

The work of salvaging and repairing the *Phoenix* took almost 18 months, and it was not until late in 1851 that the vessel was able to resume its trade to the Clarence River, now commanded by Captain J. Benaud. Sadly the reprieve was to be brief, as on 14 April 1852 the *Phoenix* was totally wrecked on the Clarence River bar, when commanded by Captain Bernard. The vessel was attempting to enter the river by the south channel against a strong running tide, and grounded, following which her machinery was stopped and could not be restarted. Her stream anchor was let go, but the warp parted, and according to an eyewitness, 'water poured into her in all directions, through the stern windows, port holes, hatches etc., and she drifted onto the middle of the North Spit where, without breaking up, she became so deeply embedded in the sand that it was impossible to release her'. None of her 40 passengers was lost, although all their belongings and some livestock being carried was. The remains of the *Phoenix* and her historic engine still lie buried on the beach, just north of Yamba.

The original master of the *Phoenix*, Captain Wiseman, had been sent to England in 1850 to oversee the building of a new steamer for the Clarence River and bring her out to Australia. Named the *Clarence*, she arrived in Sydney in the middle of 1852, but the owner received a huge offer for the steamer from a Tasmanian syndicate, and was quick to accept. Instead the veteran *William the Fourth* was placed on the Clarence trade. Commanded by Captain Wiseman, she was scheduled to make one trip from Sydney every fortnight, but had trouble maintaining such regularity. One trip in December 1854 took 13 days in one direction, and she was clearly well past her prime.

There was considerable dissatisfaction among the residents along the Clarence with the steamer service being provided, so on 24 January 1854 a group of local gentlemen formed the Grafton Steam Navigation Co., whose first auditor was Mr David Jones, who later founded the Sydney retailing firm that still bears his name. The new company immediately ordered a steamer to be built in Britain, which was named *Grafton*. This iron-hulled, 316-gross-ton vessel arrived in Sydney in April 1855, bringing out 30 passengers and about 100 tons of cargo. She entered the Clarence trade, and remained on the route until 1876. It is reported that in 1855, the one-way fare on the *Grafton* was £7.

The northern region of New South Wales was developing rapidly, and interest grew in establishing steamer services. The Illawarra Steam Navigation Co., which was really a south coast operator, placed its *Kiama* on a service from Sydney to the Manning River in 1857. This attempt to break into the north coast trades was not a success, and the vessel returned to the south coast trades. It was also during 1857 that the Australasian Steam Navigation Co. entered the northern rivers trade, when it purchased the *Clarence*. As mentioned previously, this vessel had been built in 1852

*Phoenix* was fitted with the engine removed from *Sophia Jane*.

The fine lines of *Brighton* are shown to advantage in this painting. (GA)

*Coonanbarra* on the patent slip at Cape Town during her delivery voyage. (GA)

*Kookaburra Queen* was completed in 1987.

*Boronia Princess* operates regular excursions on Lake Wendouree.

Painting of *Hygeia* by A.J. Gregory, used as a promotional postcard. (RWB)

A.V. Gregory painting of *Weeroona* on promotional postcard. (RWB)

Deane Taylor painting of *Ozone, Weeroona* and *Hygeia*, sold as a postcard on board all three vessels. (RWB)

The Hovell Tree at Albury.

Cairn at Mannum commemorating the voyage by Captain Sturt.

*Pevensey* has been restored at Echuca.

*Diamantina* was wrecked at the mouth of the Manning River in 1881. (IF)

for the trade, but was sold to Tasmania. The ASN purchased *Clarence* and opened a new service from Sydney to the Clarence, Macleay and Manning Rivers. However, the vessel did not operate to a regular schedule and was often withdrawn to relieve on the main Brisbane route. Gradually the interests of the ASN centred on services to the Manning River, on which various paddle-steamers were used. However, in 1866 the ASN withdrew from the Manning River trade completely.

In 1857 the directors of the Grafton Steam Navigation Co. decided to expand its sphere of operation to encompass the Richmond River as well, and the name of the company was changed to The Clarence & Richmond Steam Navigation Co. The first new vessel to be built by them for the Richmond River trade was the *Urara*, in 1859, which operated to both the Clarence and Richmond rivers, until being wrecked on the Clarence River bar on 1 May 1866.

The steamer *Rainbow* was built on the Macleay River by William Marshall in 1860. This 110-gross-ton, wooden-hulled vessel was owned by its builder until 1863, when bought by the Clarence & Richmond River S.N. Co. *Rainbow* spent most of her career operating to the north coast rivers, only to be wrecked off Sugar Loaf Point on 2 June 1864, when seven lives were lost.

The Clarence & Richmond Rivers S.N. Co. continued to flourish, and in 1866 added the 439-gross-ton, iron-hulled *Agnes Irving* to their fleet. She developed a reputation for being one of the finest and most successful steamers ever to work the New South Wales north coast. In 1866 the company added the 299-gross-ton *Ballina* to their fleet. In 1864, the *Florence Irving* had been built in Britain for the Clarence & Richmond Rivers S.N. Co., but she was sold almost immediately to the ASN Co., who employed her on the northern rivers trade until 1873.

In March 1870, the 285-gross-ton *Diamantina* was purchased from the ASN Co., which had previously operated the vessel on the Manning River trade. The Clarence & Richmond Co. also placed her on the Manning River trade, but there was considerable local resentment to the operation of this vessel, and in January 1875 she was sold to the newly formed Manning River Steam Navigation Co. *Diamantina* continued to operate to the Manning for another six years, but on 31 March 1881 she was wrecked on the bar at the entrance to the river. Salvaged in May 1881, she was reduced to a lighter, and not scrapped until 1907.

In 1876 the Clarence & Richmond Rivers Steam Navigation Co. produced their last, and finest paddle-steamer, the *City of Grafton*. Built by the famous Scottish firm of A. Stephen & Sons in Glasgow, *City of Grafton* was 825 gross tons, and on arrival completely outclassed all other tonnage operating to the north coast region. *City of Grafton* operated solely on the trade to Grafton and enabled the Clarence & Richmond firm to become the dominant trader to the north coast. Their ships were not only serving the Clarence and Richmond rivers, but calling at intermediate towns en route, including Port Macquarie and Coffs Harbour, as well as serving the Macleay River.

Unfortunately, 1879 was to be a very bad year for the company, with the loss of two of their main ships, *Ballina* and *Agnes Irving*. The *Ballina* ran aground on the north spit at the mouth of the Hasting River in Port Macquarie on 13 February 1879, and broke her back. The wreck was not salvaged, and eventually was covered by sand. The *Agnes Irving* was lost on 28 December 1879, on the bar at the entrance to the Macleay River. The vessel was entering the river on an ebbing tide when a huge wave drove her onto South Spit. All aboard were safely brought to shore, but within a short time the *Agnes Irving* began to break up. The master at the time, Captain McGee, had his certificate suspended for three months following an inquiry.

Despite the loss of these two fine vessels, the Clarence

*City of Grafton,* finest of all the North Coast paddle steamers. (GA)

Droghers were shallow draft vessels that operated on most of the rivers in northern New South Wales. They were also used to a lesser extent on rivers in southern New South Wales, Victoria and the Gippsland Lakes. The design of droghers was very basic, being little more than a self-propelled barge. Most were never registered, so their names are not recorded. Paddle droghers often had twin wheels at the stern, such as the one illustrated here. (GA)

The North Coast Steam Navigation Co. operated a large fleet of droghers on various rivers. These photographs of an unidentified drogher with one stern wheel were taken at Grafton, on the Clarence River, in 1942. Droghers were used on the Clarence to transport many different cargos, including sugar cane from the fields to the mill on Harwood Island. The cane filled the shallow hold, was piled high on deck, and sometimes dragged in the water, so the laden drogher looked like a small hill moving slowly down the river. (LW)

The remains of a paddle drogher at Tea Gardens, on Port Stephens. (GA)

& Richmond Co. continued to prosper, though their fleet consisted increasingly of propeller-driven vessels, as did those of their main competitors, Nicoll Bros and Nipper & See, which later was renamed John See & Co. In December 1888 the name of the firm was changed again, to the Clarence, Richmond & Macleay Rivers Steam Navigation Co. Ltd; while *City of Grafton* remained one of its prime ships. On 13 August 1891 the Rivers Co. merged with John See & Co. to form the North Coast Steam Navigation Co. Ltd, and shortly after bought out Nicolls Bros.

The *City of Grafton* continued to ply her way to the Clarence, the only paddlewheeler left in the fleet, apart from small droghers employed as towing boats on the various rivers. One of the last of these type of vessels to be built was the *Euroka*, in 1897. This 170-gross-ton vessel was designed to operate from Sydney to the Nambucca and Bellinger rivers, which had particularly shallow and dangerous bars at their mouths. *Euroka* was sold in 1910 and wrecked on Long Reef, near Manly, on 19 October 1913. The *City of Grafton* remained in service until 1913, when she was laid up. Following service during the war years as an accommodation ship, the vessel was reduced to a hulk in 1920 and scrapped in 1930.

The withdrawal of the *City of Grafton* brought to an end the use of paddle-steamers on the longer New South Wales coastal trades, though paddlers continued to serve the Hunter River for a further 20 years.

## South Coast Services

To the south of Sydney, an area known as the Illawarra, extending from Wollongong to Eden, was being opened up by settlers. This stretch of coast was particularly difficult for shipping, as there were no natural harbours, apart from Jervis Bay, and few rivers.

The first steamer to visit the area was the *Sophia Jane*,

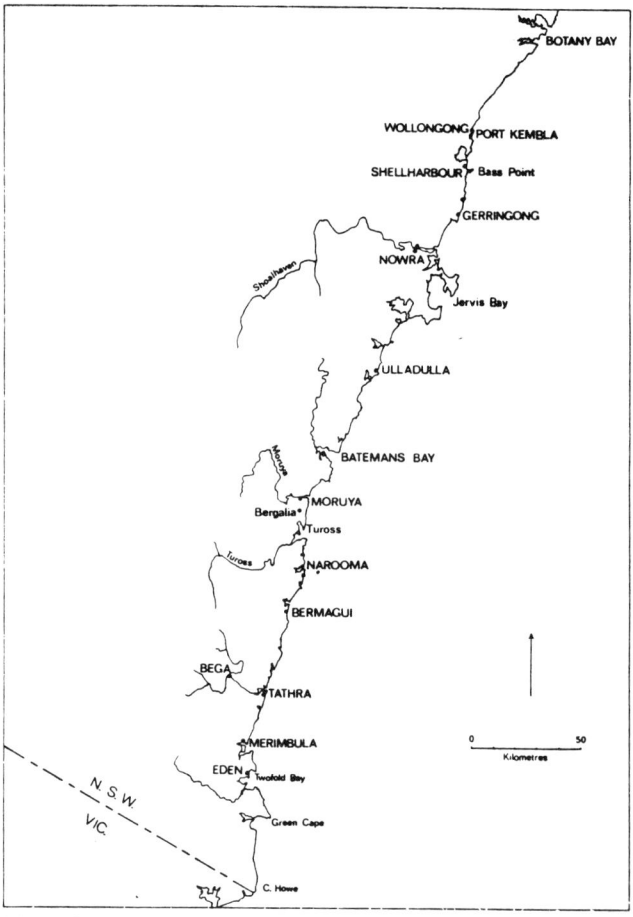

Map of NSW South coast (BP)

which in 1834 went to Wollongong, but due to the lack of a safe anchorage, the experimental voyage was not a success. During 1836 the *William the Fourth* made a number of trips to the Illawarra region. However, this vessel then traded to the north coast for several years, before returning to the south coast again.

At the beginning of 1838 a regular service of sorts was started to the Illawarra by Edye Manning, a businessman with substantial land holdings in the region. He ordered the construction of the second ocean-going steamer to be built in Australia, the *Maitland*, which was completed in Sydney at the end of 1837. Originally Manning had intended to place the 140-gross-ton vessel in service to the Hunter River, but when commissioned, the *Maitland* began making alternate trips to Morpeth on the Hunter and to Wollongong.

The first attempt to form a shipping company to provide a regular service to the Illawarra region was made by Mr T. Shadforth, who issued a prospectus on 15 May 1839. By 5 June the entire offering of 20,000 shares at £50 each had been taken up, and the Illawarra Steam Packet Co. was formed. It immediately purchased the *Maitland* from Edye Manning, and on 19 June commenced operations from Sydney to the Illawarra. Within weeks of its formation, the Illawarra Steam Packet Co. merged with another newly formed organisation, the Brisbane Waters Steam Packet Co., which had been planning to start a service from Sydney to the Gosford region. The combined concern was renamed the General Steam Navigation Co., and it soon purchased the *William the Fourth*, which was operated in conjunction with the *Maitland*. In 1840 the GSNC also bought the *Sophia Jane* and *Tamar*. These two steamers had been owned by one J.T. Wilson, who disappeared suddenly in October 1839, owing more than £30,000 in debts. The GSNC placed both the *Sophia Jane* and the *Tamar* on the Hunter River trade, as it hoped to expand into that region.

On 19 June 1841, the *Sophia Jane* left Sydney on her first voyage to the far south coast, going to South Huskisson on Jervis Bay, where it was hoped a cargo of wool could be obtained. A rough road connected the settlement with sheep stations inland, but was in such poor condition the wool wagons had great difficulty moving along it. In the end the *Sophia Jane* tired of waiting and returned to Sydney empty.

The formation of the Hunter's River Steam Packet Association in 1839, and their resultant introduction of new ships on the Hunter trade, had a serious effect on the operations of the GSNC, whose *Tamar* was quite outclassed by the new vessels. The *Sophia Jane* and *William the Fourth* remained on the south coast trade, but the *Tamar* was laid up, while the *Maitland* began operating to Port Macquarie. However, as 1841 progressed it became apparent that the GSNC was in financial trouble, and at a general meeting held on 15 November 1841, it was agreed that the firm be wound up. Once again, steamer services to the south coast became erratic, with *William the Fourth*, now owned by Edye Manning, and *Sophia Jane* being the main vessels in the trade. The first section of the sheltered harbour being built at Wollongong was opened in 1844, but in April that year the *Sophia Jane* grounded on a reef off Wollongong. With a badly strained hull, the pioneer steamship in the colony was not considered worth repairing, and in 1845 she was broken up. The *Tamar*, now owned by the Hunter's River Co., was placed on the Wollongong route, but only for a short time, so that the only regular trader to the Illawarra region was the *William the Fourth*.

The development of the south coast trade then seemed to stagnate for almost a decade, due to a combination of economic depression in Australia and the lack of suitable harbours along the coast. It was Edye Manning who revived the trade, when he ordered a new vessel to be built by the C.J. Mare shipyard at Blackwall, on the River Thames. The 166-gross-ton *Illawarra* was specifically intended for the trade from Sydney to Wollongong, which she entered in 1853.

In 1847 moorings had been laid at Kiama to induce ships to stop at this prospering town, but no regular service eventuated. The people of the Kiama region were so dissatisfied by the service they received that, in 1853, they formed the Kiama Steam Navigation Co. and ordered a steamer from Britain. Completed in August 1854 as the *Kiama*, the 104-gross-ton vessel arrived in Sydney on 4 April 1855, after a delivery voyage under sail lasting 144 days. The *Kiama* was placed in service between Sydney and Kiama, on which she operated for many years.

Also in 1853, the Shoalhaven Steam Navigation Co. had been formed, again through the dissatisfaction of residents of Nowra with the service they were being offered. Instead of ordering a new vessel, the Shoalhaven company purchased the *Nora Creina*, which had been built at Waterford in Ireland in 1839 for the Waterford Commercial Steam Navigation Co., for service from Waterford to Bristol. *Nora Creina* left Waterford on 6 October 1853, bound for Australia, and began operating to the Shoalhaven region early in 1854. One of the main backers of the Shoalhaven company was Edye Manning, who had most of his land holdings in the area.

In 1857 the Shoalhaven and Kiama firms combined their resources and formed the Illawarra Steam Navigation Co., operating both the *Nora Creina* and the *Kiama*. In January 1858 the new Illawarra Co. purchased the *William the Fourth* from the Twofold Bay Pastoral Co., which had owned the vessel for several years. The initial services operated by the new company were from Sydney to Wollongong, Kiama and the Shoalhaven region, with calls also at Gerringong, Batemans Bay and Nelligen.

It was also during 1857 that gold was discovered at Kiandra, and a trade developed from Sydney to the Clyde River, which provided access to the new strike. In November 1857 the *Nora Creina*, carrying about 80 passengers, ventured up the Clyde River to within 53 kilometres of Braidwood. This brought the region within 20 hours of Sydney, instead of the several days required for an overland trip. However, the Clyde River was quite shallow, and not suitable for regular navigation. Though a public meeting was held to raise support for the construction of special steamers for the river, nothing happened, and regular steamer services terminated at Batemans Bay.

The discovery of gold, and the resultant influx of prospectors, also attracted more steamers to the south coast. In January 1858, Edye Manning purchased the *Mimosa*, a 163-gross-ton iron-hulled steamer built in 1854, which had been operating in Tasmania. *Mimosa* was placed in service between Sydney and the Clyde River. In June 1858 the new

The second *Illawarra* was the last paddler on the South Coast trades.

Illawarra Co. faced more opposition when the *Hunter* was purchased from the Hunter River New Steam Navigation Co. by R. Haworth & Partners, of Camden. This iron-hulled steamer of 170 gross tons was superior to both the *Kiama* and the *Nora Creina*, not to mention the veteran *William the Fourth*, so to maintain their position in the trade, the Illawarra Co. ordered another new steamer from Britain.

Launched on 18 August 1860, the 325-gross-ton steamer was named *Kembla*. She was very fast, having a speed of 14 knots. It was usual for vessels built in Britain to make their delivery voyage to Australia under sail, but it was decided that *Kembla* would make the voyage under steam. On passing into the North Atlantic, the vessel was badly damaged by the seas and had to put back to Cork for repairs. There she was rigged with sails and completed the voyage under canvas. By the time *Kembla* arrived in Sydney early in 1861, the gold rush at Kiandra had failed and the trade disappeared almost overnight. The Illawarra Co. decided to try and sell the vessel in New Zealand, at which time she was transferred to the ownership of Edye Manning, while his *Mimosa* and *Illawarra* were transferred to the Illawarra Co., which now had a monopoly on the south coast trade. The *Kembla* was not sold in New Zealand, and on her return to Australia she began operating to the south coast for the Illawarra Co., and also was chartered to the Australasian Steam Navigation Co., for which she made numerous trips to Brisbane. On 1 December 1862, *Kembla* collided with the *Hunter* south of Sydney Heads, but neither ship was badly damaged.

In the early 1860s, the Illawarra Steam Navigation Co. found itself with too many ships. In 1861 the *Nora Creina* was withdrawn and dispatched to China, where she was sold. In 1862 the *William the Fourth* and the *Illawarra* followed her to the East. *Illawarra* left Sydney on 2 April 1862 for Hong Kong, and later went to Shanghai, to operate on the Yangtse and Ningpo rivers. *William the Fourth*, the first ocean-going steamer built in this country, departed Sydney for the last time on 13 June 1862, and after a stop at Newcastle, voyaged to Hong Kong, where she was sold in 1863. The *Kembla* operated spasmodically, but was frequently laid up. On 19 September 1863 the *Mimosa* was wrecked when on a voyage from Merimbula to Sydney. The steamer struck an uncharted rock 11 kilometres north of Tathra and attempts to refloat her were unsuccessful. The rock is now known as Mimosa Rock.

To replace the *Mimosa*, the Illawarra Co. had built in Sydney the 117-gross-ton wooden-hulled *Mynora* in 1864. This vessel was destined to have a very short life, as on the night of 6 April 1864 she was wrecked at St Georges Head, south of Jervis Bay. As a replacement, the Illawarra Co. purchased the *Illalong* in June 1864 from the Australasian Steam Navigation Co. This 294-gross-ton iron-hulled vessel had been built in 1854 for service to the Hunter River. Another replacement steamer was also ordered, which was completed in 1865 as the *Comarang*. This vessel also had a wooden hull, and was 198 gross tons, but only served in the fleet until 1869, then was sold to New Zealand. It was also during 1865 that the Illawarra Co. took delivery of a small shallow-draft stern-wheeler, the *Coolangatta*, designed to operate along the Shoalhaven River from the mouth to Nowra and further upstream, as the stream was blocked to larger vessels by rocks.

Going into the 1870s, the Illawarra Co. was operating the four paddlers, *Hunter, Illalong, Kiama* and *Kembla*. In 1873 the Illawarra Co. offered four departures every Friday, one to Wollongong, another to Ulladulla and the Clyde River, a third to Kiama and the Shoalhaven, while a fourth went to Batemans Bay. In addition, there was a Tuesday sailing from Sydney to Merimbula, Eden and Tathra. In 1874, the *Kembla* was sold, and joined the Hunter River trade. On 27 September 1876 the new harbour at Kiama was officially opened, with *Hunter* being included in the first group of ships to berth there.

In 1878, the Illawarra Steam Navigation Co. took

delivery of its last large paddle-steamer, the second *Illawarra*. Built by Wigham Richardson at Newcastle in England, she was a splendid vessel of 522 gross tons, 190 feet (57.9 m) long, with a speed of 15 knots. On the arrival of the *Illawarra* in Australia, the *Illalong* was withdrawn from service, and broken up the following year.

From time to time a few small operators tried to enter the south coast trades, most in specialised fields. The Gerringong Co-operative Steam Ship Co. and the Shellharbour Co-operative Steam Ship Co. combined to offer regular service to Gerringong and Shellharbour, using small vessels. In 1878 they took delivery of a small paddler, called *Our Own*, of just 73 gross tons. In 1880 they were offering a weekly service to Shellharbour and Gerringong on the screw steamer *Dairymaid*, and another weekly service to the Shoalhaven and Broughton Creek with *Our Own*, assisted by the screw steamer *Rocket*. Unfortunately, *Our Own* was wrecked on 21 August 1880 while on a voyage from Sydney. Passing Bass Point, the steam-engine of *Our Own* broke down and she drifted ashore, becoming a total loss. On 12 March 1881 the *Kiama* was disabled by a broken shaft off Cape St George and had to be towed into Jervis Bay, and then to Sydney for repairs.

Having built up its business using paddle-steamers, the Illawarra Co. took delivery of several propeller-driven vessels during this period, including the *Allowrie* in 1880. During 1880 the company provided departures from Sydney for Wollongong every Monday, Tuesday and Friday at 11 p.m., and 9.30 a.m. on Wednesday and Friday. There was a sailing every Friday for Ulladulla, Moruya, Batemans Bay and Nelligen. Kiama was served by a departure on Monday at 11 p.m., while on Tuesday and Friday a vessel departed for Kiama and Shoalhaven. The sailing for Merimbula, Eden and Tathra left on Wednesday at 9.30 a.m. and Friday at 11 p.m. The south coast was opening up rapidly, and attracted more competition for the Illawarra Co., including Huddart Parker Ltd, which placed two cargo ships on services from Sydney to Gerringong, Shoalhaven and Berry. However, the Illawarra Co. was still thriving, and gradually added more propeller ships to its fleet. In 1887, the *Hunter* was sold, and finished her career as a hulk owned by the Adelaide Steam Ship Co., being scrapped in 1904. The *Kiama* was used less and less in the 1890s, and was eventually sold in August 1896. She too was reduced to a hulk, and broken up about 1914.

This left the *Illawarra* as the sole paddler in the fleet of the Illawarra Steam Navigation Co. at the turn of the century. In 1904, the company was reconstituted as the Illawarra & South Coast Steam Navigation Co., by which time the *Illawarra* was only in use as a spare ship, all regular sailings being taken by propeller vessels. In 1908 the *Illawarra* was withdrawn altogether, and broken up during 1910.

# 4 Intercolonial Trade

In the early 1830s, when steamships were pioneering trade along the Australian coastline, the country comprised three colonies: New South Wales, Western Australia and Van Diemen's Land, with South Australia being extracted from New South Wales in 1836. It was not until 1851 that Victoria became a separate colony, followed by Queensland in 1859. With the establishment of steamer services from Sydney to the Hunter River, the trade gradually expanded to include settlements further distant from Sydney, though still in New South Wales. Paddle-steamers were not really suited to long journeys in open water, and after the initial establishment of services, propeller-driven vessels were soon favoured by shipowners.

The first voyages that can be considered as intercolonial occurred in 1837. They were made by the wooden-hulled *James Watt*, a 110-foot (33.8 m) paddler built in England in 1824 and the third steamer to be imported into Australia. Owned by Sydney businessmen James Grose and Thomas Street, the *James Watt* arrived in Hobart Town from Sydney on 31 March 1837. It was intended that the vessel would operate regularly on this route, but the fact she took 10 days in each direction did not make her a success. She then voyaged from Sydney to Melbourne, where she arrived on 4 July 1837, becoming the first vessel to enter Port Phillip Bay, but this was not the start of a regular service. Later in 1837, the *James Watt* went north from Sydney to become the first steamer to visit Brisbane, though not actually entering the river, but anchoring off Dunwich in Moreton Bay. Unfortunately, none of these pioneering voyages led to the establishment of regular services for some years. The *Sophia Jane* also made a voyage to Brisbane, in 1839, but again this was an isolated instance.

On 5 October 1840 there arrived in Sydney the large wooden-hulled paddle-steamer *Clonmell*, of 598 gross tons. Built at Birkenhead in 1836, the *Clonmell* had been operating across the Irish Sea to Waterford from Liverpool until being purchased by prominent Sydney businessman, Edye Manning, and dispatched to Australia under sail, a voyage that lasted nearly five months. She was by far the largest and finest steamer yet seen in Australia, being 156 feet (47.5 m) long and powered by a 220-horsepower steam-engine. *Clonmell* was intended to operate from Sydney to Melbourne and Tasmania. The fares charged were quite high, from Sydney to Melbourne being 15 guineas (£15 15s. 0d.) for a cabin, or £9 for deck accommodation. In December 1840 *Clonmell* made her first intercolonial voyage, from Sydney to Launceston and Melbourne and return.

On her second voyage, *Clonmell* departed Sydney for Melbourne, but on 2 January 1841 the vessel ran aground. Passengers and crew were able to reach the shore safely, and had to camp ashore under the sails while a rescue crew set off for Melbourne in the ship's whaleboat. It took them three days to reach Port Phillip Heads, and a further seven days before the stranded survivors were rescued by a sailing boat. The *Clonmell* was a total loss, so a brave attempt to establish an intercolonial trade came to a premature end.

It was in 1841 that one of the truly legendary names from the early days of Australia, Benjamin Boyd, came to prominence in shipping circles. Of Scottish ancestry, Boyd was filled with ambitious plans, which he put into effect rapidly following his arrival in Sydney in August 1842. He subsequently opened the Royal Bank of Australasia, bought huge tracts of land in the Monaro district and built his own township, Boydtown, on Twofold Bay near Eden. Here he established a whaling industry and ruled over his domain. Prior to coming to Australia, Boyd wanted to establish a steamer service along the east coast, and to this end he bought three large paddle-steamers.

The three steamers, *Seahorse*, *Juno* and *Cornubia*, had all been owned by the St George Steam Packet Co., with which Boyd may have had some connection. The first to be sent to Australia was the *Seahorse*, a 439-gross-ton, wooden-hulled vessel built at Dundee in 1837. *Seahorse* left London under sail on 3 October 1840, carrying passengers, cargo and some livestock. After a long journey, she arrived in Hobart Town on 17 April 1841. Refitted as a steamer, the *Seahorse* set off for Sydney, taking five days for the passage, arriving on 1 June. She was described in the local press as having 'two engines of 125 horsepower each. Her cabins are very roomy and her accommodation altogether of a very superior description. She makes up 70 beds.' In July the *Seahorse* commenced a fortnightly service to Melbourne, but in April 1842 was withdrawn, due to rising costs and lack of support. In August 1842, after Boyd arrived in Australia, the *Seahorse* began operating again, to Melbourne, Launceston and Hobart. *Seahorse* was the first steamship in Australia to be awarded a mail contract, receiving £200 for every trip to Melbourne with the mails.

The second of Boyd's steamers to arrive in Australia was the *Juno*, 621 gross tons, built in 1836. *Juno* departed London on 26 June 1841 under canvas, and arrived in Sydney on 25 March 1842. Amazingly, this steamer lay at anchor in Sydney Harbour for five years, then made the first crossing by a steamer of the Tasman Sea, as described elsewhere.

*Cornubia*, the third of Boyd's purchases, was a much

smaller vessel, just 160 gross tons, built in 1832. *Cornubia* arrived in Sydney on 6 June 1842, and like the other pair, spent most of her time idle.

The *Seahorse* was the most regular of Boyd's traders, but on 5 June 1843 she ran aground in the Tamar River, at George Town. As the tide dropped, the vessel heeled over, straining the hull, but at the next high tide she floated off, and arrived back in Sydney on 11 June. There was no dry dock in Australia large enough to take the ship, which Boyd claimed as a total loss. His insurers refused to pay on the claim, and lengthy court litigation followed until, in November 1849, the *Seahorse* was sold at auction for just £850 and converted into a wharf hulk.

By the time the *Seahorse* was sold Benjamin Boyd's other enterprises in Australia—the Royal Bank of Australasia and the Boydtown settlement and whaling station—had all failed. In 1848 he had sold the *Juno*, and the following year he disposed of *Cornubia*. Boyd left Australia in 1851 for the Solomon Islands, and subsequently vanished.

Prior to being sold, the *Cornubia* had been chartered in October 1846 by the Colonial government to take Colonel Barney and a group of settlers to Gladstone, in Queensland. During November 1846 *Cornubia* had made several trips between Brisbane and Gladstone, the first such voyages along the Queensland coast. The purchaser of *Juno*, one W.S. Boyd, who was not related to Benjamin, placed the vessel on a service between Sydney and Adelaide. Boyd had hoped to receive a subsidy from the South Australian government, but this was not forthcoming and the service was soon abandoned. Both *Cornubia* and *Juno* were disposed of to overseas owners.

The next entrant into the intercolonial trade was the Hunter's River Steam Navigation Co., which had three new steamers delivered from Britain. The last of this trio, the *Shamrock*, arrived in Sydney on 18 October 1841 and spent a short time operating to the Hunter River. However, in early 1842 the *Shamrock* began operating from Sydney to Moreton Bay, then in September 1842 she began running to Launceston and Melbourne, in competition with the *Seahorse*. The *Seahorse* was a veritable coal-eater, while the *Shamrock* was an economical vessel to run and could charge a fare of just £10. Following the loss of the *Seahorse*, *Shamrock* was the only steamer engaged in the trade, operating on a fortnightly schedule for many years. In January 1852 the *Shamrock* completed her hundredth round voyage to Melbourne, and the Melbourne *Argus* of 7 June 1852 referred to her as 'this favourite steamer, now advancing in years, still keeps up her character for regularity and despatch. Her last trip to Sydney occupied only 72 hours, during five of which she was detained at Twofold Bay.'

In 1842 the Hunter's River Co. also began sending the *Rose* and *Thistle* on occasional trips to Brisbane. The same year they bought the *Sovereign* from James Grose and placed her on the Hunter River trade. In 1843 the *Sovereign* began making regular voyages to Brisbane, being joined by the *Thistle* in the same year. She was replaced by the *Tamar* in 1845, which worked the route with the *Sovereign*.

The entrance to Moreton Bay used by the early steamers was through the South Passage, which included crossing a dangerous bar off Amity Point. On 3 March 1847 the *Sovereign* left Brisbane for Sydney, having on board a number of Brisbane's leading citizens among her 28 passengers, as well as 26 crew and a full cargo of hides, wool and tallow, much of which was carried on deck. Crossing Moreton Bay, a southerly gale forced Captain Henry Cape to seek shelter, and it was not until 11 March that the voyage was continued. Heavy seas were still breaking over the bar as the *Sovereign* attempted to make her way out to sea, and after breasting through two waves, the force of the water wrenched the paddle shaft from its bearings. Losing way, the rudder chains parted and deck cargo broke adrift as the crew fought to raise sails. It was a desperate situation, as

*Shamrock*, built for the Hunter trade, mostly ran between Sydney and Melbourne.

waves pounded the doomed vessel, which sank in four fathoms of water. Of those on board, 44 were lost, while the 10 survivors, including the captain, were rescued from the surf by local Aborigines. The loss of the ship, and so many prominent citizens, was a shattering blow to Brisbane, and the South Passage route was abandoned in favour of a longer one around the northern end of Moreton Island.

To replace the *Sovereign*, the Hunter's River Co. ordered a new steamer, which was built at Chowne's shipyard in Pyrmont, Sydney. Launched on 23 August 1848 and named *Eagle*, the vessel was placed on the Brisbane service, which she operated single-handed.

The Hunter's River Steam Navigation Co. had been formed in 1839 with the intention of providing a service between the Hunter River and Sydney. All the vessels built for the company had been designed to operate along the Hunter River, but as they expanded their interests to the intercolonial trades, these vessels were really not suitable for such services. They only succeeded through lack of competition, a situation that could not last. Despite this, an order was placed with the famous Denny shipyard in Dumbarton, Scotland, for the construction of two vessels, suitable to navigate the Hunter, for delivery in 1852. However, events in Australia were moving fast and the Hunter's River Steam Navigation Co. was wound up on 30 June 1851. The next day, the Australasian Steam Navigation Co. came into existence, taking over the business as a going concern. The new title more accurately reflected the spheres in which the company operated.

The two ships being built in Scotland, *Waratah* and *Yarra Yarra*, arrived in Australia in 1852. *Waratah* was 256 gross tons, and arrived in Sydney on 26 March 1852, while *Yarra Yarra*, which was 337 gross tons, arrived on 5 April. On her delivery voyage to Australia, *Yarra Yarra* brought out the 98-gross-ton steamer *Ballarat* in sections, which were assembled in Sydney.

Shortly before the arrival of the *Yarra Yarra* and *Waratah*, gold had been discovered in Victoria, and both ships were quickly placed in service from Sydney to Melbourne. They were the best appointed ships serving in Australia, and the first to offer increased headroom for passengers in public spaces. The saloon was still placed aft, but steerage quarters were placed right forward for the first time. Both ships proved to be slower than had been hoped, but they were useful additions to the ASN fleet.

Soon the Melbourne trade was being catered for by all available ASN ships, including *Yarra Yarra* and *Shamrock*, while *Waratah* began operating between Melbourne and Hobart. However, in 1852 the Launceston Steam Navigation Co. was formed, and quickly gained a stronghold in the Bass Strait trade with their screw steamers. The *Waratah* was withdrawn from the route before the end of the year and went to other trades.

The Victorian gold rush seriously depleted the steamer services to Brisbane, which did not please the Queenslanders at all. They formed the Moreton Bay Steam Navigation Co., but could not raise sufficient capital to start operations, and the venture folded early in 1853. The ASN realised it needed more ships and by 1855 nine vessels had been added, some

new, others bought second-hand, but most were propeller-driven.

Of these new ships, several were intended for the service to the Hunter River, or in Brisbane or Melbourne. However, three of the vessels were designed for the intercolonial trade, but only one, the *Telegraph*, was a paddler. The other two, *City of Sydney* and *Wonga Wonga*, were the first propeller vessels actually ordered by the ASN, with the *Wonga Wonga* being noted for her economical coal consumption. However, the *Telegraph* proved to be a real flyer, and set many records that stood until the 1880s.

The *Telegraph* arrived in Sydney on 9 January 1855, after a 109-day delivery voyage from Scotland, and was immediately placed in the trade between Sydney and Melbourne. As built, she was 352 gross tons, but in 1859 the vessel was lengthened from 194 feet (58.1 m) to 221 feet (67.3 m). This was accomplished at the ASN yard at Pyrmont, and was the biggest job of its kind yet attempted in Australia. *Telegraph* returned to service on 25 June 1859, and the press reported on 'the really tasteful manner in which this steamer has been fitted and painted'.

The Australasian Steam Navigation Co. had enjoyed a complete monopoly on the intercolonial trades since its formation, but in December 1853 a competitor was established, the Sydney and Melbourne Steam Packet Co., no doubt attracted by the demand for passages to the Victorian goldfields. The new company purchased the American-built paddler *New Orleans*, which was renamed *Governor General*, and placed her in service between Sydney and Melbourne. This 682-gross-ton paddler had arrived in Sydney from San Francisco in May 1853 and was then offered for sale. No doubt the availability of this large ship, which could carry about 600 passengers, was a major factor in the formation of the S&M Co. A second paddler bought by the company was the wooden-hulled *London*, of 687 gross tons, built in 1837 for the Dundee, Perth & London Shipping Co. Although large, this vessel was a real veteran, and outclassed by the ASN ships of the day. The S&M Co. also purchased a propeller-driven vessel, the *Hellespont*, giving them a rather unbalanced fleet.

Initially the Sydney & Melbourne Steam Packet Co. enjoyed good returns, as there was still a huge demand for coastal passages. This encouraged some of the directors so much they ordered a new vessel from Britain, which was to be the largest and fastest steamer on the Australian coast. The vessel was built at Millwall by the John Scott Russell shipyard, which at the same time was constructing the giant *Great Eastern*. The vessel was named *Pacific*, and was 1,469 gross tons, with a length of 248 feet (75.5 m), and provided accommodation for 100 first-class passengers, and 300 in second class.

The British government offered to buy the *Pacific* to use as a transport for the Crimean War, but the generous offer was turned down, and with a full passenger complement, the *Pacific* steamed out to Australia, arriving in Sydney on 26 February 1855. The huge vessel was immediately placed in service between Sydney and Melbourne, but the high hopes of the directors of the S&M Co. were soon dashed. Although large, the *Pacific* was no flyer, and had an excessive

*Pacific* was a great failure on the Australian coastal trade.

connection with the Cunard trans-Atlantic service. In 1847 the *Unicorn* was sold to the Pacific Mail Steam Ship Co. and operated out of San Francisco until dispatched to Australia, arriving in Sydney on 22 August 1853. Offered for sale, the *Unicorn* was bought early in 1854 by Edye Manning and began operating between Sydney and Melbourne. Though large, *Unicorn* was too expensive to operate, and on 15 December 1854 she left Sydney for Hong Kong, where she was sold.

The end of the gold rush to Victoria in the mid-1850s caused a reshuffle in intercolonial traders. The ASN Co. once again had the trade to itself and was determined to restore the Queensland trade to its former importance. The service from Sydney to Melbourne was entrusted to the *Telegraph* and the *Wonga Wonga. Yarra Yarra* and *Waratah*, along with the propeller-driven *City of Melbourne*, were placed on a new service, from Sydney to Wide Bay (Maryborough) and Port Curtis, with no call at Brisbane. In fact there would not be a service between Brisbane and Wide Bay until 1860. Eventually this route would be extended south to Melbourne, to become the longest service ever operated by paddle-steamers in Australia.

In 1860, the ASN Co. obtained a contract from the Queensland government to carry the mails from Brisbane to all parts as far north as Rockhampton. This aroused the ire of numerous prominent Queenslanders, and in March 1860 a meeting was held at Ipswich, which led to the formation of the Queensland Steam Navigation Co., one of whose backers was Robert Towns, who was responsible for the founding of Townsville four years later. By the end of 1860 a paddle-steamer had been ordered from the Barclay, Curle & Co. shipyard in Glasgow, which was launched on 16 September 1861 and named *Queensland*. Arriving in Brisbane on her delivery voyage on 3 June 1862,

appetite for coal. The ASN Co. scheduled its *Telegraph* opposite her at every sailing. The *Telegraph* not only offered faster passages, but a cheaper fare, though at considerable cost to the ASN finances. In December 1855 the S&M Co. was forced out of business. The *Pacific* was sent back to Britain, seeking a buyer, and eventually operated across the Atlantic for the Galway Line. The *London* and *Governor General* were both offered at auction in July 1856 and bought by the ASN Co., which employed them on their service between Sydney and Melbourne.

Another paddler worthy of mention that appeared in Australia at this time was the *Unicorn*. This wooden-hulled, 903-gross-ton vessel had been built in 1836 in Scotland for G. & J. Burns, to run between Glasgow and Liverpool. In 1840 she was purchased by the Cunard Line and sent across the Atlantic to Halifax in May 1840, to operate a mail service between there and Pictou, Nova Scotia, in

*Lady Young* operated from Brisbane to southern ports. (IF)

*Leichardt* was the largest iron-hulled paddler to be built in Australia. (IF)

the *Queensland* was placed in service along the Queensland coast, in direct competition with the ASN ships. A fare war erupted, which quickly halved the fares from Brisbane to places like Rockhampton and Maryborough. Despite being a one-ship operation fighting a giant, the QSN prospered, being well supported by the people of Queensland, and in 1863 two further paddle-steamers were ordered. The first to arrive in Brisbane, in June 1864, was the *Lady Bowen*, of 527 gross tons, while her identical sister, *Lady Young*, followed three months later. This pair were then placed on the Queensland coastal trade, as the QSN had just secured the mail contract from the ASN, while the smaller *Queensland*, of 373 gross tons, began operating between Sydney and Brisbane. In this way the QSN was able to offer a regular intercolonial service, and more direct competition to the ASN Co.

Rate wars continued between the two companies, with occasional truces that were soon broken. By January 1867 the QSN Co. was in serious financial difficulties, but it managed to struggle on to the end of the year. The ASN Co. then offered to buy out the QSN Co., and in January 1868 the deal was finalised. Once again, the ASN had overwhelmed an opponent, and added their ships to its fleet.

During this period the ASN Co. built a number of new ships for their fleet, including some notable paddle-steamers, the *Coonanbara* in 1862, followed in 1864 by the *City of Brisbane* and the *Cawarra*, then the *Leichardt* in 1865. The *Cawarra* was built for the Hunter River trade, but was also employed on various services to Queensland. The *City of Brisbane* was also placed on the intercolonial trades, mostly on secondary routes.

The best of the four was the *Coonanbara*, a sleek, two-funnelled, three-masted steamer of almost 900 gross tons, and 223 feet (67.9 m) long. Built by the C.J. Mare shipyard at Blackwall, on the River Thames, *Coonanbara* ran into heavy weather in the South Atlantic during her delivery voyage, when her rudder and steering gear were carried away, and much damage was done to her fittings. She had to put in to Cape Town for repairs, where luckily there was a slip big enough to take her. On her arrival in Australia, *Coonanbara* was soon considered the crack steamer on the coastal trades, and became very popular.

Unlike the other three, the *Leichardt* was built locally, at the ASN Co. shipyard in Pyrmont. She was the largest iron-hulled paddle-steamer to be built in Australia, being 368 gross tons, with a length of 188 feet (57.3 m). *Leichardt* looked very smart, with two widely spaced, raked funnels and two masts. She operated on the various east coast trades, but was mainly involved with services to the northern part of New South Wales, or within Queensland. It was during April 1865 that the ASN Co. added another paddler to its fleet, the *Florence Irving*, which had been built the previous year in England. This vessel was also used extensively on the northern rivers trade, but saw some service on the intercolonial routes.

The pace of development and change on the Australian coastal trades was so fast that paddle-steamers soon fell out of favour for the intercolonial trades, being supplanted by propeller-driven vessels. The *Cawarra* was operating to Queensland when she was wrecked off Newcastle on 12 July 1866. On 9 October 1867 the *Telegraph* was wrecked off Camden Head, on a voyage from Sydney to Queensland.

Just five years after her arrival, the *Coonanbara* was relegated to the Hunter River trade, where she spent many successful years. The *City of Brisbane* operated along the east coast of Australia until 1870, then joined *Coonanbara* on the Hunter River trade, later being renamed *Sydney*. In 1873 both the *Leichardt* and the *Florence Irving* were rebuilt, and converted into propeller-driven vessels. *Yarra Yarra* was sold in November 1874 and converted into a collier. *Queensland*, *Lady Bowen* and *Lady Young* survived into the 1880s, but were relegated to local services within Queensland. By 1875, no paddle-steamers were being employed on the intercolonial trades.

# 5 Overseas Traders

Although several of the early paddle-steamers to operate on the Australian coast came from Britain, their only overseas voyages were during delivery. Even then, some of the vessels came out under sail, rather than using their machinery. In 1842 the Australian-built paddle-steamer *Victoria* was sold to owners in India, and in subsequent years a number of vessels voyaged from Australia to foreign ports following their sale. The enormous distances involved in steaming to Australia from Europe or North America effectively precluded the establishment of regular steamship services for many years.

Even the shorter service across the Tasman Sea to New Zealand was difficult for steamers. The first commercial voyage was made by the paddler *Juno*, of 621 gross tons. Built at Greenock in 1841, the *Juno* had come out to Australia under sail, but then was laid up until 1847, when her machinery was installed. On 13 June 1847 the *Juno* left her berth in Sydney, but did not pass through Sydney Heads until the following day. She carried nine passengers, 1,000 sheep, 79 head of cattle, and an unknown number of horses. The horses all survived the trip, but only 670 sheep and 48 cattle made it to Auckland, as the voyage was beset with difficulties. For the first few days the *Juno* battled a heavy north-east gale, which eased on the evening of 23 June. However, the wind then veered to the west, causing a nasty cross sea, which put such a strain on the pintles of her rudder that they broke, and the rudder was lost. For three days the seas were too rough to attempt any repairs, but on 26 June a temporary rudder was put in place. Reaching the Bay of Islands safely, further repairs were carried out to the rudder, then on 4 July the *Juno* headed for Auckland. Again rough seas were encountered, which destroyed the temporary rudder, so the vessel returned to the Bay of Islands, where another rudder was fashioned and fitted. Departing again on 6 July, *Juno* reached Auckland in just 15 hours, despite battling a strong headwind, the voyage having lasted 23 days. *Juno* attempted to start her return trip to Sydney on 22 August, but suffered more problems and did not get away until 11 September. It was not until 1854 that a regular steamer service was started to New Zealand, using propeller-driven vessels.

In 1852 the P&O Line commenced the first service to Australia from Britain. The discovery of gold in Victoria at this time induced other companies to enter the trade, amongst them the Liverpool & Australian Navigation Co., which despatched the famous iron-hulled screw steamer *Great Britain* from Liverpool to Australia in August 1852. Another Liverpool concern to enter the Australian trade at this time

was Millers & Thompson, managers of the Golden Line of Packets, which dispatched the screw steamer *Antelope* on 8 March 1853, for Adelaide, Melbourne, where she arrived on 18 August, and Sydney. Six months later the Golden Line of Packets advertised that the American paddle-steamer *Golden Age*, of 2,864 gross tons, would depart Liverpool on 26 November 1853, for Melbourne and Sydney.

The *Golden Age* had been built at New York by William H. Brown. She was laid down as the *Adriatic* for the Collins Line, which already owned four similar-sized paddlers, *Atlantic, Pacific, Arctic* and *Baltic*. During construction, however, the vessel was sold to the New York & Australian Navigation Co., which planned to use her on a new service from Panama to Sydney. On completion she was renamed *Golden Age*, and crossed the Atlantic to Liverpool to prepare for a voyage to Australia, from where she would commence her trade to Panama.

The New York & Australian Navigation Co. had been formed early in 1853, and during that year despatched two vessels on trans-Pacific voyages. The first of these was the 768-gross-ton screw-propelled *Monumental City*, built in 1852, which became the first steamer to cross the Pacific to Australia. Unfortunately, she was wrecked near Mallacoota Inlet, on the Victorian coast, on 15 May 1853. The second vessel was the paddle-steamer *New Orleans*, of 682 gross tons, built in 1848 in New York. From early in 1850, *New Orleans* operated between San Francisco and Panama, until being despatched to Australia from San Francisco on 10 March 1853.

Following a voyage lasting 64 days, *New Orleans* arrived in Sydney on 14 May. En route, she had called at Nukahiva, Tahiti, Tongatabu and Brisbane, becoming the first steamship from overseas to visit the port. Time spent in port during the voyage was 22 days 13½ hours, including 8 days 20½ hours at Brisbane, so the actual running time was 41 days 14½ hours. The month following her arrival in Sydney, the *New Orleans* was advertised for sale. A description of the ship showed that she had accommodation for 160 passengers in the saloon, 60 in the ladies' cabin and 400 in steerage, which seems quite a lot, but maybe they did not all have berths. *New Orleans* was bought by the Sydney & Melbourne Steam Packet Co., renamed *Governor General*, and spent the next six years plying the Australian east coast. In January 1861 she was steamed to Hong Kong and sold for service on the Yangtse River, becoming the third foreign vessel to reach Hankow.

The *Golden Age* departed Liverpool on 28 November 1853, but collided with the North Wall on the Birkenhead

*Golden Age* made just one voyage to Australia.

shore and had to return for dry-docking. Repaired, she sailed again on 5 December, and after calling at the Cape Verde Islands and Cape Town, arrived in Melbourne on 14 February 1854, and in Sydney on 23 February. *Golden Age* then spent three months making coastal voyages between Sydney and Melbourne, one in a record time of 44 hours.

The *Golden Age* had a wooden hull, the lower frames being oak while the top frames were locust-wood and cedar. The entire hull was double-diagonally braced with iron bars. She was equipped with all the latest devices, and special attention had been paid to the ventilation. She was powered by a beam engine of the American type, in which an upright cylinder, said at the time to be the largest yet placed in a ship, worked direct to one end of a massive, stoutly braced beam, which swung on heavy trunnions above her deckhouse. The idea of these upright engines was to save space and fuel. *Golden Age* was fitted out with accommodation for 1,200 passengers, 200 first cabin, 200 second and 800 third class. There were three saloons, panelled in rose, satin and zebra woods, two having crimson and gold plush furnishings, while the upper saloon had white and gold furnishings. Five hundred tons of cargo could be carried, and 1,200 tons of coal.

Despite a report in the *Sydney Shipping Gazette* that the vessel 'was originally intended to trade between Panama and Sydney, but it is now intended that she shall ply between San Francisco and Sydney', the *Golden Age* departed Sydney on 11 May 1854, bound for Tahiti and Panama, this being the second voyage by a paddle-steamer eastwards from Australia. On board were over 100 passengers, mail and some general cargo. *Golden Age* arrived in Tahiti in 13 days 6 hours, departing again on 30 May, taking 19 days to reach Panama, on 17 June, having consumed 2,600 tons of coal on the voyage from Sydney. The high price and poor quality of coal obtained in Tahiti resulted in the voyage showing a considerable financial loss, although the mails, sent across

Panama and on to London on another steamer, arrived in just 65 days.

The New York & Australian Navigation Co. had previously announced plans to place five steamers on the trans-Pacific run, but the commander of the *Golden Age*, Lieutenant Porter, suggested that the voyage would only be a success if operated in two stages, each maintained by two vessels. However, the company decided not to continue with the trade, and *Golden Age* was sold.

It is worth recording the voyages of the *Pacific* in this chapter, even though they were not intended to be on a regular basis. The Sydney & Melbourne Steam Packet Co. was the first company formed to provide a service to link the two cities. In 1853 several directors of the company decided to order a paddle-steamer, which would be the largest on the coastal trade, and completely overwhelm any opposition. Built on the Thames at the Milwall yard of John Scott Russell, the builders of the famous *Great Eastern*, the 1,469-gross-ton vessel was named *Pacific* when launched in 1854. Fitted out with accommodation for 100 first-class and 300 second-class passengers, *Pacific* took on a full complement for the delivery voyage to Australia. Prior to her departure, the owners had been offered a large sum for the ship by the British government, which was seeking suitable transports for the Crimean War. The offer was declined, as it was felt the *Pacific* would reap huge returns on the Australian coast.

*Pacific* was probably the first paddle-steamer to make the long voyage from Britain to Australia entirely under steam, and made a triumphal entry into Melbourne and Sydney. However, all did not go according to plan. On the coastal trade, *Pacific* proved to be quite uneconomical, and the shareholders of the Sydney & Melbourne Steam Packet Co. refused to allow the company to purchase the ship from the directors. They tried to sell her to the opposition Australasian Steam Navigation Co., but in vain. So the

*Pacific* was sent back to England, in the hope that the British government would still be interested in her, but this proved futile. *Pacific* was the only paddle-steamer to make a round voyage from Britain to Australia and back. However, this was not intended to be a regular service, but the voyages of the *Pacific* were significant events in Australian maritime history.

In June 1855 an attempt was made to establish a regular steamer connection between the east coast of Australia and Singapore. The paddler used was the *Phoenix*, which had been built at Greenock in 1842 for service in South African waters. On 18 October 1852 the 240-gross-ton *Phoenix* departed Cape Town for Melbourne, with a full complement of gold diggers aboard. On arrival in Melbourne, the vessel was sold to local identities. An attempt to run the ship to Adelaide was unsuccessful, so she was resold in May 1855 to Robert Towns, of Sydney.

Apparently the vessel was in very poor condition, as the *Sydney Gazette* in June 1855 reported that the *Phoenix*, after 'extensive repairs, on Saturday took a trial trip down the harbour'. The report went on to state the ship had 'entirely new boilers in her, is newly decked fore and aft; her engines have been thoroughly overhauled, and the entire expense of the repairs have not been less than £9,000'. As to her future employment, 'Messrs Towns & Darley purpose sending her about the 15th of this month to Singapore, with the view of meeting the Indian mail'.

On 23 June *Phoenix* left Sydney for Singapore, having on board only five passengers, but a large amount of mail for England. On 8 July she struck a reef in the Prince of Wales Channel in Torres Strait. All aboard, and the mails, were safely removed, but the *Phoenix* was a total loss. So ended the attempts by the fledgling colony to establish its own links with Singapore. In future, it would have to rely on foreign-owned ships.

By the mid-1850s, paddle-steamers were being replaced on international trade routes by screw-propelled vessels. The frailty of the paddlewheels in open oceans made them less than reliable, though some quite large paddle-propelled vessels were still built in later years, particularly in America. The last paddlers to operate from overseas ports to Australia were *Nebraska*, *Nevada* and *Dakota*, built in the mid-1860s for William H. Webb, who had hoped to sell them on completion to the United State government for use as transports during the Civil War. Instead they were only chartered, and on its expiry, Webb tried the trio on various routes, the last being across the Pacific.

In 1870 William Webb and Ben Holliday formed the California, New Zealand & Australia Mail Steamship Co. in San Francisco. They planned to establish a four-weekly service via Honolulu, using the three large paddlers. The first voyage was taken by the *Nevada*, which departed San Francisco on 8 April 1871 for Honolulu, Auckland, Wellington, Lyttleton and Port Chalmers. The first voyage to Australia was that of the *Nebraska* in May 1871, going to Sydney and Melbourne. The third ship, *Dakota*, had slightly different engines from the other pair, and suffered endless mechanical problems. She was on the east coast of America when the service was commenced across the Pacific, undergoing engine repairs, and did not depart New York until 10 August 1872, proceeding via Cape Town to Melbourne, then Auckland and Honolulu. Once these three ships had completed their initial voyages, they operated only from Honolulu, as the smaller *Moses Taylor* and *Mohongo* were used on the connecting service to the mainland.

*Nevada*, *Nebraska* and *Dakota* were the largest paddle-

*Nebraska*, one of three paddlers that came to Australia between 1871 and 1873.

steamers ever to visit Australia, but they were hopelessly out of date and really not suited to the trade at all. They had hulls built of oak and hackamack double-planked timber, 10 centimetres thick and strapped with iron. There were four decks, and while the accommodation was roomy for those times, it was very cramped by modern standards. The San Francisco *News of the World* described them thus:

> Running along the centre of the deck are 20 staterooms, each having a close and a Venetian door, and a window 32 inches square. These staterooms are all double, with doors on each side and ventilators on top. Right aft is the ladies' sitting room, well fitted up, private, and well ventilated. Forward of this is the smoke room, fitted up with a degree of comfort seldom seen on board ship. On the main deck is the grand saloon, 90 feet long, 28 feet wide and 8 feet high. On each side of this saloon is a row of staterooms, opening on the deck and accommodating 80 passengers, with 2 bridal chambers in the forward part of the saloon. The berth deck is occupied by the third class passengers and will accommodate 620. Abaft of this there are 40 well-ventilated staterooms for second class passengers. For extinguishing fire, an iron pipe leading the whole length of the ship has some 15 branches of hose always connected, and water and steam are available. There are lifebuoys in each berth, and boats capable of carrying 830 passengers.

The writer went on to say that the ships would 'average a speed of 340 miles a day when working up to full power', but with their antiquated single-cylinder beam engine they seldom manage more than 10 knots. The ships had an enormous appetite for coal, about 30 tons per day. Coal could be obtained quite cheaply in Sydney, and more would be taken on in Auckland, but it was very expensive to purchase in the Pacific Islands.

*Nebraska* was easily the best of the three, while *Nevada* was the source of numerous problems. In October 1872 *Nevada* collided with the small barque *A.H. Badger* in the Tasman Sea, but did not stop. The barque sank a few hours later, her complement being rescued by another sailing ship some time later. On arrival in Sydney, the captain of the *Nevada* did not report the incident, which only came to notice when the survivors were landed. Following an inquiry into the collision, *Nevada* was held at fault and her captain condemned for not stopping. It is said that subsequently he dared not show himself in the streets of Sydney, for fear of being hooted. Later the *Nevada* was the subject of an inquiry by the Australian and New Zealand postmasters-general, as to her fitness for carrying passengers, due to severe boiler problems. When the Ship Subsidy Bill was being considered by the American Congress in 1873, the mail subsidy granted to the company was withdrawn.

By the beginning of 1873, all three vessels were reported to be in extremely poor condition. The withdrawal of the mail subsidy effectively killed the economic viability of the three ships on the trans-Pacific route. They were obtaining very little cargo, so revenue was almost entirely dependent on passengers and the mail subsidy. In 1874 the service was terminated, the last departure from Sydney being taken by the *Nebraska* in April 1874. So ended the operation of paddle-steamers on overseas services to Australia.

*Adelaide* is the oldest surviving steamer in Australia.

Restored *Ada* barge on right, with B22 awaiting restoraion, at Echuca.

*Industry* and derrick barge near Renmark. (FT)

*Murray Queen*, a small boat with a grand name.

# 6 Bass Strait Services

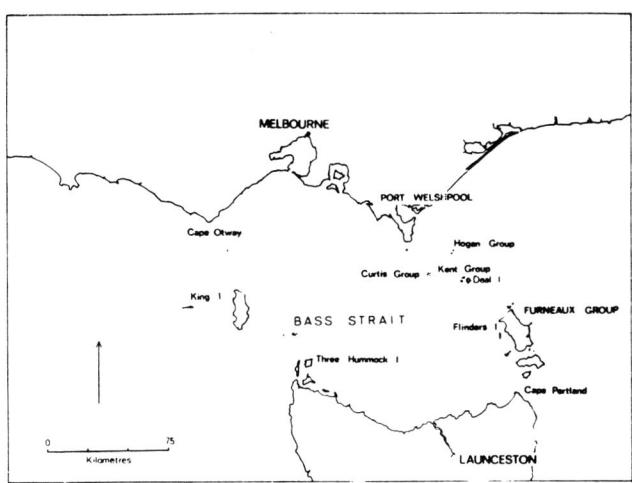

Map of Bass Strait (BP)

Bass Strait is a dangerous, often stormy stretch of water that separates the island state of Tasmania from mainland Australia. From the days of earliest settlement in Tasmania, or Van Diemen's Land as it was originally known, it was essential that shipping services be established as quickly as possible, especially with the other main settlement, Sydney. For many years this was maintained by sailing ships. With the development of a settlement on the shores of Port Phillip Bay, which became Melbourne, a much shorter connecting service with the mainland became possible.

In June 1837 came the first attempt to establish a steam connection between the mainland and Tasmania. The *James Watt*, which had arrived in Sydney from Britain in February 1837, departed Sydney on 19 June, bound for Launceston, then Port Phillip Bay. The arrival of the vessel in Launceston on 26 June was reported in the *Launceston Advertiser* three days later:

> The steam-ship *James Watt* arrived in this port on Monday, having put in to Twofold Bay for coals. Seven days were occupied (this stoppage inclusive) in the passage from Sydney. She leaves this morning for Port Phillip, returning hither in about a week or ten days, when she will start again for Sydney. We most heartily wish the proprietor success.

*James Watt* made a second voyage to Tasmania in September 1837 and returned again in January 1838, but then was sent elsewhere.

It was almost three years before a second steamer, the *Clonmell*, was placed in service from the mainland to Tasmania. It was intended that the *Clonmell*, described as the largest of the colonial steamers, would operate a triangular service similar to that run by *James Watt*, only going to Melbourne first. *Clonmell* arrived in Launceston for the first time on 10 December 1840, but on its second voyage was wrecked near Wilsons Promontory while bound from Sydney to Port Phillip Bay.

For several months there was no further connection, then in October 1842 the *Corsair* was chartered by the Port Phillip Steam Navigation Co. and began operating between Melbourne and Launceston. Unfortunately, the paddler's engines gave a lot of trouble and the vessel was often under repair, losing £1,000 for her operators in the first four months of the service. At the same time, the large paddle-steamer *Seahorse*, owned by Benjamin Boyd, was running between Sydney and Melbourne, and the timetables of the two ships were arranged to provide a through connection. However, in August 1842 the *Corsair* ceased trading, and it was then arranged for the *Seahorse* to call at George Town on her way from Sydney to Melbourne.

Then a second ship was added to the Bass Strait service, the *Shamrock*, owned by the Hunter's River Steam Navigation Co., which later became the Australasian Steam Navigation Co. This vessel had been built in 1841 for the service between Sydney and Newcastle. However, in 1842 the vessel began running between Sydney and Melbourne, while a call at Launceston was added to the itinerary in September 1842. *Shamrock* provided formidable opposition for the *Seahorse*, which had a prodigious appetite for coal, while *Shamrock* was very economical and could charge a lower fare. The period of competition between the two paddlers was of brief duration, as on 5 June 1843 the *Seahorse* ran aground in George Town Cove. At low water the vessel listed heavily, straining the hull, and though floated off at the next high tide, returned to Sydney and was laid up.

The *Shamrock* continued to call in to Launceston en route every three or four weeks for several years, but in 1846 the itinerary was changed to allow for a return trip from Melbourne to Launceston before returning to Sydney. At times in 1845 and 1846, *Shamrock* was replaced by her sister ship, *Thistle*, for short periods. In 1847 Benjamin Boyd returned to the route again with another of his paddle-steamers, the *Cornubia*, which traded regularly between Melbourne and Launceston. In an attempt to attract custom, the fare charged for travel on the *Cornubia* was reduced to just 5s., but the *Shamrock* still retained its popularity and in 1848 the *Cornubia* was withdrawn.

*Shamrock* remained the main steamer connecting Tasmania to the mainland for many years, but in 1851 was faced with stiff competition. The *City of Melbourne* was the first propeller-driven steamer to be built in Australia, and the Launceston *Examiner* of 4 June 1851 commented on the advantages of the new type of propulsion thus: 'In smooth water the screw has less power than the paddle, but in rough weather it has a decided advantage, as, unlike the paddle, it is always under water, and the vessel is not encumbered with those unseemly appendages—the paddle boxes'. *Shamrock* and *City of Melbourne* maintained regular schedules across Bass Strait, but with the discovery of gold in Victoria the demand for passages increased and the small paddler *Waratah*, owned by the Australasian Steam Navigation Co., also joined the route for occasional trips. At the same time, no fewer than 15 sailing vessels of varying types and sizes were also engaged in the Bass Strait trade.

On 6 August 1852 the *City of Melbourne* ran ashore on King Island, and though refloated, never returned to the Tasmanian trade. The owners of the *Shamrock* seized this opportunity to place their new paddler *Yarra Yarra* on a regular service between Melbourne and Launceston, replacing *Shamrock*. The 555-gross-ton *Yarra Yarra* had been built in Scotland in 1851 and was a great improvement on the *Shamrock*. Entering service in September 1852, the vessel carried 51 cabin and 350 steerage-class passengers.

In 1852 two shipping companies were founded in Tasmania, the Tasmanian Steam Navigation Co., in Hobart, and the Launceston Steam Navigation Co. The latter was formed specifically to operate a direct service between Launceston and Melbourne, but rather than order a new steamer, it purchased the *Clarence*. This paddle-steamer, which had been completed in Britain in December 1851, was built for service from Sydney to the Clarence River in northern New South Wales. On arrival in Sydney, the vessel was inspected by representatives of the Launceston company, who no doubt saw a golden opportunity to fill the gap left by the loss of the *City of Melbourne*. They made a huge offer for the ship, certainly far more than it had cost to build. The owner had no hesitation in accepting, and after a hurried overhaul, the *Clarence* began running between Launceston and Melbourne in October 1852.

At 346 gross tons, the *Clarence* was smaller than the *Yarra Yarra*, but very well fitted out. From the start, there was an intense rivalry between the two paddlers, commencing with the very first voyage made by the *Clarence*. The ASN scheduled the *Yarra Yarra* to leave Melbourne at the same time as its new rival, and the pair were still together when they entered the Tamar River at 7 a.m. There now began a race up the river, for the honour of being the first to berth. Reaching a section where the channel narrowed, the *Clarence* closed in on the *Yarra Yarra*, which made no effort to get out of the way, and a collision resulted, with the *Clarence* losing her figurehead while the *Yarra Yarra* lost a portion of her bulwarks. Although this type of incident was not repeated, the two ships competed fiercely for the available trade, in which they also had competition from three smaller propeller steamships, the *Pirate*, *Queen of the Netherlands* and *Lady Bird*. By 1854 the first two had left the scene and the *Lady Bird* had been purchased by the Launceston Steam Navigation Co., which also added two other propeller-

powered steamers, the *Black Swan* and *Royal Shepherd*. In April 1854 the *Yarra Yarra* was withdrawn from the Bass Strait trade, ending the ASN Co. interest in Tasmania, leaving the Launceston company as the only major operator on the route. Its four ships were scheduled to make 18 crossings to Melbourne per month. This only required three ships, so the *Clarence* spent a considerable period laid up, then was offered for sale, it being considered that propeller ships were better suited to the strait service than the paddler.

From time to time new competitors appeared on the Bass Strait trade, one being the paddler *Fenella* of 261 gross tons. Built in 1846 for service in the Irish Sea, the *Fenella* was sent to Australia in 1856, hoping to find a buyer. For a short time she operated between Melbourne and Launceston, but soon went on to other trades. In 1857 the 453-gross-ton paddler *North Star* also joined the trade. Built in Britain in 1843, *North Star* had also been sent to Australia for sale in 1854. After three years lying idle at anchor off Sandridge Pier in Port Phillip Bay, *North Star* was purchased by a Captain Lawrence, who placed the ship in service between Melbourne and Launceston. However, after only a few months the ship was dispatched to Shanghai and offered for sale there.

To counter this opposition, the Launceston Steam Navigation Co. engaged in a price-cutting war, that had a disastrous result for the company, which went into liquidation. The *Clarence* was sold in 1856 and a new company, the Launceston & Melbourne Steam Navigation Co., took over the Bass Strait trade, though using only propeller steamships.

The Bass Strait trade developed over the next 30 years, but the Launceston & Melbourne Steam Navigation Co. did not prosper and was eventually taken over by the Tasmanian Steam Navigation Co. In 1878 the Union Steam Ship Co. of New Zealand also entered the Tasmanian trade, following their purchase of the Australian shipping firm, McMeckan, Blackwood & Co. Then, in August 1889, Huddart Parker Limited decided to enter the Bass Strait trade as well, but the vessel it wished to use, the Port Phillip Bay steamer *Coogee*, needed to be altered to suit it for the trade. In the interim, Huddart Parker chartered the paddler *Newcastle* to run between Melbourne and Launceston.

The *Newcastle* had been built in 1884 for the Newcastle Steamship Co., to operate between Sydney and Newcastle. At 1,251 gross tons, the vessel was larger than those being operated by the Tasmanian Steam Navigation Co., and Huddart Parker also reduced their fares to £1, forcing the TSN to do the same, their previous fare having been £3 5s. 0d. *Newcastle* was quite an imposing-looking vessel, with an unusual arrangement of three yellow-painted funnels, two closely spaced forward of the paddlebox, with a third stack further aft. The *Newcastle* was scheduled to make three return trips a week across Bass Strait, under the command of Captain H.C. White, formerly of the TSN Co.

Advertised as 'the fastest steamer in the colonies, with accommodation for 400 passengers, and engines of 4,000 hp', the *Newcastle* faced its main competition from the propeller steamer *Pateena* of the TSN, and the two were of

*Newcastle* was chartered by Huddart Parker for their Bass Strait service. (RWB)

similar speed. *Newcastle* departed Melbourne for her first crossing of Bass Strait on the afternoon of 26 October 1889, arriving in Launceston the following morning. In order to maintain her schedule, the *Newcastle* used to spend only about nine hours in Launceston, then depart for Melbourne the same evening. Initially *Newcastle* worked alongside the larger Huddart Parker steamers *Burrumbeet* and *Elingamite*, but in November 1889 they were withdrawn. *Newcastle* subsequently also made a fortnightly trip to ports on the north-west coast of Tasmania, Burnie and Devonport.

Sometimes *Newcastle* and *Pateena* would engage in a race, but the pair were very evenly matched.

The only problem with the *Newcastle* was her enormous appetite for coal to enable a speed of about 16 knots to be maintained. The Newcastle Steamship Co. had been hopeful that Huddart Parker would be sufficiently impressed with the *Newcastle* to buy the ship, but when the *Coogee* was ready in April 1890, the *Newcastle* was handed back to its owners. This brought to an end the use of paddle-steamers on the Bass Strait services.

# 7 Tasmania

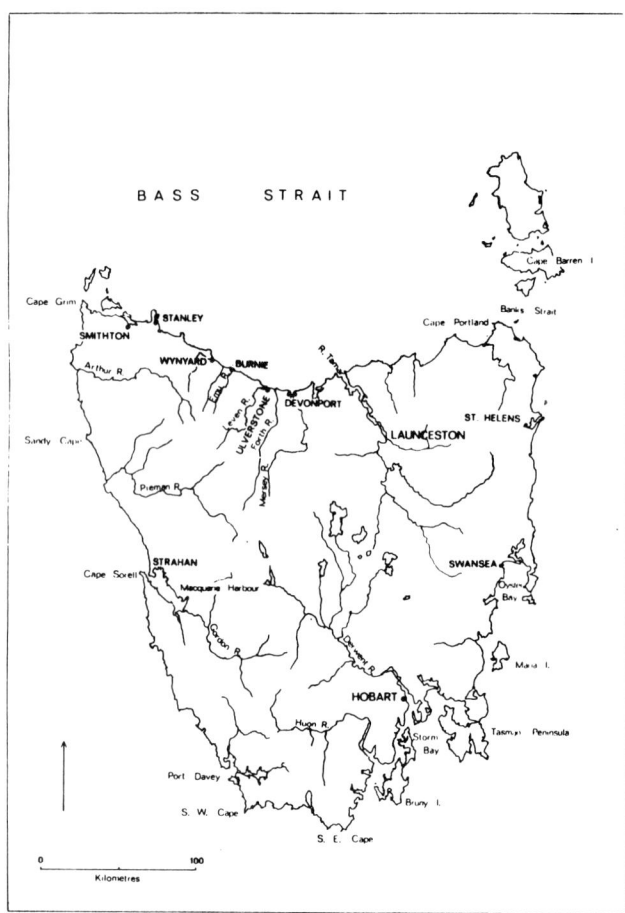

Map of Tasmania (BP)

Tasmania, which was known as Van Diemen's Land until 1856, became a colony independent from New South Wales in 1825. Initial settlements had begun at Hobart Town on the Derwent River in the south of the island in 1803, and at Launceston on the Tamar River in the north in 1804. In later years the island was notorious for its brutal penal settlements, at Macquarie Harbour on the west coast and Port Arthur near Hobart. However, free settlement was encouraged in the main centres of Hobart and Launceston. Hobart was quite a thriving centre, second only to Sydney, so it is not surprising that within a year of the first steamship arriving in Sydney, there was a steamer operating in Hobart.

The first person to operate steam vessels in Tasmanian waters was Dr Alexander Thomson, who made six voyages to Australia as a ship's surgeon, then decided to settle in Van Diemen's Land. Prior to departing England with his wife and young daughter, Dr Thomson placed an order with a shipyard on the River Thames to construct a paddle-steamer for him, to be shipped in sections to Hobart. It appears that, during a visit to Hobart in 1830, an agreement with Lieutenant-Governor Arthur was arranged whereby, if Thomson obtained a steamer for service on the Derwent, he would receive a grant of land.

By the time Thomson arrived in Hobart as a settler in December 1831, the system of free grants of land had been discontinued. However, Thomson petitioned the Land Board, citing his agreement with the governor and claiming that his steamboat was being shipped to Hobart at that time, and his claim for a land grant was approved once a steam vessel under his ownership had operated on the Derwent for one month. Instead of having to wait many months until his new boat was completed, Dr Thomson was able to obtain his land grant quite early in 1832. The pioneer Australian-built paddle-steamer *Surprise*, completed in Sydney in May 1831, had not been a success on Sydney Harbour, so in January 1832 its owner, Henry Smith, voyaged to Hobart with the intention of selling the vessel. The *Surprise* arrived in Hobart under sail on 1 February 1832 and was purchased by Dr Thomson. The paddles were reassembled, and on 20 February *Surprise* made the first voyage by a steam boat in Tasmanian waters, from Hobart across the Derwent to Kangaroo Point, now known as Bellerive.

Once the vessel built for Dr Thomson in England arrived in sections in Hobart, work began on its assembly. The *Colonial Times* reported on 9 May 1832 that 'Messrs Callaghan are now building for Mr Thomson a steam boat of sixty-five feet from stem to stern and eighteen in breadth of beam. The vessel came in frame from England, consequently it will shortly be afloat.' Despite the last statement, the vessel did not make its first voyage until 10 September 1832. Thomson named his new boat *Governor Arthur* and the *Hobart Town Courier*, reporting on the first voyage, stated:

> when the paddles were put on and the anchor weighed, the vessel made two or three turns about the harbour, and then darted across the ferry to Kangaroo Point, a distance of 3 miles which she performed in 12 minutes, although a considerable portion of the power (14 horses) was not put on... Dr Thomson deserves universal praise and encouragement of the colonists at large for being the first introducer of this noble addition to human power and comfort in our island...the advantages it affords are manifold, not the least of which will as a matter of course be the saving of many lives which have been hitherto annually lost in crossing in sailing boats.

Thomson operated the *Surprise* and *Governor Arthur* on a ferry service across the Derwent, and also up the river to New Norfolk.

On 1 June 1833, with Dr Thomson on board, the *Governor Arthur* left Hobart, bound for Launceston, this being the first voyage by a steamer along the Tasmanian coast. Encountering heavy seas, the vessel was forced to put into Georges River, now St Helens, for repairs. When the voyage continued, the vessel steamed past the Tamar and reached Circular Head before the mistake was realised and she turned back to reach Launceston. More repairs were required, then the vessel was advertised for sale in the *Launceston Advertiser* on 26 September 1833, described as

> that new, substantial Thames built steam boat, the *Governor Arthur*, now laying in the harbour and ready for instant service. She is of 50 tons burthen and 14 h.p. schooner rigged, coppered and copper fastened. . . she is well found in sails, chain cables, anchors, etc. This vessel is admirably adapted for a store for supplying the settlers on the Tamar or coast, and bringing their produce to port in return; and would yield a handsome profit to the owner in the sale of wines etc.

No sale eventuated, which might not have been surprising, as previous attempts to interest the people of Launceston in steam vessels had been singularly unsuccessful.

Dr Thomson was in serious financial trouble, and the failure to sell the *Governor Arthur* was a major blow for him. He managed to secure a cargo of flour and returned with his vessel to Hobart. Thomson then petitioned Governor Arthur for a further grant of land, stating he was £7,000 in debt due to his steamboat ventures, and wished to return to farming. Although the date is unknown, Thomson did manage to dispose of the *Governor Arthur*, probably early in 1834, as during that year a new engine was built for the vessel in Hobart. On 24 October 1834, the *Hobart Town Courier* reported that the

> new steam engine for the *Governor Arthur* steam boat is, we are happy to observe, nearly finished. . . The wheel which produces the blast revolves at the astonishing rate of 1,500 times in a minute. When the engine is complete, it is intended that the vessel shall be established as a passage boat between Hobart Town and New Norfolk, leaving town every morning and returning in the evening. . . making the distance between the two places, including all stoppages, in about 3 hours.

Dr Thomson also disposed of the *Surprise*, which is believed to have been converted into a topsail schooner. During 1835, Thomson left Hobart and took his family to live in the new settlement founded on the banks of the River Yarra, which became Melbourne. He later moved to Geelong, and became the first mayor in 1850.

While Dr Thomson was pioneering steam vessels in Hobart, a group of five businessmen from Launceston were interested in getting a steamboat onto the Tamar. On 1 May 1832 a public meeting was held at the Launceston Hotel for the purpose of 'forwarding the establishment of a Steam Vessel upon the River Tamar', but the public response was disappointing. The *Launceston Advertiser* stated on 9 May that: 'we are very sorry to find the public of Launceston did not exhibit that degree of interest in the establishment of a steam vessel at this port, which we expected, and that it is now left to a few gentlemen, who have however determined upon carrying the thing into effect'. By the end of 1832 the Steam Navigation Co. had been formed, later renamed the Tamar Steam Navigation Co. The *Launceston Advertiser* on 23 May 1832 stated that the aim of the company was to 'be the means of opening a regular intercourse with George Town. . .cause a constant supply of timber, stone, slate, lime, fish, etc., the produce of the river and its banks, to be brought to market'. The advantages of a steamer operating along the Tamar were further extolled, as an engine would

> enable ships to get down the river at all times and at all seasons with safety and expedition. Nothing but a steamer could effect this object, in consequence of the winds prevailing from the north-west so much as they do. Such a wind, being directly up the river, frequently prevents vessels from getting out to sea for days and days after they have broken ground, as there is no room for a heavy vessel to beat against the wind.

In 1834 the Steam Navigation Co. engaged a Captain Wales to travel to Britain, purchase a suitable vessel and bring it to Launceston. Wales found a suitable vessel in Glasgow, where it had been built in 1833, probably on a speculative basis. Named *Tamar*, the vessel was 96 feet (29.3 m) long, and powered by a 60-horsepower side-lever jet-condensing steam-engine. The *Tamar* left Glasgow in ballast, with 12 passengers, making the long voyage under sail and arriving in Launceston on 8 September 1834. The *Advertiser* on 11 September described the new arrival as 'a fine vessel of her class; is very strongly built and well finished in every respect', but went on ominously, 'rumour stated that she is immediately to be sent to Sydney for sale'. The *Tamar* was apparently not welcomed with the expected enthusiasm, as on 30 October the *Advertiser* mentioned 'the advantages that would be derived from steam navigation on the River Tamar, particularly as regards the towing of vessels, and trust sufficient encouragement will be given to enable the owners of the steam vessel purchased purposely for the river, to continue her upon it.'

During November 1834 the *Tamar* did make a few trips along the river, but then it was sold to Samuel Bryan. On 29 November 1834 Bryan left Launceston in the *Tamar*, bound for Sydney, where he sold the vessel.

For some years, interest in steam ships waned in Tasmania, though a few schemes were promoted to establish steamship companies, but none came to fruition. One was given the grand title of the Hobart Town, Launceston & Port Phillip Steam Navigation Co., but one that did actually operate a vessel was the Derwent Steam Navigation Co. In April 1840 it took delivery of the first steamer to be totally built in Tasmania, the *Derwent*. A wooden vessel of 49 gross tons, the *Derwent* operated between Hobart and New Norfolk. Shortly after, the second Tasmanian-built steamer was completed, by John Watson in Hobart. Named *Native*

Steaming down the River Derwent towards Hobart is the *Monarch*, which was built in 1846 at Renfrew in Scotland. Rigged as a three-masted schooner, *Monarch* made the voyage from the Clyde to Tasmania under sail in 100 days during 1854. For the next forty years, *Monarch* plied regularly between Hobart and New Norfolk. *Monarch* had an iron hull, and was fitted with a steeple steam engine. (LR)

*Youth*, she ran between Hobart and Kangaroo Point, and later became the first steamer to travel on the Huon River. Meanwhile, in Launceston, the River Tamar Steam Navigation Co. was formed in 1840 and ordered a paddle-steamer to be built in Sydney. Delivered in March 1842, the 80-foot (24.4 m) vessel was named *Gypsy*. Initially the *Gypsy* ran three trips a week from Launceston to George Town and Kelso, but within a month this had been reduced to two. During the winter of 1844 the service was suspended, then resumed for several months with a trip every Saturday. By 1845, *Gypsy* operated only when required, and in 1847 she was sold and left Tasmania.

The first iron-hulled steamer to arrive in Tasmanian waters was the *Thames*. Build in England, at Blackwall on the Thames, she was owned by the Derwent Steam Boat Co., and at 110 gross tons was far larger than any previous vessel in Tasmania. The *Thames* was brought to Australia under sail, the voyage lasting four and a half months, arriving in Hobart on 10 November 1843. The *Thames* was more of a general trader than a ferry, and pioneered many short sea routes, but was never really successful, so in December 1847 she was sold to a Melbourne syndicate.

Over the next few years the number of paddle-steamers in Tasmanian waters slowly increased. Some vessels were imported from other states, such as the *Kangaroo*, built in Sydney in 1840, which arrived in Hobart in 1847, being owned by the Tasmanian government. Among the locally built steamers was the *White Hawk*, completed early in 1850. This vessel had a very short career, as in June 1850 she

caught fire while berthed overnight at Battery Point and was totally destroyed.

In 1853 there was a notable arrival, the *Culloden*, which was purchased from Britain by the Derwent & Huon Steam Navigation Co. This 145-gross-ton paddler had been built by Caird & Co. at Greenock in 1845 for the well-known British firm, G. & J. Burns. *Culloden* operated on its trades across the Irish Sea, then went through several other British owners. On being sold to Tasmania, *Culloden* was fitted out as a sailing ship for the delivery voyage. This was not without incident, as the vessel had to put into Mauritius with a damaged rudder. Arriving in Hobart in September 1853, *Culloden* was refitted as a steamer and entered service from Hobart, mostly as a ferry and excursion vessel, and also for short coastal services.

A rival to the *Culloden* appeared in 1855, when the *Mimosa* arrived under sail from Britain, having been ordered by another new Tasmanian shipping firm, the Eastern Steam Navigation Co. The *Mimosa* came out under sail in 130 days, arriving in Hobart in December 1854, and entered service on the east coast trades early in 1855. *Mimosa* and *Culloden* were both considered fast vessels, and in a race between the two from Hobart to Huon, *Mimosa* was victorious. Unfotunately, the east coast trade was not strong enough to support the ship, which was sold to Sydney owners in January 1858.

One of the last paddlers to enter service in Tasmania was the *Natone*. Built by Mort's Dock & Engineering Co. Ltd at Balmain, *Natone* was a 186-gross-ton iron-hulled, double-ended vessel, with a rudder at each end, owned by the Tasmanian Steam Navigation Co. Designed as a tender to service the larger Bass Strait vessels *Pateena, Mangana* and *Corinna* on the 22-kilometre section between Rosevears and Queen's Wharf, Launceston, *Natone* could carry 800 passengers, and arrived in Launceston on 29 October 1884. A cracked boiler plate resulted in the vessel being laid up for six months before repairs could be effected. *Natone* was never a success on the Tamar, and in October 1885 she returned to Sydney, then was sold for service in Queensland.

The longest surviving of all the paddle-steamers to ply the waters of Tasmania was the *Kangaroo*, which served for 70 years across the Derwent. The Tasmanian government placed the order for the vessel, which was built at Goldsmith's Domain Slip in Hobart. The design was unique, consisting of two separate hulls joined together by wooden planking across the top to form a single deck, in effect an early catamaran. Construction commenced in 1854, and the 30-horsepower two-cylinder steam-engine arrived in February 1855 from England, having been built by Seaward & Cappel of London. The engine was placed on the deck amidships, and a single paddlewheel, 18 feet (5.5 m) in diameter and 6 feet (1.8 m) wide, installed between the two hulls. The steering arrangement was quite awkward, with a tiller being located at each end. On completion, the *Kangaroo* was 109 gross tons, being 110 feet (33.5 m) long with a beam of 11 feet (3.4 m). She was placed in service as a vehicular ferry, in those days transporting horses and carriages from Hobart to Kangaroo Point.

Although the *Kangaroo* cost the Tasmanian government £18,000 to build, she was never an economic success. In 1857 the government sold her to Mr A. Morrison for just £1,800, but he had no success with the vessel either. In May 1864 Morrison gave the vessel away, to Captain John Taylor, for whom the operation of the ferry became more a way of life than an economic exercise. Taylor continued to operate *Kangaroo* as a ferry, but to no regular timetable. He was also not averse to using the vessel for towing jobs, especially when sailing ships were becalmed in the Derwent River. Sometimes he would offer his services for towing while passengers were aboard, and not deliver them to their destination until the tow was completed.

The eccentric operation of *Kangaroo* by Captain Taylor made both him and the vessel notorious in Hobart. In the late 1800s Taylor allowed the Tasmanian Engineers to use *Kangaroo* during mine-laying exercises in the Derwent. In 1903 he sold the *Kangaroo* to the O'May Bros, well-known Hobart shipping identities, who made a number of improvements to the vessel, including the installation of proper wheelhouses to replace the tillers. The O'Mays operated *Kangaroo* across the Derwent, and in 1912 sold her to the Rosny Estate and Ferry Co. Ltd, who ran her from Hobart to Bellerive. In 1925 the Tasmanian government purchased *Kangaroo*, but by then her days were numbered. New ferries were being built for the Bellerive trade, and on 29 March 1926 *Kangaroo* made her final crossing of the Derwent. The old vessel was laid up and her engine removed. Despite her considerable historic significance, the *Kangaroo* was left to rot, and eventually sank, the remains later being blown up.

Today there is one paddlewheeler operating in Tasmanian waters, the *Lady Stelfox*, which runs excursions from Penny Royal World in Launceston along the Tamar River and through the Cataract Gorge. A very attractive

*Natone* spent a short time as a tender at Launceston. (RWB)

*Kangaroo* on the Domain Slip at Hobart, with paddle wheel removed. (GA)

little excursion boat, *Lady Stelfox* was built during 1982 and entered service early in 1983. Although powered by a Volvo Penta diesel engine, there is a simulation of a working steam-engine visible to passengers, with all parts moving. In addition to the paddles, *Lady Stelfox* also has a propeller, which is needed to push her along when the river is flowing quickly. *Lady Stelfox* makes hourly excursions along the river for most of the year, and is very popular with visitors to Launceston.

# 8 Queensland

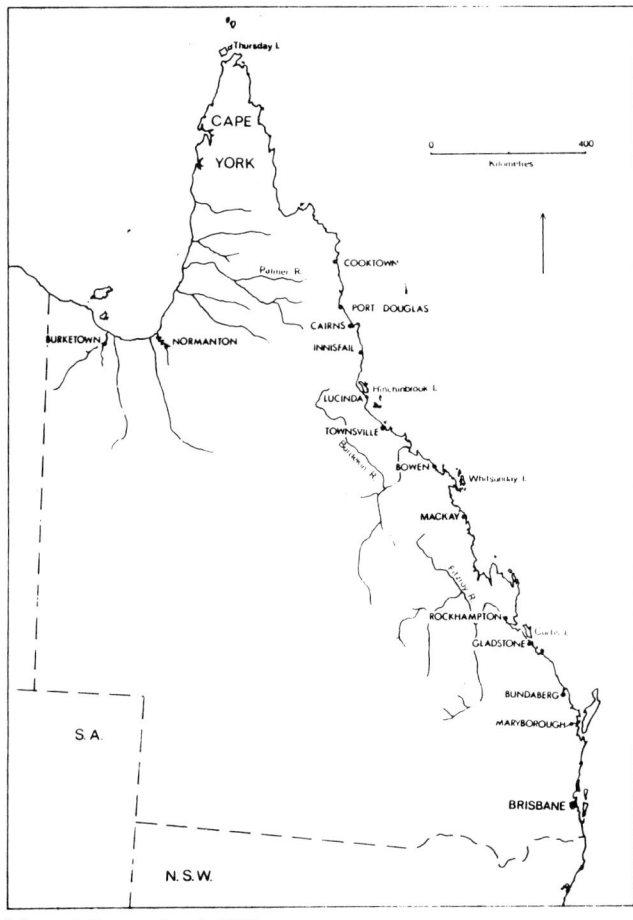

Map of Queensland (BP)

The first steamer to enter Queensland waters was the *James Watt*, in 1837, on a passage from Sydney to Moreton Bay. This paddler had recently arrived from Britain, the second to make the long ocean journey, but was not destined to enjoy any success on the Australian coast. In 1838 the pioneer paddler *Sophia Jane* was the second steamer to enter Moreton Bay, having been sent there to transfer the occupants of the penal establishment to Sydney. Following this, the Moreton Bay area was populated only by free settlers and became established as a new centre of commerce.

The major settlements were along the banks of the Brisbane River, within easy reach of Moreton Bay. In 1842 regular trading between the Moreton Bay settlements and Sydney commenced, when the *Shamrock* was placed on the trade, later being joined by the *Rose, Thistle* and *Sovereign*. In 1846 the Brisbane region could boast a population of only 829, while further upriver there were 103 persons living at a place called Limestone, now known as Ipswich. Despite

these small numbers, the first regular ferry services on the river were started in 1846, using the paddler *Experiment*.

The *Experiment* had been built in 1832 for service on Sydney Harbour, being originally propelled by horses. In 1834 a steam engine was installed, but she was well past her best when despatched north to open a service between Brisbane and Ipswich. The first trip departed Brisbane on 22 June 1846, but the river was not well charted and *Experiment* grounded near Goodna. Refloated the next morning, she completed the trip to Ipswich, receiving a gala welcome. *Experiment* then settled down to a regular three trips per week, though she was described in the local press as 'leaking and wheezing'.

On 21 January 1848 the *Experiment* sank at her moorings in Brisbane. The owners of the *Experiment* decided to have a new vessel built in Brisbane by Taylor Winship, which was completed in 1849 as the *Hawk*. The *Experiment* was raised, her engines being removed and placed in the new steamer, as such machinery was still very rare in the colony. The wooden-hulled *Hawk* served on the Ipswich ferry service for many years. Another vessel operating to Ipswich in 1849 was the *Raven*, built in Sydney in 1848 for the Hunter's River Steam Navigation Co. Originally intended to operate on Sydney Harbour, the *Raven* instead was sent to Brisbane, and ran regularly to Ipswich. In October 1850 the *Raven* was sent back to Sydney, but was wrecked on the bar at the entrance to the Macleay River on 7 October.

In 1849 the Bremer Steam Navigation Co. was formed, operating the *Hawk* and the similar *Swallow* on the trade to Ipswich. Despite dredging and charting, the river still could be quite dangerous, and on 31 August 1855 the *Swallow* struck rocks and broke in two while travelling downstream.

As trade developed, more steamers were built. In 1855 Taylor Winship completed the 78-gross-ton *Bremer*, which also did duty as a towing boat when required. In January 1857 the iron-hulled *Brisbane* arrived from Britain, having been built for the Moreton Bay and Brisbane River trades, while in 1857 the *Breadalbane*, which had been serving on Port Phillip Bay, arrived in Brisbane. In 1860 the wooden-hulled *Ipswich* was built in Sydney for the river trade. In 1859 Queensland was separated from New South Wales and became a separate colony.

Probably the most interesting of all the steamers employed on the Brisbane River during this period was the *Settler*, a 381-gross-ton stern-wheeler. *Settler* had been built in Adelaide, to the order of two Americans, and resembled an American river steamer of the era. The hull was built of Puget Sound pitch pine, specially imported, and hog beams were incorporated above the main deck, a feature of most American boats. This was done to prevent the wooden hulls 'hogging', or sagging, as the engines were placed aft, with the boilers forward. On completion, *Settler* entered service on the Murray River, but had great difficulty negotiating many of the tight bends. In December 1862 she returned to Adelaide, to be prepared for a voyage to New Zealand as a schooner. Departing Adelaide on 19 February, the *Settler* made slow progress, but then surprised everyone by arriving in Brisbane on 14 May 1863.

Just how this change came about is unknown, but the *Settler* was refurbished as a steamer and entered service in the Brisbane area. Her main duties were carrying passengers and the mails to and from ships anchored in Moreton Bay. The *Settler* also operated ferry services and was used for excursions on public holidays. About 1884 the *Settler* was run ashore on the mud at Bulimba, and left to rot away.

Other paddle-steamers engaged in the Ipswich trade during this period were the *Gneering* and a small vessel with a most unusual name, the *Tadorna Radjah*. In 1864, the *Emu* was shipped out to Brisbane in sections and assembled at Kangaroo Point. This 270-gross-ton iron-hulled vessel was originally owned by the Queensland Steam Navigation Co., and later passed into the fleet of the Australasian Steam Navigation Co. The completion of a railway line between Brisbane and Ipswich in 1875 reduced the river trade considerably, though it was 1928 before the last service ended. *Emu* was sold to become the *Brightside* of the Port Jackson Steam Boat Co., while other vessels were forced to find alternative employment.

Just five years after the establishment of Queensland, the State government took delivery of a 'Government Yacht', the paddle-steamer *Kate*. Built in England, this 147-gross-ton iron-hulled vessel was brought to Brisbane under sail as a three-masted schooner. The *Kate* was used for various government duties, and in 1868 carried the first royal visitor to the State, the Duke of Edinburgh. In 1881 she carried more royalty, the Duke of Clarence and Prince George, during their visit to Brisbane. In 1885 the *Kate* was sold and used for towing duties and as a tender until being sunk on 11 November 1890 after a collision with the steamer *Burwah* near Pile Light.

The Queensland government replaced the *Kate* with a much larger and grander vessel, probably the most notable paddler ever to churn the waters of the State. The *Lucinda* was built by Wm Denny & Bros at Dumbarton, with a steel hull. She was 301 gross tons, 172 feet (52.5 m) long, and had two decks. Launched on 7 October 1884, the *Lucinda* left Britain for Queensland on 17 January 1885. For the delivery voyage, a crew of 31 was carried, and the vessel duly arrived in Brisbane on 7 May.

*Lucinda* was given a schooner rig, with masts and spars of pitch pine, and a figurehead, giving her the appearance of a yacht. Sleeping accommodation was provided for up to 40 passengers and 11 crew, though there were only four cabins. The 'Denny List' states that the forward saloon was 'fitted with sofas all round with turn up backs so as to afford sleeping accommodation for 20 persons. The after saloon

*Lucinda* **was owned and operated by the Queensland Government. (RWB)**

was fitted as a social hall. An oval shaped deck opening in the centre, with stained glass skylight, gave light and ventilation.' The forward part of the deckhouse contained the smoking room, while the after part was fitted out as a ladies' withdrawing room, with side panels of Japanese tapestry. *Lucinda* was the first paddle-steamer in Australia to be fitted with electric lighting.

During her career as a government yacht, *Lucinda* was used to transport ministerial parties to many parts of Queensland, sometimes going as far as the Gulf of Carpentaria to visit Burketown and Normanton. On one occasion she went to New Guinea, when Queensland Premier Sir Samuel Walker was a guest of the administrator. These trips were not always enjoyed by the participants, as the report of one journey in 1885 to Townsville indicates. The *Lucinda* ran into heavy weather, and was 'pig jumping' along, which resulted in most of the dignitaries aboard getting seasick and being most relieved to reach dry land.

In 1891 Sir Samuel Walker and his advisers were conveyed by *Lucinda* to Sydney, where he served as chairman of a conference drawing up the first draft of an Australian Federal Constitution. To provide a secluded spot for the discussions, they were held aboard *Lucinda* as she cruised through Broken Bay and along the Hawkesbury River. In 1898 *Lucinda* made a second visit to Sydney, during which the final draft of the Constitution was signed in the forward saloon. In 1901 the Duke and Duchess of York, later King George V and Queen Mary, visited Brisbane. The royal party were carried by *Lucinda* from their ship anchored in Moreton Bay to the centre of Brisbane.

When the Labor Party came to power in Queensland it considered *Lucinda* to be an extravagance. On becoming Premier in 1907, Sir Robert Philp decided to use *Lucinda* for excursions by children at state schools. All the luxurious appointments were removed, and additional deckhouses constructed, and over the next decade or so *Lucinda* carried about 50,000 children per year. In 1921 the expense of maintaining the vessel could not be justified, so she was laid up. Sold in 1923, she was reduced to a coal hulk along the river, though her classic lines remained. Many years later, the *Lucinda* was driven ashore on Bishop Island, in Moreton Bay, and left to decay.

There were very few paddlers employed in the Queens-

*Premier* shortly before being launched at Maryborough in 1898. (GA)

land coastal trades, and most were only on short runs. The *Culgoa* arrived in Brisbane from the Murray River in February 1873, and six years later was lengthened. *Culgoa* was frequently used on a service from Brisbane to Noosa Heads, but was wrecked there on 13 May 1891. A few of the other rivers in the state also saw paddle-steamer operations, but these were quite small vessels, often not registered. For example, on the Mary River there were stern-wheel droghers, which carried cargo or towed barges. In 1898 the Queensland government placed the *Premier* on a service between Gladstone and Rockhampton. This iron-hulled, 148-gross-ton stern-wheeler was brought out from Britain in sections to Maryborough and assembled there. This was a very costly venture for the government, which had refused an offer from the ASN Co. to provide a steamer for the route, which was only required until the railway line linking the towns was completed in December 1903. The *Premier* was then sold and used on the timber trade between Noosa and Brisbane until the early 1920s, being renamed *Lintrose* in 1908.

As the settlement of the Moreton Bay area expanded, so further trades were developed along the Nerang, Logan and Albert rivers. These were generally quite small vessels, sometimes with stern-wheels, and usually operated in conjunction with the timber trade. One of the earliest such vessels was the sternwheeler *Ellen*, of just 21 gross tons, built in 1866 but broken up only nine years later. The *Leonie*, built in 1865 at Fortitude Valley, was 43 gross tons and had an iron hull. She carried general cargo. On 27 September

1879 she caught fire while in Moreton Bay, but was able to reach the shore, where the fire was extinguished. It was presumed that the fire was caused by a cargo of sugar being placed too close to the boiler. In 1885 the much-travelled double-ended *Natone* arrived in Brisbane and was placed on the Southport trade by the Southport Steam Ship Co. In 1889 she was transferred to a service from Redcliffe to Brisbane, and during the 1893 floods, *Natone* was left high and dry on the Eagle Farm Flats. A few days later, a second flood tide swept through and the vessel floated back into the river.

Probably the best remembered paddle-steamer to operate from Brisbane to Southport was the *Maid of Sker*. Built in 1884 at Kangaroo Point, she had an iron hull, a crew of five and was designed as a general cargo carrier. In 1889 a railway link was completed between Brisbane and Southport, reducing the river trade, but the *Maid of Sker* continued to operate along the Nerang River until 1925. Reduced to a barge, the hull of the *Maid of Sker* managed to survive years of misuse, sinkings and abandonment, and now the vessel stands in Bishop Park at Nerang, as a memorial to all the paddle-steamers that helped build the state of Queensland.

The last bastion of paddlers in Queensland has been the Brisbane River, where for many years a side-wheeler named *Heatherington* operated the Bulimba ferry. There is no record of just when this vessel was built, as it was never registered, but it was designed as a 'horse ferry', so must have entered service around the turn of the century. The *Heatherington* was

*Maid of Sker* as she appeared during her forty years of active service. (GA)

*Kookaburra Queen* was built for excursions along the Brisbane River.

130 gross tons, with a hull 76½ feet (23.3 m) long and 33 feet (10 m) wide. The single deck extended over the bow and stern, and there were landing ramps at each end. A 24-horsepower diagonal compound condensing steam-engine, with a Scotch Marine type boiler, were located amidships, and the wheelhouse above, with a single tall, thin funnel at one end. There were covered passenger areas along each side, with vehicles being parked between.

As originally built, *Heatherington* was certified to carry 200 passengers and 14 horses and carts. Gradually motor cars replaced the horse-drawn modes of transportation, and *Heatherington* was adapted to carry them. Over the years numerous newer vessels were built for ferry services across the Brisbane River, but *Heatherington* continued to ply at Bulimba for over 60 years, operated by Brisbane City Council. Her last run was at 6.30 p.m. on 30 January 1953, following which she was withdrawn. Sold to Moreton Tug & Lighterage Co., her engine and deckhouses were removed and she was reduced to a barge. Renamed *Heather*, she survived in this guise until the mid-1970s.

In preparation for Expo 88, the site of which was on the south bank of the Brisbane River, the Lord Mayor of Brisbane declared 1987 the 'Year of the River'. The idea was to clean up the river frontage, and the waters them-sevles, in preparation for the visitors expected to throng the city during 1988. There was also an upsurge in interest in river cruises, and this resulted in the return of paddlewheel vessels to the Brisbane River. The brainchild of Brisbane entrepreneur Gary Balkin, in 1986, construction started on a large paddlewheel excursion boat at the Millkraft Thompson shipyard. The entire vessel was built of wood and named *Kookaburra Queen* when launched in February 1987. The 30-metre long vessel was powered by a pair of diesel engines and entered service during 1987, operating regular excursions along the Brisbane River.

No sooner was *Kookaburra Queen* in service than construction began on a second paddler, though in this case it was to be a stern-wheeler. Launched in February 1988 as *Kookaburra Queen 2*, she was of similar size to the earlier vessel and also diesel-powered. *Kookaburra Queen 2* entered service just in time for the opening of Expo 88, while *Kookaburra Queen* became a static floating restaurant at the Expo site. I enjoyed a morning excursion along the Brisbane River on *Kookaburra Queen 2* in September 1988, which included a delicious Devonshire tea.

With the end of Expo 88, *Kookaburra Queen* returned to active service, though it was also used as a static restaurant from time to time. During the summer months the vessel was moved to the Gold Coast, to operate excursions, and has been based there for lengthy periods since then. *Kookaburra Queen 2* continued to operate regular excursions along the Brisbane River. At the time of writing, both these vessels were for sale.

# 9 Western Australia

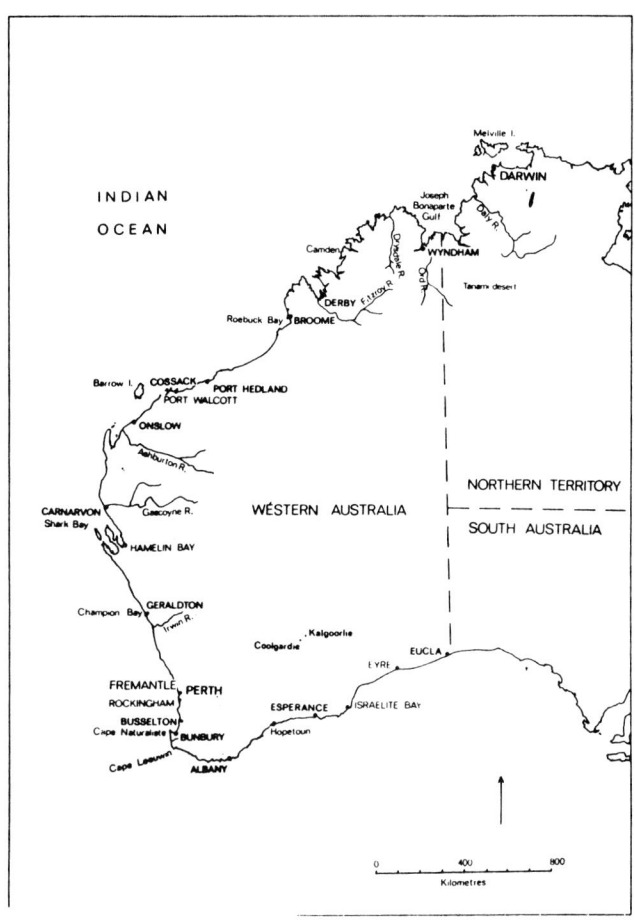

Map of Western Australia (BP)

Western Australia had fewer paddle-steamers than any other state. The first area to be settled was Albany, in 1826, but glowing reports by Captain James Stirling of the Swan River area led to free settlement there commencing in 1829, at which time the western half of the continent was proclaimed a separate colony. However, numerous problems beset the early settlers, and in 1840 the population of the area had dropped to just 1,139. The situation did not improve through the 1840s, but then transportation brought more settlers, albeit unwillingly, though in 1870 the population still numbered a mere 29,019. The gold rush of 1885–95 brought a huge influx of new settlers, so that in 1900 the population had jumped to 179,967.

The use of paddle-steamers in Western Australia was restricted almost exclusively to the Swan River, where they operated as ferries, tugs and excursion vessels. The first shipbuilding yards were established as early as 1834, on the foreshores of Eliza Bay, near Perth. For many years, these

yards turned out some fine sailing vessels, built with hulls of Australian jarrah, famed for its resistance to teredo worm attack. Over the years, further shipbuilding ventures flourished for short periods at other settlements around the coast, but none built steamers.

Vessels from Britain and Europe, bringing cargo and mails to Australia, called at Albany, from where goods, mail and passengers were transported in sailing ships to the mouth of the Swan River. The entrance to the Swan River was through a very narrow channel which at low tide was so shallow that at times it was possible to walk across on the exposed sandbars. As a result, passengers and cargo had to be landed on the sea side of Fremantle, transported across the narrow neck of land to the river, and embarked on small vessels for the final stage of the voyage to Perth. It was not until 1877 that a channel was cleared and a wharf built at Fremantle.

The first steamers appeared on the Swan River during the 1850s. The first locally built paddle-steamer was launched on 13 October 1854 from T.W. Mews' shed on Eliza Bay. Named *Speculator*, she was a side-wheeler, and her engine was built by Solomon Cook, an American engineer who had settled in Perth. The boilers were made of iron bullock-wagon tyres riveted and welded together, through which there was a constant and frightening escape of steam. The *Speculator* was placed in service between Perth and Fremantle, but she was not a success, and within a few years had been withdrawn.

During 1857, two further paddle-steamers were placed in service on the Swan River. Built in Britain, the *Lady Stirling* was brought to Australia in sections aboard the *Shanghai* and reassembled at Fremantle, being launched in February 1857. The iron-hulled *Lady Stirling* was 38 gross tons, 80 feet (24.3 m) long, and once again Solomon Cook was called in to fit the engines, funnel and paddles. On 16 May 1857 *Lady Stirling* left Fremantle with cargo and passengers on her maiden voyage up the Swan River to Fremantle, taking two hours. She remained active on the Swan River, both as a ferry and towboat, until being scrapped in 1888.

The second new vessel to embark on a career on the Swan River during 1857 was a stern-wheeler, the *Pioneer*. She was built locally with a wooden hull by Solomon Cook, no doubt based on American stern-wheelers he must have seen. Her engines, upright boiler and passenger accommodation were all located aft, with cargo being stowed forward. The *Pioneer* ran a regular service from Fremantle to Perth and Guildford. On one occasion, when returning downriver from

*Lady Stirling* was shipped in sections to Fremantle, and assembled there.

Guildford, a steam pipe burst and a number of passengers, thinking the boiler was about to explode, leapt overboard in panic and swam for the shore.

Solomon Cook built a number of small paddle-steamers for service on the Swan River, such as the *Friends*, completed in 1859. This wooden-hulled vessel was only 18 gross tons, and served as a ferry and towboat until 1872, when she was broken up.

The majority of paddle-steamers built for the Swan River trade were quite small, and many were never officially registered. The *City of Perth*, completed in August 1871, was one of the larger paddlers, being 73 gross tons. This wooden-hulled vessel was used for towing duties and as a tender in Gage Roads, as well as along the Swan River. The *City of Perth* was later converted into a lighter, and after many years work in this capacity, was abandoned in Rocky Bay, where her remains can still be seen on the western side of the bay.

Another paddle-steamer built during this period was the *Enchantress*, of 41 gross tons. Completed in 1875, she served on the Swan River until 1888, when she was broken up. In 1883 the *Florence* was completed in Perth for the Swan River trade, but she was only 28 gross tons. Some vessels were built purely for carrying freight and towing barges. The *Nerimba* is a good example of this type of vessel. She had no superstructure at all, just a hold forward, engine amidships between the paddlewheels, then the boiler and another small hold aft. There was no protection at all for the helmsman or the crew, and in many respects the *Nerimba* was more of a powered barge. Such vessels were used to transport goods from anchored ships up the Swan River to Perth for many years.

During the 1890s there was a minor resurgence in paddle-steamers on the Swan River. The *Duchess*, completed in 1890, was 71 gross tons and fitted with a 30-horsepower steam engine. She was originally owned by the South Perth

Ferry Co., and later by the State government, but in 1935 was sold to A.F. Tilley & Co., after which her career is unknown. By contrast, the tiny *Premier*, just 21 gross tons, was completed in June 1891, for service between Perth and Fremantle. Her career ended about 1908. In 1897 a land development company, Melville Water Park Estate Ltd, imported two small vessels in sections from Britain.

The *Helena* and the *Harley* were 32-gross-ton, composite-hulled double-ended ferries, which were assembled at a slipway at Coffee Point established by Melville Water Park Estate Ltd to build and maintain its boats. They were not very attractive vessels, having a large open deck with a wheel at each end and a single tall funnel not quite amidships. The *Harley* and *Helena* ran regular services from Perth to Applecross, Coffee Point and Canning Bridge, where the developers had land for sale, but the scheme failed. The vessels were abandoned on the riverbank in 1905 and eventually broken up in 1930, though some of their under-water sections still lie off Coffee Point.

One of the last paddlers to be built for the Swan River ferry trades was the *Countess*, completed in 1897, which was only 35 gross tons. She was owned by various companies during her career, which ended in 1929 when she was sunk off the coast while on a voyage from Point Cloates to Geraldton. Paddle-steamers continued to operate along the Swan River until 1927.

One of the last paddlers to enter service in Western Australia, the *Decoy*, was also one of the most interesting. This iron-hulled vessel was originally built in Scotland in 1877, and went into service on the Murray River until 1902, when she was sold and transferred to Port Adelaide. Here the *Decoy* operated as a tug, usually off the port, but sometimes towing barges to various ports in the South Australian gulfs. The early 1900s were a time when the gold diggings in Victoria were almost exhausted, but those in Western Australia were booming, causing a steady demand from prospectors for passages west.

Despite the limitations of her accommodation, the *Decoy* was commissioned to carry a group of goldminers from Port Adelaide to Fremantle in 1905. Just what the passengers must have endured as the small craft battled across the Great Australian Bight can only be imagined. On her arrival in Fremantle, the *Decoy* was offered for sale and purchased by Sunman & Tasker in September.

The new owners extensively rebuilt the *Decoy*, adding an upper deck, open at the front but covered by an awning from the funnel aft. The *Decoy* then began service as an excursion steamer on the Swan River, and for a short time was highly successful. An imported propeller steamer, the *Manx Fairy*, was rebuilt for the excursion trade in 1906, and renamed *Westralian*, while in the same year the *Zephyr* arrived in Perth from Sydney. These two ships began to dominate the excursion trade to such an extent that in February 1909 *Decoy* was sold and returned to the Murray River, where she survives as a houseboat just north of Mannum.

Today there is another *Decoy* steaming along the Swan River, an exact replica of the original. The new vessel was built by Australian Shipbuilding Industries in their yard at South Coogee, near Fremantle, to the order of Swan River

*Duchess*, built in 1890, had a wooden hull and 30hp steam engine. (GA)

*Helena* operated on ferry services from Perth across the Swan River.

*Decoy* after being rebuilt as a excursion steamer. (RM)

Paddle Steamers Ltd. Launched on 28 February 1987, with little ceremony, an official naming ceremony was held on 8 March at the Barrack Street jetty in Perth, and *Decoy* entered service on 6 April, operating excursions.

The new boat has a steel hull and upperworks, while the deckhouses are Western Australian jarrah. Of 85 gross tons, she has a length of 25.1 metres, moulded beam of 7.6 metres and a draft of 1.15 metres. She is powered by a two-cylinder direct-acting steam-engine, built in 1905 by Ransomes, Sims & Jeffries Ltd, at Ipswich in England. This machinery was obtained from a timber mill and overhauled for use in the new paddler. The first paddle-steamer to be seen on the Swan since 1927, the *Decoy* can carry 170 passengers.

*Marion* in the Randell Dock at Mannum. (LR)

*Coonawarra* has been a popular Murray River cruise boat for over forty years.

*Murray River Queen* was the first of the modern cruise boats.

*Emmy Lou* is the only steamer offering river cruises in the world.

# 10 Victoria

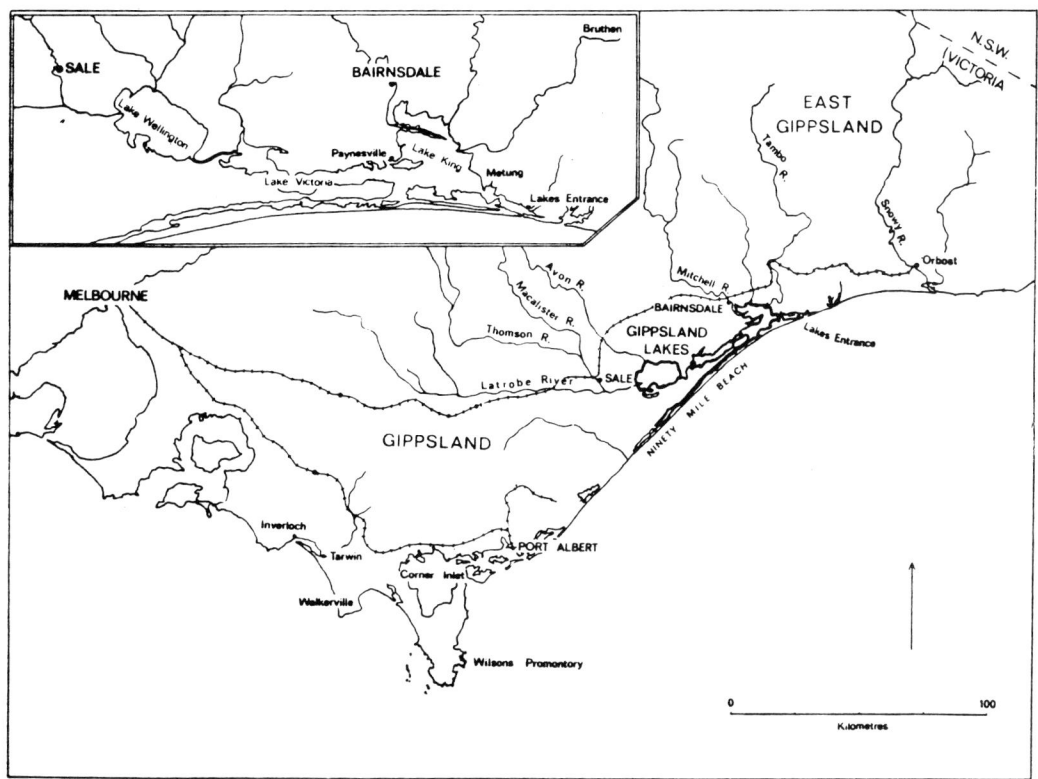

Map of Victorian coast (BP)

The coastline of Victoria was not conducive to paddle-steamer operations, with only a handful of services being established. However, a number of services ran for many years on protected waters, with some of the finest Australian paddle-steamers ever built operating on Port Phillip Bay.

The main coastal paddle-steamer service was that operated between Melbourne and the Gippsland Lakes, and also within the Gippsland Lakes. The entrance to the lakes proved difficult to navigate, and many vessels were lost trying to pass through this treacherous passage, but within the lakes, a thriving trade developed, linking the various towns and also providing excursions.

With the extension of Melbourne along the banks of the Yarra River, it was inevitable that ferry services would develop, linking outer suburbs to the main city area. There was also a booming excursion trade, and several paddlers were built specially to operate along the river. Several other boats came to the Yarra from Ballarat, where a fleet of lovely little excursion boats operated on Lake Wendouree. These boats were unique, their dimensions being governed by the limitations of operating on the shallow waters of the lake.

By far the most impressive paddlers to operate in

Victorian waters were those that ran excursions on Port Phillip Bay, which can be described as the largest harbour in the world. Paddle-steamer operations on the bay began in the 1840s, the early boats mostly being tugs which were needed to tow sailing ships. The first excursion on the bay is said to have been operated on 3 December 1842, and over the next century an impressive fleet of paddle-steamers were built to cater to this trade. A century later, on 2 March 1942, the day of the excursion paddleboat came to a sad end when the magnificent *Weeroona* operated her final trip, then went off to war.

## Coast and Lake Services

Paddle-steamer services along the coastline of Victoria were never as extensive or successful as those along the coastlines of New South Wales and Queensland. The services radiated from Melbourne, either going west to the Otway coast, or further to Warrnambool and Portland, or eastwards to the Gippsland Lakes. However, the earliest steamer services to coastal ports were usually part of a larger service between

Sydney and Adelaide. It was only later that individual companies were established to service these routes alone.

The first such service to be established was from Melbourne to Port Fairy and Portland by the paddle-steamer *Manchester* in 1853. Built in Scotland in 1851, *Manchester* was originally owned in Liverpool. She came to Australia in 1853 and was placed in the Victorian coastal trade in August, but then moved to Launceston in April 1854. In 1855 the vessel returned to the Victorian coastal trade, again going to Portland, but in April 1856 she was sold to new owners in India.

The other region to be served by paddle-steamers from Melbourne was the Gippsland Lakes. This region was first opened up for settlement following the wreck of the paddler *Clonmell* on 2 January 1841. The *Clonmell* drove ashore in Corner Inlet while on a voyage from Sydney to Melbourne. There was exploration under way at that time to find suitable grazing lands, and reports from the survivors of the wreck resulted in the Gippsland Co. being formed and settlement commencing in the area. Port Albert was named about 1842 and became an important port, as the overland journey from Melbourne was very difficult. However, Port Albert presented many navigational problems. In July 1859 the former Hunter River paddle-steamer *Thistle* was purchased from the Australasian Steam Navigation Co. and placed in service from Melbourne to Port Albert. Just five months later the *Thistle* was wrecked on the bar outside Port Albert, and this disaster spelt the end of that place as a port for the Gippsland region.

Access to the Gippsland Lakes was a major problem, as they had no natural outlet to the sea. A barrier of sand dunes separated the fresh water of the lakes from the ocean, and it was not until a channel had been cut through the dunes at Lakes Entrance that a regular steamer service could be established. One of the first steamers to trade to the Gippsland Lakes was the paddler *T. Norton*, which had been built in 1859 at Williamstown for service on Port Phillip Bay as a tug. From about 1863, this vessel began making occasional trips to Lakes Entrance. In 1864 a group of bsuinessmen and traders interested in improving transport to the Gippsland area formed the Gippsland Lakes Navigation Co., and purchased a paddle-steamer named *Charles Edward*.

The *Charles Edward* was built in 1864 by Archibald Denny at Dumbarton in Scotland, to the order of a New Zealand firm, the Otago Steam Navigation Co., which went into liquidation before the vessel could be delivered. An iron-hulled vessel of 141 gross tons, the *Charles Edward* arrived under sail in Melbourne in September 1864 and became the first regular trader to the Gippsland Lakes. A weekly service was operated from Melbourne to Bairnsdale, Sale and Stratford, but the vessel cannot have been a success, as in 1867 she was sent to New Zealand to be sold.

In 1865 the name of the company was changed to the Gippsland Steam Navigation Co. Ltd, and it purchased several small vessels, mostly for service within the lakes. In 1867 two further paddlers were added, the *Avon* and the *Murray*, which were advertised as providing services from Melbourne to Port Albert, Corner Inlet and Phillip Island as well as the Gippsland Lakes. The *Murray* usually departed on Wednesdays, and the *Avon* on Fridays.

Built in Scotland, the iron-hulled *Murray* was 229 gross tons and powered by two 60-horsepower oscillating steam-engines, and when launched on 20 January 1866 was intended for the Murray River trade. Departing Liverpool on 2 February, the vessel was brought to Australia under steam, and carried with it the sections of a small steamer, the *Platypus*, which were unloaded at Port Victor, from where the *Murray* proceeded to Adelaide. She departed on her first trip to Goolwa, at the mouth of the Murray, on 31 July, but by then had been sold to the Gippsland Co., departing Adelaide for Melbourne on 4 August. The *Murray* spent many years trading to the lakes, and in March 1881 was stranded at the entrance, being aground for over a week. When refloated, the vessel was leaking badly, but managed to get back to Melbourne for dry-docking. The following year she was sold, and began operating on the New South Wales coast.

The Gippsland Co. was not the only one interested in serving the areas east of Melbourne. In 1864 the 26-gross-ton iron-hulled *Lady of the Lake* was built in Melbourne, and operated for many years within the Gippsland Lakes. She was wrecked in June 1880, but later salvaged and repaired, and continued working in the lakes until the early years of this century. Another vessel to venture along the coast was the *Reliance*, which met a most unfortunate end.

The *Reliance* was built on the south bank of the Yarra River, opposite the old Cole's and Queen's wharves, in 1865 for Dove & Freyer. She had a composite hull, was 84 gross tons, with a length of 97 feet (29.5 m). A versatile craft, she was used for towing or trading voyages during the week, and excursion trips on Sundays and public holidays, where she became quite popular. However, in 1869 the vessel was placed on a new service, to Flinders at the mouth of Westernport Bay.

Flinders was a growing settlement in the 1860s, but had very poor communications with Melbourne. A Royal Mail coach service operated between Frankston and Flinders, but the roads were so bad the service was very unreliable. The owners of the *Reliance* seized the opportunity to provide a cheaper and more reliable service. On 6 July 1869 *Reliance* left Melbourne on her first voyage to Flinders, which proved highly successful. A week later the vessel left on her second voyage, but as she was leaving Westernport Bay on the return trip she struck a submerged rock. Although the vessel was taking water, it was not considered too serious, so the voyage continued and she duly arrived at Cowes. *Reliance* stayed there overnight, and although the next morning the inflow of water was greater, Captain Paxton decided to continue his voyage to Melbourne. At 5.30 a.m. on 16 July he set off at half speed, but when *Reliance* was near Cape Schanck the vessel began to fill at an alarming rate. At 11.30 a.m. the *Reliance* sank in 17 fathoms. She had been carrying a mixed cargo, much of which washed ashore on nearby beaches, where it was quickly grabbed by a local settler. The loss of the *Reliance* put an end to paddle-steamer services to Westernport Bay.

Whenever possible, propeller-driven vessels were built

*Reliance* was sunk off Cape Schanck during a storm in July 1869.

for the Gippsland Lakes trade, as the rough seas often encountered along the Victorian coast were not suited to paddlers. However, in 1880 the paddle-steamer *Paynesville* was built by Johnson & Co. on the banks of the Yarra for J.C. Johnson, who placed her in the Gippsland trade. Quite small at 64 gross tons and only 80 feet (24.3 m) long, the *Paynesville* was to enjoy a very short career. On 20 March 1881 she left Lakes Entrance for Melbourne, but shortly after crossing the bar was found to be leaking. The inrush of water was so great that it extinguished the fires in the boilers and the vessel had to be run ashore on Ninety Mile Beach. A tug was sent from Melbourne to try and refloat the *Paynesville*, but she broke up and became a total loss.

One of the companies operating steamers within the Gippsland Lakes, linking the various towns and settlements, was the Lakes Navigation Co. Ltd. In December 1877 it took delivery of a 100-gross-ton wooden-hulled paddle-steamer, the *Tanjil*, built on the banks of the Yarra by R. Kennedy & Sons. Powered by a locomotive type 36-horsepower steam-engine, the *Tanjil* spent her entire career on the Gippsland Lakes until being destroyed by fire at Bairnsdale on 29 January 1885.

The Lakes Navigation Co. immediately ordered a new paddle-steamer to be built at Sale by G. White & Sons. The new vessel, also named *Tanjil*, had a wooden hull, but was double-ended and smaller than her predecessor at 69 gross tons. The engines from the first *Tanjil* were salvaged and installed in the new boat, which operated the same routes as the earlier boat and remained on the lakes until the 1920s, when she was hulked.

The first captain, and also part-owner, of the second *Tanjil* was James Bull, who had been mate on the first vessel of the name. The Bull family had a long association with

steamers on the Gippsland Lakes, and later one of James Bull's sons also served as captain of the *Tanjil*, while other sons served on the vessel as deckhands. The *Tanjil* used to make three round trips a week from Bairnsdale, across the Mitchell River, across Lake King and up the Tambo River to Mossiface and Bruthen. Apart from passengers, on the outward journey the vessel would carry general cargo, mostly transhipped from the steamer *Despatch*, which connected Bairnsdale with Melbourne. On the return trip the cargo would consist of maize, wool and other produce from the farms in the district as well as ore from the mines.

The voyage up the Tambo River was full of interest. As the vessel neared the Swan Reach Bridge, her whistle would be sounded as a signal for the bridge to be raised. A short distance further on were the towering Tambo Cliffs; then the river became quite narrow and the *Tanjil* had to be pushed around sharp bends by long poles that were carried for that purpose. Captain Bull's son recalled how one bend, called Humbug Bend, was a source of annoyance to his father, as the *Tanjil* would not answer her helm and made a dive for the bank. In some stretches the river was so shallow that the paddlewheels would be pushing on the muddy bottom, sometimes causing the vessel to list quite sharply, to the terror of passengers.

On public holidays the *Tanjil* and other steamers on the lakes would run excursions to Ninety Mile Beach. These were always very popular, the decks being crowded with happy passengers, and a brass band playing. One New Year's Day the *Tanjil* filled to capacity with excursionists at the Upper Tambo wharf, and on arrival at Swan Reach there was another crowd waiting to board. Captain Bull decided not to stop and continued to Johnsonville, about 8 kilometres by river, but only 1.6 kilometres by land. When

Captain Bull saw only a few people on the wharf at Johnsonville, he pulled in, but then the shed doors were opened and dozens of people who had walked from Swan Reach swarmed out and clambered aboard. Captain Bull had no option but to take them on the excursion, though he was worried all day that the police might count heads when he returned, and fine him for carrying more passengers than his licence allowed.

Another story told of the *Tanjil* concerns a Sunday School outing to the Back Beach, a stretch of Ninety Mile Beach. *Tanjil* ran aground on a sandbank and was held fast, so several groups of passengers were taken to the shore in a small boat. Then the pastor, who was a particularly large man, decided he would go ashore too. As soon as he stepped into the boat *Tanjil* floated free, to the great amusement of all present.

About 1900 the *Tanjil* was taken off the Tambo River trade for a season and operated from Marlo to Lakes Entrance. This area was enjoying a boom at the time, with maize being brought down the Snowy River from Orbost, in barges towed by a small tug, to Marlo on the coast. There the four-bushel bags would be loaded onto *Tanjil* and other steamers, and carried 45 kilometres down the coast to Lakes Entrance, where it was transhipped for Melbourne. Captain Bull was once asked what he would do if was caught in a southerly buster and unable to reach shelter. He replied he would simply run the *Tanjil* onto the beach and step ashore, which he could do as she had a very shallow draft.

Captain James Bull was also involved when the Murray River paddle-steamer *Burrabogie* was brought to the Gippsland Lakes in 1882. Built in 1874 at Echuca, the *Burrabogie* worked on the Murrumbidgee and Murray rivers as a tow boat. Captain Bull navigated the vessel from the Murray River to the Gippsland Lakes, where it was refitted as a 'floating palace', being described as the first luxury vessel on the Gippsland Lakes. Unfortunately, the land boom in the area burst in 1887 and the *Burrabogie* was relegated to operating as a freighter, carrying timber on the lakes. At some later date she was converted to propeller propulsion and remained in use until 1950. In 1974 her hull was lying at Paynesville and restoration moves were said to be afoot, but nothing was done.

Another Murray River paddler to operate on the Gippsland Lakes was the *Ethel Jackson*. Built at Echuca in 1876, she was originally owned by W. McCulloch & Co., and when new was claimed to be the longest vessel yet built for the Murray, being 115 feet (35 m) long. Unfortunately, she proved to be too long and deep for the river and was not a success. In 1884 much of the top hamper was removed, but in 1886 the *Ethel Jackson* was sold.

Bought by D. Munro & Co. Ltd, the *Ethel Jackson* left the Murray River and was steamed around the coast to the Gippsland Lakes to join the growing fleet of steamers trading out of Bairnsdale. After some years in the Gippsland Lakes, the *Ethel Jackson* was sold and steamed up the east coast to Townsville, where she ended her days as a hulk.

Another small paddler employed on the Gippsland Lakes was the *Nell*, built in 1878 at Brisbane Water, near Gosford in New South Wales, as a ferry for Sydney Harbour. In

*Ethel Jackson*, with *Burrabogie* astern, berthed in the Gippsland Lakes. (FT)

1883 the *Nell* was sold to Gippsland interests, but ran aground on Gabo Island during a storm on her delivery voyage. The vessel had been seeking shelter in a bay, but was driven ashore on 1 November 1883 when her anchors parted. During salvage work, a new stem and stern post had to be fitted, and the keel repaired, and she was not refloated until 8 August 1884. *Nell* then completed her voyage to the Gippsland Lakes, where she operated until 1897. During this time she passed through several owners, one being the Snowy River Shipping Co. The *Nell* finished her life as a sailing ship, not being broken up until 1931.

# Yarra River Boats

The Yarra River, which flows through the City of Melbourne, was discovered in 1803. It was originally called the Freshwater River, being given its present name in 1835. Yarra is a corruption of an Aboriginal word for something that flows or ripples. The Yarra is quite a small river, and has a tributary, originally known as the Saltwater River, but renamed in 1913 the Maribyrnong River. The two rivers meet a short distance from where the Yarra empties into Hobsons Bay. Passage by boats up the Yarra was affected by two natural barriers; in the lower reaches by a reef across the river at the site of present day Queens Bridge, while further upstream Dights Falls proved to be an impassable obstacle to vessels. However, over a number of years there was a thriving ferry and excursion trade along the Yarra, and also the Maribyrnong. This section deals only with the vessels that remained within the Yarra and Maribyrnong rivers. Those that operated on the lower end of the river to Williamstown and Port Phillip Bay are covered in the next section.

Within a short time of first settlement in April 1835, Melbourne grew rapidly, with the first bridge to span the Yarra being completed in 1845. Settlement expanded along the banks of the Yarra, into areas known today as Richmond and Collingwood, and in 1853 the first pleasure park,

The *Curlip* is pictured near Orbost, where it was built in 1890 from locally grown mahogany. Owned by the Snowy River Shipping Co., *Curlip* towed barges between Orbost and Marlo, where their cargo was transferred to coastal vessels. On 3 March 1919, *Curlip* was wrecked at the mouth of the Snowy River. (LR)

Cremorne Gardens, was opened at Richmond. However, the new attraction lay some two miles from the centre of Melbourne, and while rowing boats and some small screw-driven steamers provided a ferry service, it was not very efficient.

It was decided that a large steamboat was needed, so in 1853 the grandly named Upper Yarra Steam Gondola Company was formed, with the object of building and operating a suitable vessel. Built by Robertson & Co., whose yard was just downstream from the Cremorne Gardens, the vessel was launched with considerable ceremony in March 1854, being named *Gondola*. It was 60 feet (18.3 m) long with a 12-foot (3.7-m) beam, and had a wood-burning tubular boiler which powered two horizontal two-cylinder steam-engines, producing 14 horsepower, and driving the 8-foot (2.4-m) side-wheels. In appearance the vessel was unique, with curved lines and pronounced extensions of the bow and stern. There was space on board for 200 people, and almost that number crammed on board for the first trial trip, on 8 April 1854. *Gondola* began operating regular services to the Cremorne Gardens from her berth just above Princes Bridge near the centre of Melbourne, the journey taking less than half an hour. The master of the *Gondola*, whose name was Liddle, was a stickler for maintaining

schedules and anyone delaying their departure from the gardens at night could well miss the last service back to Melbourne.

Over the next few years several more vessels were built for this service, but none of them was a paddler. At the same time, the network of railway lines around Melbourne was expanding rapidly and on 12 December 1859 the first train arrived at Cremorne. Within a short time, the ferries serving Cremorne Gardens were all put out of service and sold. The *Gondola* was also sold, but the new owner converted her into a sailing ship, under which guise she saw many years of service on Hobsons Bay. In 1863 the Cremorne Gardens also closed.

For many years, passenger services on the Yarra River languished, relying almost exclusively on the excursion trade. By 1898 two new attractions had brought patrons back to the river, the Glen Tea Gardens and the Hawthorn Tea Gardens. A number of new boats were built, but they were all screw-driven. One of the major operators of ferries at the turn of the century was Valentine Cole, who in 1907 bought a paddle-steamer for service on the Yarra.

The *Alexandra* had been built in 1884 at Ballarat for excursion service on Lake Wendouree. She was typical of the boats built for that trade, being 52 feet (15.9 m) long

Artists impression of *Gondola*, first steamer on the Yarra. (CJ)

and less than 10 feet (3 m) wide, with a single deck covered by an awning. However, *Alexandra* had an iron hull which made her too deep to operate on Lake Wendouree effectively. During the 1890s, Ballarat was badly affected by the Depression, so Cole was able to buy the *Alexandra* quite cheaply. He had the boat brought to Melbourne, where it proved very popular, usually operating excursions up the Yarra to Hawthorn. For the next quarter of a century, *Alexandra* was the sole paddleboat operating on the Melbourne rivers.

Early in 1934 another major ferry operator, Lou Harding, whose firm was known since 1933 as Melbourne Ferries (Hardings) Pty Ltd, also purchased a paddleboat from Ballarat. The excursion trade on Lake Wendouree had been once again affected by depression, and although there were only four vessels still operating, the largest, the 65-foot (19.9-m) *Fairyland*, had to be taken out of service and laid up in her shed. Purchased by Lou Harding, the *Fairyland* was loaded onto a truck and taken to Geelong, where it was relaunched and towed across Port Phillip Bay and into the Yarra. Before being allowed to operate on the river, a number of modifications had to be made to the vessel, the work being done by Robison Bros, of South Melbourne. These included the insertion of 42 40-gallon (182-litre) drums under the deck, to make her unsinkable. New regulations had been introduced, banning vessels with coal-fired engines from the river, so the original machinery was taken out and replaced by a 40-horsepower petrol engine taken from a truck.

*Fairyland* entered service on the Yarra River in March 1934, with a capacity of 156 passengers. Her regular run was from Princes Bridge upstream to Dights Falls, with calls

*Alexandra* was originally an excursion boat at Ballarat. (CJ)

at the Botanic Gardens, South Yarra, Twickenham Ferry and Hawthorn. With the full trip costing just 2*s.*, the boat was very popular and well patronised.

Among those impressed by the *Fairyland* was the Hicks family, who operated a fleet of excursion boats up the Maribyrnong River to the Riverview Tea Gardens, which Daniel Hicks opened in 1909. By the 1930s the family had extended their operation to include some services on the Yarra River, and also into Hobsons Bay, although the Maribyrnong River trade remained their main interest. It was at this time that the Hicks decided to add a paddleboat

*Fairyland* came from Ballarat to the Yarra in 1934. (CJ)

*River Queen* ran excursions along the Maribyrnong and Yarra rivers. (CJ)

to their fleet. They built it themselves at Riverview, with the help of an elderly German craftsman, who used an adze to shape the timbers for the 65-foot (19.9-m) long hull, which had a beam of 16 feet (4.9 m). When completed in 1935, the vessel was named *River Queen*, becoming the largest excursion boat on the river, with a capacity of 209 passengers. Originally *River Queen* had only a canopy, and chain wire around her bulwarks, which earned her the nickname of 'the hen coop'. Later, a more permanent cover with two squat dummy funnels was added, along with solid bulwarks, which greatly improved her appearance. *River Queen* used to operate from Princes Bridge to Riverview, with some excursions on the Yarra as well.

The two paddlers would only operate together on the rivers for a few years, as the *Fairyland* was involved in two serious accidents, the second one leading to her destruction. On the night of 24 May 1936 the *Fairyland* was returning downstream from the Hawthorn Tea Gardens with 149 passengers and a crew of two. Visibility was reduced to almost nothing by a heavy fog and near the Grange Road Bridge the *Fairyland* hit a rock. Water began gushing in and while there was enough buoyancy to prevent the vessel sinking, Vic Harding at the helm decided to run her aground on a sandbank. This caused some of the passengers to panic and a rush to one side caused the boat to list heavily, until its deck was under water. Passengers then climbed onto the roof, but that collapsed under their weight. Over 100

passengers ended up in the icy waters of the river, and many had to be rescued by strong swimmers. Eventually everyone clambered ashore, soaked but unhurt. As for the *Fairyland*, damage was minimal and she was soon back in service.

Less than a year later, disaster again overtook the *Fairyland*. On the afternoon of Saturday, 13 March 1937, the boat was again returning from Hawthorn with a full load of excursionists when the engine failed just above the Church Street Bridge. This time Lou Harding was at the helm and he steered the disabled boat into the river bank. The passengers were transferred to another Harding vessel, the *Bay Ferrie*, and carried to their destination. *Bay Ferrie* then returned upstream to assist the *Fairyland*, the two vessels being secured side by side for the trip downstream.

With the *Fairyland* in motion again, Harding though it might be possible to restart the engine, using the paddlewheels to turn it over. When this was attempted, there was a backfire, then the engine burst into flames. The two men on board *Fairyland* were slightly injured, but were able to escape onto the *Bay Ferrie* as the *Fairyland* was engulfed in flames. Cast adrift, the paddleboat drifted down the Yarra, ablaze from end to end, then the petrol tank blew up and some of the 40-gallon tanks installed for buoyancy also exploded. By the time the flames were extinguished, the lovely *Fairyland* was a blackened wreck, though much of the hull still appeared to be sound. At first it was thought the boat could be rebuilt, but in the end it was decided she was beyond repair and the hulk was scuttled, a sad end for a lovely little vessel.

This left *River Queen* as the only paddleboat operating on the Melbourne rivers for several years. However, Lou Harding was still keen to have a paddler in his fleet, so, using the insurance money received for the *Fairyland*, he had a replacement built in 1938. The new vessel was smaller than its predecessor, being 60 feet (18.3 m) long and 17 feet (5.2 m) wide, with seats for 144 passengers. It was built in the Williamstown boatyard of Jack Savage, who had to enlarge his building shed to accommodate the vessel, which was the largest he had built to that time. On completion the new boat was named *Mississippi* and it made its maiden trip on 1 November 1938, which was also Melbourne Cup Day. The paddles were driven by a petrol engine, but the *Mississippi* proved to be very slow, so after a few years a second engine and propeller were installed to supplement the paddles, which improved her speed. In appearance, the *Mississippi* was almost identical to the *Fairyland*, but was fitted with two short funnels, similar to those on *River Queen*.

During the 1930s the Maribyrnong trade declined rapidly, so in 1938 *River Queen* and three other boats owned by the Hicks family were moved permanently to the Yarra, where business was also not as good as before. *River Queen*, which had proved very comfortable to handle on the placid waters of the Maribyrnong, was a different proposition on the Yarra, where the faster flowing water made her difficult to handle. To alleviate this problem, twin screws were added, powered by their own 100-horsepower auxiliary engines, but the paddlewheels were retained, which made *River Queen* very fast.

All the excursion boats were now operating from berths

*Mississippi* was built in 1938. (CJ)

near Princes Bridge, and competition was intense. Each company employed barkers, who would compete with each other to gain custom for their boats. A round trip to Hawthorn, which lasted about two hours, could be had for 2s. 6d., and there were also shorter trips available. Certain boats seemed to be more popular, with *River Queen* often being the first to fill up and get away ahead of the rest. The boat would cruise upriver for 45 minutes to the Hawthorn Tea Gardens, where passengers would go ashore for a look around, then return to the boat for the return trip. During the war years, the excursion trade flourished, especially when the Americans were in town.

In the years immediately following the end of the war, the Yarra River excursion trade underwent numerous changes associated with a decline in patronage. In 1947 the Hicks family decided to end their association with the river. By this time their fleet had been reduced to just four vessels, including the paddler *River Queen*. The vessels and the company name were leased for 10 years to two long-time river identities, Harold Anderson and Bob Atchison. *River Queen* was the pride of their fleet, and Harold Anderson was not averse to an occasional unofficial race with some of the screw-driven vessels owned by the opposition, in which the paddler performed very well.

In 1948 Melbourne Ferries was purchased by Julian Dyson, who subsequently bought out several other Yarra excursion and ferry firms, to become the major operator on the river, his only competition being the Hicks boats. Among the vessels now owned by Julian Dyson was the paddler *Mississippi*, which provided competition for *River Queen*. At one time Dyson considered transferring the *Mississippi* to Echuca, on the Murray River, but this did not eventuate. Several years later Dyson did send one of his screw-powered boats to Echuca, but it was not a success.

In 1949, when petrol rationing ended, the excursion trade began to decline as more people purchased cars. Without adequate income to maintain them, the boats began to deteriorate and some were taken out of service, though the two paddlers, *River Queen* and *Mississippi*, managed to keep going. One good source of income was group charters, which provided a reasonable return during the summer months. On 8 February 1952 the *Mississippi* was chartered by a group of 132 Ukrainian migrants for a picnic trip to Hawthorn. Prior to this trip, the boat had been out of service

for a while, the engine having been removed for refit. During this time the vessel had been riding quite high in the water, allowing the wooden planks in the hull to dry and shrink.

*Mississippi* left Princes Bridge bound for Hawthorn, but as she neared her destination it became apparent that water was pouring in through gaps in the planking and the vessel was slowly sinking. The passengers began to panic and swarmed to one side of the boat, causing it to roll over. Many people were flung into the water, including one man who hit his head on a paddlewheel and drowned. Fortunately, the river was very shallow and the vessel rested on the bottom, with most of one side still showing above water. This enabled the survivors to cling to the boat until rescue arrived. One of the first boats on the scene was *River Queen*, which had been heading back downstream from Hawthorn and, rounding a bend, almost collided with the sunken *Mississippi*. The paddler was salvaged and subsequently returned to service, but the incident did not help the excursion trade.

In 1957 the lease on the former Hicks family fleet held by Harold Anderson and Bob Atchison came to an end. They did not wish to renew the arrangement, which enabled Julian Dyson to achieve his ultimate ambition and control the entire Yarra River excursion trade. His firm, Melbourne Ferries, bought the two largest boats, including *River Queen*, while the smaller pair were placed on the Yarraville ferry service. Unfortunately, Dyson did not have any plans to use the *River Queen* and, much to the dismay of the Hicks family and Harold Anderson, the popular paddler was scuttled in 1958. This left only four excursion boats still operating on the Yarra, including the *Mississippi*. In 1960 the Hawthorn Tea Gardens closed, though they reopened in a different guise in 1971. In 1961 the *Mississippi* was taken out of service.

The Yarra excursion trade went through a long period of depression, but in December 1976, in an attempt to revive the trade, a new boat was built. In February 1978 another new excursion vessel entered service, a rather unattractive concoction named *Saona*. Built with a catamaran hull and a single deck, the 44-foot (13.4-m) long vessel was fitted with twin funnels forward, in the style of Mississippi riverboats, and had a large paddlewheel at the stern. However, this was purely for effect, as the vessel's engine was connected to a propeller. Owned by John Good and operated by the Yarra River Boat Co. Pty Ltd, *Saona* ran excursions from Princes Bridge to the Botanic Gardens, and also for a while experimented with a morning and evening commuter run between Como Park and Princes Bridge, but this only survived four months. On the night of 28 July 1988, *Saona* was destroyed by fire while berthed at South Wharf.

# Lake Wendouree

Undoubtedly the least known of Australian paddle-steamers are those that plied the waters of Lake Wendouree, at Ballarat in Victoria.

Located 113 kilometres west of Melbourne, the Ballarat

region first came to prominence in the late 1830s, when cattle were sent there for grazing during a major drought. In 1851 gold was found in the area and the population of the region grew rapidly. By 1854 there were 27,000 people living in Ballarat, and in the same year occurred the armed rebellion by miners, culminating in the battle at the Eureka Stockade, in which 30 men died. Gradually Ballarat developed into a major country town, and by the 1870s the population had grown to 48,000 living in a fine city, with superb boulevards, parks and cultural centres. On the western edge of the city lay Lake Wendouree, which was a popular destination for outings.

During the 1860s the local council decided to improve the foreshores of Lake Wendouree. The work was done by prisoners, who each morning were marched from the gaol by their warders, pulling small carts carrying spades, axes, picks and other tools. They cleared the foreshores right around the lake, chopping down the old gums and planting elms, pines and willows.

The very attractive Botanical Gardens were developed at the western end of Lake Wendouree and became a popular picnic spot on Sundays and public holidays. It was quite a long walk from the town to the Botanical Gardens, so in 1865 a syndicate including Thomas Gill and James Ivey built a paddle-steamer to carry passengers from one end of the lake to the other. Built by the Soho foundry in Ballarat, under the supervision of an engineer named Ebrington, this pioneer vessel was named *Victoria*. It had an iron hull and a simple steam-engine, but proved to be a complete failure on the lake, being far too heavy and totally unsuited to lake conditions. At this time the lake had still not been cleared of reeds, which covered much of the surface.

In 1869, when the level of the lake was down due to a drought, the reeds were burnt off. At the same time, prisoners were used to cart mining debris to the north-eastern corner of the lake, to build a dam to confine the waters of the lake.

Thomas Edward Gill was a prominent citizen of Ballarat. Born at Douglas in the Isle of Man in 1839, and apprenticed to a coachbuilder at an early age, he arrived in Melbourne as an immigrant in 1853 and caught the paddle-steamer *Citizen* to Geelong. From there he walked to Ballarat, there being no roads except the bush tracks between Ballarat and Geelong at that time. Gill went to the goldfields for a short time, but then reverted to his former profession of coachbuilding. Subsequently he expanded into boatbuilding, and built many dinghies from Tasmanian Huon pine and New Zealand kauri, which were hired out from the boatshed at the eastern end of the lake.

In 1875 Thomas Gill erected a popular hostelry, known as Gill's Lake View House, on the shores of Lake Wendouree. In the same year he completed the first successful paddle-steamer for Lake Wendouree, named *Wendouree*. This vessel ran regularly from a wharf near Gill's boatshed, in front of his hotel, to the Botanical Gardens. The *Wendouree* had a wooden hull and was a well-appointed, elegant steamer, though quite small. The vessel was also used for evening moonlight cruises in the summer months.

Over the next few years a number of small steamers were placed in service on Lake Wendouree, owned by various people, including Thomas Gill, James Ivey, and a Mr Sutton. Among these vessels were the *Queen, Prince Consort, Princess, Lord Roberts* and *Gem*, as well as the *Ballarat*, owned by Thomas Gill, and the *Lady of the Lake*, owned by James Ivey, who operated as the Garden City Steam Boat Co., which claimed its fleet could carry '690 souls'. Only one paddle-steamer on the lake had two decks, but it was very tender, due to the shallow draught, heeling over when the winds got under the awning.

On 16 June 1885 a third vessel for Thomas Gill was launched as the *Golden City*, entering service a few weeks later. This vessel was described as the prettiest of all the lake steamers and immediately became very popular. On 6 August 1885 James Ivey wrote to the Town Clerk of the City of Ballarat, George Perry: 'Sir, I desire to have the name of my steamer *Lady of the Lake* changed to that of *Golden City* and hereby make application having that object in view. Trusting it will be acceded to.'

It is not known why Ivey wished to change the name of his vessel to be identical with the new Gill boat, though there must have been considerable rivalry between the pair. However, the name change was approved, and in October 1885 the Steam Boat Inspector for the City of Ballarat, W. Sewell, inspected both boats. He was then prompted to write to the Town Clerk on 20 October: 'Sir, you will see by the enclosed that there are two steamers of the same name, namely the *Golden City*. I think it very unwise to have two boats of the same name as it may lead to some confusion with the public.' This advice went unheeded, so Lake Wendouree had two vessels named *Golden City* in operation, though Gill's boat seems to have become known as the *New Golden City*.

'Sydney may have its Harbour and Melbourne its Bay, but Ballarat has Lake Wendouree,' ran an advertisement in 1905. Although in size there could be no comparison, the lake became immensely popular as a relaxation and recreation place, with a fleet of paddle-steamers ferrying passengers from View Point to the Botanical Gardens, the fare being 3d. each way. There were also evening trips, some including bands. With so much competition, there was also a certain amount of racing between the boats, which resulted in some collisions and caused the council to introduce a nautical by-law proclaiming speed and loading limits.

In October 1907 four of the Lake Wendouree boats were sold to a Melbourne syndicate. Among these was the *Golden City* owned by James Ivey. On 4 October 1907 the Ballarat *Courier* reported that 'Mr Scotney has arrived with his team of 15 horses and by 2 p.m. today he expects to start his journey to Melbourne, which will be reached on Monday'. The *Golden City* was hauled out of the water by eight horses, following which the engine and paddles were removed. It was then loaded on the jinker with the other three boats, and on arrival in Melbourne they entered service on the Yarra River. *Golden City* was run by Hardings Ferries from Princes Bridges, but about seven years after leaving Lake Wendouree the vessel was swept by fire and burnt to the waterline.

*Ballarat* was typical of the Lake Wendouree excursion steamers. (GA)

*Golden City* decorated for the 1938 Ballarat Centenary celebrations. (CDG)

This left the original *Golden City*, now owned by Thomas Gill's son, Douglas, still operating on Lake Wendouree with a few other steamers. In 1932 Gill sold the *Ballarat* to Melbourne owners. The vessel was hauled out of the lake by a traction engine at St Patricks Point and transported by road to Melbourne, where it served on the Yarra River. In 1935 the steam machinery in the *Golden City* was replaced by a petrol engine. The thirties saw a marked decline in the Lake Wendouree steamer trade, and some boats were abandoned on the lake shore, leaving only three in service. The fare was still 3*d.* for adults and 1*d.* for children.

In 1945 Lake Wendouree almost dried out in a drought. Douglas Gill was suffering ill health and in 1946 he sold the *Golden City* to Roy McCrae and Campbell McArthur, who continued to operate the vessel on the lake. Since being built, the *Golden City* had been kept in a boathouse when not in operation and the new owners continued this practice. In this way, the old vessel remained in superb condition.

During the 1960s conditions on Lake Wendouree changed considerably. The lake had become increasingly popular as a swimming spot, making it dangerous for the boat to use its regular wharf. At the same time, a growing accumulation of floating weeds further impeded the operation of *Golden City*. A new wharf was built and a revised itinerary established, which took the boat on circular excursions to the north shore of the lake, but in 1966 *Golden City* was again sold. The purchaser was Archie Spooner, who owned the Carribean Gardens recreation park outside Melbourne. On Sunday, 23 January 1966, the *Golden City* made its final run on the lake, and several days later it was lifted out of the water and placed on the back of a truck for the long journey to its new home.

For the first time in a century, there was no paddleboat operating on Lake Wendouree, However, after a few years, a new boat was built for the lake by Lyle Brown. Named *Sarah George*, it lacked the classic lines of the old steamers but proved adequate for the trade. In the early 1980s the *Sarah George* was sold to Mr Bob Cocks, who ran it for several more years. Cocks then built a new boat for the Lake Wendouree excursion trade, the *Boronia Princess*, and the *Sarah George* was sold, becoming a houseboat on the Murray River.

In June 1987 the *Golden City* was advertised for sale in the Melbourne papers. The Apex Club of Ballarat expressed an interest in purchasing the boat and returning it to Lake Wendouree. The arrangement was finalised, and on 27 June the *Golden City* arrived in Ballarat on the back of a truck and was lowered gently into the lake by a crane. In July 1988 the Golden City Steamer Museum Society was formed, to restore the vessel and return it to full excursion service on the lake.

# Port Phillip Bay

Port Phillip Bay is a huge drowned valley, that can be described as the largest harbour in the world. There is only one entrance, on the southern side, known as the Rip, through which the waters can race at up to 8 knots, making it very dangerous. The distance to Melbourne in the north-

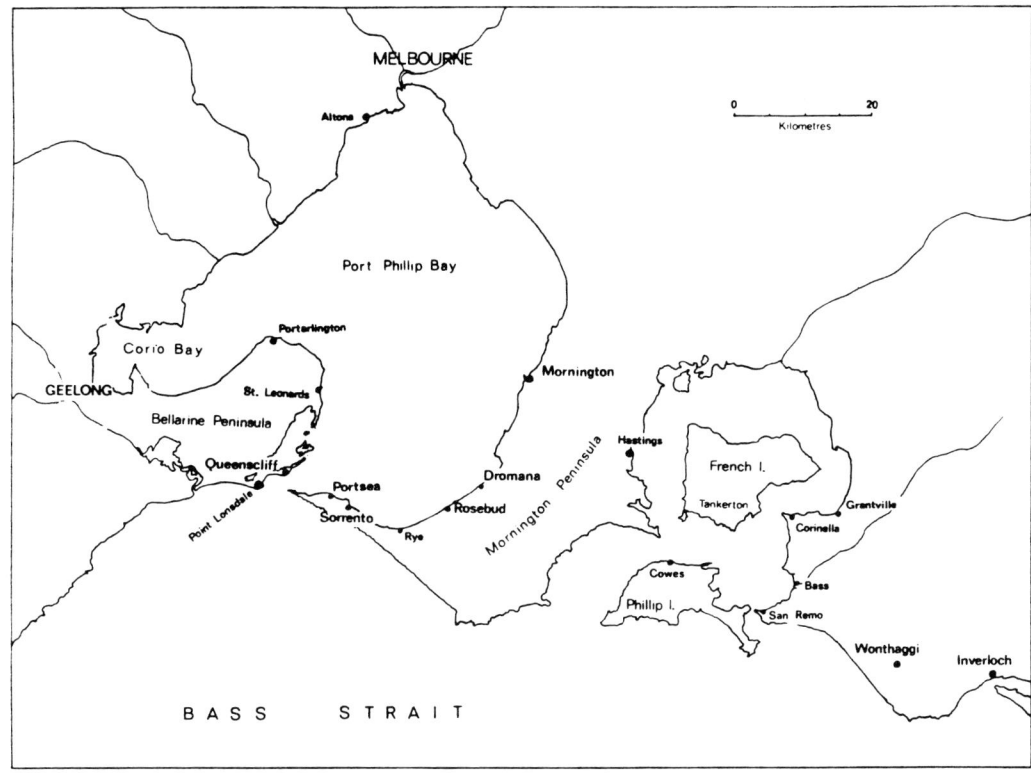

Map of Port Phillip Bay (BP)

west corner is about 65 kilometres. It was on this huge stretch of water that some of the finest paddle-steamers seen in Australia operated excursions.

In 1835 John Batman and a group of settlers from Tasmania established the first settlement on Port Phillip Bay, a short distance up from the mouth of the Yarra River on the site where Melbourne was proclaimed in 1837. The area developed very quickly and by the 1840s the suburbs of St Kilda and Brighton had been founded on the shores of Port Phillip Bay. At the mouth of the Yarra River the suburb of Williamstown also grew. Due to the shallow water in Hobsons Bay, off the mouth of the Yarra, visiting ships had to anchor out, with goods and passengers being taken ashore at Williamstown.

The first steamship to disturb the waters of Port Phillip Bay was the *James Watt*, on 4 July 1837, returning there again in September 1837 and January 1838. The first regular steamer service to operate in the area was between Melbourne and Williamstown. The first steamer was called the *Fire Fly*, about which very little is known. It is believed to have been built in Sydney in 1837 and taken to Melbourne under sail. The *Port Phillip Patriot* of 27 October 1838 stated that the '*Fire Fly* will commence running tomorrow between Melbourne and Williamstown, W. Pearson, Master'. The vessel is believed to have operated only until February 1840, at which time the engine was removed and installed in a sawmill at Brighton. Apparently the *Fire Fly* did not meet with the approval of everyone, as in *Chronicles of Early Melbourne*, written in 1888 by Edmund Finn, he said 'this apology for a steam boat was a half rotten composition of an old submarine more disposed to buzz than to fly and with more smoke than fire'.

The second steamship to operate on the Yarra River was

the *Fairy Queen*, which was launched on 3 April 1841, being owned by a Mr Manton. It is believed this steamer was erected from preconstructed parts shipped out from England. *Fairy Queen* began operating along the Yarra between Melbourne and Williamstown on 8 July 1841, and she appears to have remained in service for quite a few years.

During 1841 two other steamers of importance arrived in Melbourne. The first was the *Governor Arthur*, on 20 January from Tasmania. Assembled in Hobart in 1832 from parts shipped out from England, this vessel had operated a variety of river trades in Tasmania before crossing Bass Strait, where she began operating between Melbourne and Williamstown. On 23 December 1841 the *Governor Arthur* was gutted by a fire at Queens Wharf, and sank. Raised and reconditioned, she resumed running on the Yarra in September 1843, only to be withdrawn in February 1844. Her engines were placed in a new paddle-steamer, the *Diamond*.

The second new steamer to arrive in Port Phillip Bay in 1841 was the *Aphrasia*, built on the Clarence River in New South Wales. Her first owners are reported to have been the Geelong Steam Navigation Co., although her registered owners are shown as the Port Phillip Steam Navigation Co., but it is known that *Aphrasia* was built for the trade between Melbourne and Geelong, in Corio Bay. *Aphrasia* was 131 gross tons, 100 feet (30.4 m) long, and powered by a pair of 40-horsepower side-lever steam-engines. From time to time *Aphrasia* would also be used as a tug, and on ferry work close to Melbourne.

The development of new settlements around the shores of Port Phillip Bay proceeded apace. Near Port Phillip Heads, on the Nepean and Mornington peninsulas, several small communities were developed, including Portsea,

Sorrento, Dromana and Mornington. The population in the area grew rapidly, as did the number of ships entering the Bay. Geelong, on Corio Bay to the south-west of Melbourne, had been settled at almost the same time, and at one time seemed a rival for the title of major port on the Bay. *Aphrasia* made her first trip to Geelong on 5 July 1841, and operated regular trips on Monday, Wednesday and Friday. From 1 September 1841 she also carried all the mails to and from Geelong.

In 1842 there arrived in Port Phillip Bay the wooden-hulled paddle-steamer *Corsair*. Built in Britain in 1827 and originally owned in Ireland, *Corsair* left London on 10 October 1840, bound for Adelaide, which was reached on 3 March 1841. An attempt was made to start a steamer service between Adelaide and Melbourne, but this soon failed and *Corsair* ended up on Port Phillip Bay. This vessel is considered to be the first steamer in Australia to be designated as a tug, and she performed towing duties for sailing ships in Port Phillip Bay.

*Corsair* is also claimed to be the first steamer to run an excursion on Port Phillip Bay. This occurred on 3 December 1842, though there is little doubt that other steamers had carried passengers around the Bay previously. However, this trip by the *Corsair* was the first to be designated an excursion, and it set a precedent that would be followed for the next 100 years, of excursions around Port Phillip Bay on paddle-steamers. Unfortunately, the *Corsair* was not a successful ship in Australian waters. In 1843 she went on to Sydney and when a sale did not eventuate there, her owners dispatched her to Hong Kong in December 1845, where she was sold, but withdrawn from service in 1850.

The first iron-hulled vessel to be registered in Melbourne was the *Vesta*. Imported in sections from Britain and assembled in Melbourne, the *Vesta* was owned by George W. Cole and completed in December 1842. Mainly employed on towing duties on Port Phillip Bay, on 22 August 1843 *Vesta* made her first voyage en route to Geelong, services being offered on Tuesday, Saturday and Sunday. Together, *Vesta* and *Aphrasia* provided Geelong with an almost daily service, to the delight of the citizens, but then *Vesta* altered her arrangements, and ran on the same days as *Aphrasia*, leaving Melbourne at 6 a.m. The fares for both steamers were 15s. cabin class and 9s. steerage. Later *Vesta* was a regular trader from Melbourne to Mornington and Queenscliffe, until sold in 1864 to New South Wales owners.

The trade between Melbourne and Geelong was growing at a steady pace, and on 20 December 1847 the steamer *Thames* was also placed on the route. Built in London in 1842, the *Thames* had taken four and a half months to sail to Hobart, where she spent the next few years, until bought by a syndicate of Melbourne businessmen. The ship was immediately placed in the Geelong trade in competition with the *Aphrasia* and *Vesta*, but at times was also used for towing and some excursion work.

There were also several other steamers involved in the Geelong trade, though not on a regular basis. George W. Cole owned a fleet of vessels and had the *Diamond* and *Maitland* running to Geelong when necessary. Cole bought the *Maitland* early in 1851 from the Hunter's River Co. and used it mainly as a tug. On 7 February 1852, while lying at Cole's wharf in Melbourne, the *Maitland* suddenly sank, almost drowning the captain. The vessel was raised the following month and returned to service. Both *Maitland* and *Diamond* ceased running to Geelong at the end of 1852.

The year 1852 was an unfortunate one for both the *Thames* and the *Aphrasia*. On 19 February the *Thames* was on a voyage to Geelong when she encountered heavy weather off Point Cook. The captain changed course to close the shoreline in search of sheltered water, but the ship struck a rock and had to be quickly run ashore to prevent her sinking. All aboard were saved, but on 6 March a severe storm ripped through the area and *Thames* was smashed to pieces. On 17 October 1852 the *Aphrasia* ran aground near Corio Bay, at a time when she had 200 passengers on board and no lifeboats. For several hours the vessel remained stranded, with no way of communicating with the shore, but eventually she was freed and resumed her service. *Aphrasia* remained in Port Phillip Bay until 1861, then was sold to New Zealand interests.

The discovery of goldfields in the Ballarat and Bendigo areas in 1851, and the resultant gold rush, made Melbourne into a major port within a few years. Prospectors came from all over the world, others came to share in the prosperity, Port Phillip Bay was always filled with ships and the settlements around the bay rapidly grew into towns and cities. From 1852 a steady stream of steamers, new and old, arrived in Port Phillip Bay, hoping to cash in on the boom. However, not all were successful.

On 5 March 1852 a meeting was convened at Geelong, from which a committee was selected, resulting in the formation of the Geelong Steam Navigation Co. The chairman of the committee was one Duncan Hoyle, and he placed orders for two paddle-steamers to be built in Scotland. The first steamer completed was *Melbourne*, and it joined the Geelong trade in March 1853. The *Melbourne* offered lower fares than the others, 15s. in saloon instead of £1, and 7s. 6d. in the fore cabin against 12s. 6d.

This increased to five the number of steamers operating regularly to Geelong: the paddlers *Melbourne*, *Vesta*, *Aphrasia* and *Victoria*, another recent arrival, and the propeller steamer *Keera*. Unfortunately there was a shortage of wharf space, and on days when two steamers arrived, a race developed to secure the only berth. On 26 April 1853 the captain of a beaten ship was accused of deliberately hitting the stern of his rival, the *Melbourne* while the passengers were disembarking. The *Melbourne* was pushed 40 feet along the wharf by the impact and suffered some damage, though only one passenger was injured.

Completed early in 1853, the second steamer for the new Geelong Co. was named *Duncan Hoyle*, and it arrived in Geelong in June, after a 98-day delivery voyage. When the *Duncan Hoyle* entered service in July 1853, the *Vesta* was withdrawn. However, also in July 1853, the iron-hulled *Prince Albert*, which came to Melbourne from Scotland for R. & S. Raleigh, joined the Geelong trade. A fare war broke out, the rates being reduced to 8s. 6d. in saloon, and just 6s. in the fore cabin.

In 1854 the *Aphrasia*, *Melbourne*, *Victoria* and *Prince Albert* were all taken off the Geelong trade, being replaced by four other vessels—the paddlers *Breadalbane* and *Citizen* and the propeller vessels *Express* and *Shandon*. The *Breadalbane* was an iron-hulled steamer sent to Melbourne from Scotland shortly after being completed in 1853, with the intention of finding employment in the Bay trades. The *Citizen* was built in Scotland in 1852 and originally named *Glasgow Citizen*. She arrived in Port Phillip Bay in October 1854 and the following month was bought by the Geelong Steam Navigation Co. for £7,000. The *Breadalbane* was sold after a short time and went to Sydney, while the *Duncan Hoyle* and the *Melbourne* were both disposed of in 1855 and the Geelong Steam Navigation Co. went out of business. The *Duncan Hoyle* spent about three years operating from Melbourne to Tasmania, then was sold to Hong Kong owners, while the *Melbourne* ended her days in South Australia, being wrecked at the Murray mouth in 1859. Also in 1855, the new *Geelong* arrived in Melbourne for W. Locke & Partners and operated to Geelong until December 1856. From that time on the Geelong trade was conducted almost exclusively by propeller-powered vessels, though the *Citizen* continued to operate until September 1861.

The Australasian Steam Navigation Co. imported two paddle-steamers from Britain in 1852, the large *Yarra Yarra* for coastal work and a smaller vessel which was brought out in sections by the *Yarra Yarra* on its delivery voyage. The smaller vessel was assembled by the ASN shipyard at Pyrmont, in Sydney, the engines installed being those salvaged from the *Raven*, which was wrecked in 1850. Originally intended for service between Brisbane and Ipswich, the vessel was to be named *Brisbane*. However, the demand for vessels in Port Phillip Bay was so great the vessel was instead named *Ballarat* when launched in February 1853 and sent south. Unfortunately, *Ballarat* was not really suited to the Bay trades, and in 1856 went to Queensland, and later to New Zealand.

Probably the most interesting vessel to enter the Port Phillip Bay trades at this time was the *Governor Wynyard*, which was the first steamship to be built in New Zealand, in 1851. She was just 26 gross tons, 54 feet (16.4 m) long and 12 feet (3.7 m) beam. Built at Freemans Bay in Auckland, the hull of the vessel was pohutukawa timber, and the planking kauri. The engine was a locally built steeple type, while construction of the boiler posed major problems, as Auckland had then only been established for 10 years and was little more than a large village, with no skilled boilermakers. A passenger on an American barque in port said he was a boilermaker and improvised a rolling machine by hollowing out a clay bed in a yard. After heating the plates, he hammered them to the mould of the clay. An advertisement for the strongest man in the land brought forth a huge labourer, who punched every rivet hole by hand.

Launched on 24 December 1851, the *Governor Wynyard* ran trials on 19 January 1852, from Auckland to the Tamaki River. Unfortunately, the *Governor Wynyard* was ahead of her time, and in March 1853 she was sold to J.M. Bryant, of Melbourne.

With her paddlewheels and boxes removed, the *Governor Wynyard* crossed the Tasman Sea under sail, then was reassembled on the Yarra River. Her small size made her an ideal boat to act as tender to the many sailing ships that thronged the harbour, but in 1854 the boom had burst and the prospects for the future were not so bright. *Governor Wynyard* was sold to Launceston owners and spent the rest of her career operating along the north coast of Tasmania. Her engine was removed in 1859 and she operated as a sailing ship until being wrecked on Circular Head on 20 July 1873.

A number of other paddle-steamers entered service on Port Phillip Bay during this period. One of the largest vessels to arrive was the 453-gross-ton *North Star*, a wooden-hulled paddle-steamer built in Aberdeen in 1837 for the Aberdeen Steam Navigation Co. Arriving in Melbourne in 1853, the *North Star* saw some service, but spent most of the time laid up off Sandridge Pier. The vessel was offered for sale on 17 June 1854, but no offers were forthcoming and she remained idle until May 1856, when sold to a Captain Lawrence for just £1,000. After a very brief spell of service between Melbourne and Launceston, the *North Star* was sent to Shanghai, where she arrived on 26 March 1857 and was then sold. More successful was the 97-gross-ton wooden-hulled *Hercules*, which had been built at Dundee in 1849 for the Dundee, Perth & London Shipping Co. Ltd and arrived in Melbourne in August 1853. *Hercules* went through a number of owners over the years, being longest in the hands of companies controlled by Captain James Deane, and ended her days as a lighter in the 1920s. Another vessel that would later be associated with James Deane was the *Black Eagle*, which also arrived in Port Phillip Bay in 1854, and spent 30 years trading there.

Two former Sydney ferries came to Melbourne in the 1850s and spent some years operating as ferries on Port Phillip Bay. The *Comet* was a wooden steamer built in 1843 for the service between Sydney and Parramatta. In 1854 she was purchased by George W. Cole, and on arrival in Port Phillip Bay was placed on the ferry service on the Yarra River between Melbourne and Williamstown. A railway line was under construction from the city to Sandridge, on the shores of the Bay. When the railway was completed, *Comet* became the first vessel to operate the new ferry route to Wiliamstown from Sandridge, which was renamed Port Melbourne.

The other former Parramatta River ferry to join the Bay trades was the *Kangaroo*, a wooden-hulled vessel dating from 1840, when it was built by John Korff at Raymond Terrace. In 1847 the *Kangaroo* was sold to the Tasmanian government and ran as a ferry in Hobart until 1857, when she was purchased by George W. Cole and brought to Melbourne. Cole bought the *Kangaroo* as a dual-purpose ferry and tug, though her usefulness as a towing vessel was limited. However, it is known that the *Kangaroo* did service such famous sailing vessels as the *Lightning*, *James Baines* and *Donald McKay*.

The 32-horsepower steam-engine in the *Kangaroo* was built by John Struth in Sydney, and was somewhat unusual. Captain Hartley R. Watson wrote of the *Kangaroo*:

the engine room of this square-sterned, old paddler was an austere spot, devoid of shining brass or copper. The engine itself was a baffling contrivance which often left the skipper in doubt about what was going to happen next. High grade lubricating oil had no place in this engine room. In its stead was an old iron kettle which was kept simmering on the top of a big cylinder, emitting the pungent reek of boiling tallow.

The Victorian gold rush came to an end in the early 1860s, but at the same time gold was discovered on the South Island of New Zealand, and a new rush began. Vessels of every size and description were flung into the trans-Tasman trade, carrying thousands of eager prospectors to the new goldfields. There was also a great demand for steamships to operate around the New Zealand coast, and many of the Port Phillip Bay paddlers made the voyage to New Zealand, where they were offered for sale. Among the first paddlers to go were the *Geelong* and the *Aphrasia*, which left Port Phillip Bay in December 1861. The *Citizen*, which was withdrawn from the Geelong trade in 1861, was first sold at auction, the new owner deciding to send the vessel to New Zealand for resale. The *Comet* was also sold, to two brothers who also wished to send the vessel to New Zealand for resale.

The captain of the *Comet*, Robert Watson, refused an offer to take the vessel across the Tasman Sea, claiming that the proposed voyage was dangerous to the point of madness for such a small vessel. The *Comet* was only 87 gross tons, and 92 feet (28 m) long. Watson was an experienced ocean seaman, but his view was dismissed by the owners of the *Comet*, who found themselves another captain. Both the *Comet* and the *Citizen* were advertised to take passengers on the voyage to New Zealand, and the berths were quickly filled with prospectors. On 15 October 1862 the two boats left Port Melbourne together for the trip across the Tasman, but neither was ever seen again.

Having refused the fatal trip on the *Comet*, Captain Robert Watson remained in Melbourne and took command of the *Kangaroo*, which replaced the *Comet* on the ferry service between Port Melbourne and Williamstown. The *Kangaroo* was of a similar size to the *Comet*, and also offered little cover for passengers, while the open bridge forward of the funnel afforded the captain and helmsman no protection whatsoever. Things improved greatly in 1868, when the last of these ferries was built on the banks of the Yarra, a double-ended wooden vessel named the *Gem*. She was quite unlike anything else that had been seen on Port Phillip Bay, with a pair of tall funnels set side by side, as in the American river steamers. Originally owned by Captains G.W. Cole and A. Devlin, the *Gem* passed through a number of owners until 1911, when she was towed to Adelaide. Amazingly, during her entire period of service on the bay, the *Gem* had only one master, Captain Robert Watson. In the 1880s, the *Gem* was given a white hull, and the funnels painted red with black tops, which made her stand out in an era when most ships were painted black.

The ships that came to Port Phillip Bay had varying backgrounds, one of the most unusual being that of the paddle-steamer *Luna*, which arrived in 1866. A 252-gross-ton iron-hulled vessel, the *Luna* had been built in London in 1864 as a blockade runner for the Southern States in the American Civil War. This was a very profitable but highly dangerous undertaking, but twice the *Luna* successfully ran the blockade of Confederate ports by the Unionists. In 1866 the *Luna* was purchased in London by J. & D. Parker & Co., who in 1853 had sent Thomas James Parker to Geelong to establish a branch of their merchant business. The *Luna* was sent out to Port Phillip Bay and operated a variety of trades, including excursions, her master being Captain Thomas Webb. In 1876 Thomas J. Parker and Captain Webb would join up with John Trail and James Huddart to form the famous shipping firm, Huddart Parker Ltd.

The *Luna*, under the command of Captain Webb, was involved in a major accident off Williamstown Pier on 16 July 1867. Travelling at about 12 knots, she collided with the steamer *Black Swan*, carrying passengers and cargo for Launceston, causing that ship to sink in four fathoms. Fortunately no lives were lost and the *Black Swan* was refloated and repaired. However, the ramifications were more serious, as Captain Webb had his certificate suspended for nine months, his ship being held to be in the wrong. The accident also incurred debts for the owners that they could not meet, so the *Luna* was seized and sold at auction. After a short spell in Sydney, the *Luna* was sold to the government of New Zealand and finished her days as a coal hulk on the other side of the Tasman, being broken up in 1902.

Mention was made earlier of Captain James Deane and the various vessels he owned and operated on Port Phillip Bay. Captain Deane was born in England in 1829 and arrived in Australia in the 1860s, and in subsequent years owned 15 paddle-steamers, many of them tugs, on Port Phillip Bay. He was also instrumental in the establishment of the regular excursion trades that would become extremely popular on the Bay over many years. During the 1870s

The double-ended ferry *Gem* was built in Melbourne in 1868.

*Mystery* operated as both a tug and an excursion boat on Port Phillip Bay.

Profile drawing of *Williams*. (PN)

Captain Deane lived aboard a former storeship, the *Sir William Molesworth*, which was moored at Williamstown. The interior had been elaborately fitted out as a private residence, where he was very comfortable, until one day the ship was badly damaged by fire. Forced to move out, the resourceful Deane converted the hulk into a marine blacksmith's shop, which was extremely successful. In 1904 Deane purchased another fire-damaged vessel, the former three-masted sailing ship *Habitant*, and converted it into a floating dock at Williamstown, which eventually became the Hobson's Bay Dock & Engineering Co. Pty Ltd. In 1884 Deane combined with Hugh Reid, Captain James McIntyre and David Syme to form the Melbourne Coal Shipping & Engineering Co. Ltd, later renamed the Melbourne Steamship Co. Ltd, which owned a fleet of coastal vessels.

In 1867 James Deane purchased the *Mystery*, for use as both a tug and an excursion vessel. Built at Northam in Kent, *Mystery* was a wooden vessel of 105 gross tons, with two tall funnels set very close together, and a foremast only. She was powered by a 60-horsepower grasshopper side-lever steam-engine, and had a speed of about 9 knots. For 15 years, *Mystery* operated in British waters as a tug, then in December 1867 was sold to Captain Deane.

On her arrival in Melbourne the *Mystery* was used as a tug, but Deane also fitted some passenger accommodation to make the vessel more suitable for excursion work. At that time there were a number of tugs offering excursions occasionally, but they had very basic accommodation for passengers. During the peak summer holiday period, especially around Christmas, numerous other vessels would be made available for excursions, including some of the larger coastal traders which ran trips to the resorts near Port Phillip Heads. *Mystery* was the first vessel to offer excursions on a regular basis and became very popular. She was also employed for a couple of years on the regular trades to Portarlington and Geelong. Deane sold the *Mystery* in 1874 and she spent the next 25 years on Sydney Harbour.

Buoyed by the success of the *Mystery* in the excursion business, Deane purchased another vessel in 1872, intended exclusively for this trade. The vessel he obtained was the *Williams*, built in 1854 in Scotland for the Hunter River New Steam Navigation Co. Ltd, an iron-hulled paddle-steamer of 218 gross tons. The *Williams* operated a passenger and cargo service between Sydney and the Hunter River until 1862, then was sold to the Australasian Steam Navigation Co., and for the next 10 years operated in Queensland waters, mostly on the route from Brisbane to Maryborough and Rockhampton. When James Deane purchased the *Williams* he had her rebuilt, including lengthening by 11 feet (3.3 m) to 166 feet (50.5 m). In addition, the mainmast was removed and a more extensive superstructure fitted, the top deck being covered by an awning along its entire length. These changes increased her size to 322 gross tons. Surprisingly, the open bridge forward of the funnels was retained, leaving the poor helmsman with no protection from the weather. The vessel was then given a light grey hull, while the two funnels had a red base, black top and wide white band.

On 9 November 1872 the *Williams* ran her first trial trip down Port Phillip Bay, with invited guests on board. They were all amazed at the comfort offered by the vessel, which was vastly superior to anything provided previously. The promenade deck was 90 feet (27.4 m) long, with space set aside for dancing to the best bands in Melbourne. The main deck was of the same length as the promenade deck, while the quarter deck ran half the length. The main saloon was 50 feet (15.2 m) long, ran the full width of the vessel and was resplendent with luxurious fittings, including mirrors and gilding. There were also comfortable seats spaced around the other decks, and ample open deck space for walking or taking the sea air. A report in the *Argus* also stated

> a new feature in the excursion trips, and one which was highly spoken of, was the catering on board, a very appetising cold collation being obtainable at the moderate figure of one shilling per head. This in itself will be a perfect boon to those who heretofore have borne the burden of providing sandwich baskets and packages of refreshments.

On this first trip, the *Williams* averaged 11 knots, far better than any previous excursion vessel.

The *Williams* operated primarily as an excursion vessel, but was used in the off-season for towing duties. Her regular route was from Port Melbourne to Queenscliff, Portsea and Sorrento, but calls were also made at other resorts from time to time. Deane had also purchased the tug *Black Eagle* in 1872, and on holidays he operated her on shorter excursions to St Kilda and Brighton, and occasionally to Schnapper Point (Mornington). In this way, Deane was able to dominate the excursion trade in Port Phillip Bay, with the *Williams* being the finest vessel then in service.

Of course it was a situation that could not last for ever, and in December 1874 a rival appeared, the *Golden Crown*, operated by the Sorrento & Queenscliff Steam Navigation Co. Ltd. This company had been formed in 1874 by the Hon. George Coppin, who had settled in Sorrento in the 1860s. Coppin was a vigorous promoter and investor, and he developed Sorrento into a major tourist destination. Aware of the enormous success, and financial rewards, being enjoyed by Captain Deane with his superb excursion steamer, Coppin and Robert Stirling formed their own steamship company and sought a suitable ship to purchase. They found what they were looking for in New Zealand, buying the *Golden Crown* in October 1874.

The *Golden Crown* was built in Auckland in 1870, and at 330 gross tons was the largest and finest vessel yet constructed in the country. Noted marine authority Dickson Gregory claimed that the *Golden Crown* was to have had an iron hull, the plates and frames being cut in England and sent to New Zealand by a steamer which was lost on the way. However, other authorities state the vessel was always intended to have a wooden hull, the timber for which was cut three years prior to construction commencing, then left to season. The machinery was imported from Scotland; two oscillating, direct-action steam-engines of 140-horsepower, built by J. & G. Thomson in Glasgow. On trials in December 1870, she reached 13 knots. *Golden Crown* was built for Mr J.S. McFarlane, who placed her in service from Auckland to Thames, where gold had been discovered, and

*Golden Crown*, built in New Zealand, spent many years on the Bay. (RWB)

*Murray Princess* is designed along the lines of a Mississippi River boat.

*Avoca* has been operating excursions for sixty years.

*Canberra* was originally built as a fishing boat.

*Melbourne* is the only steamer operating excursions at Mildura.

*Rothbury* is now fitted with a diesel engine.

*Pyap* runs regular daily excursions from the Swan Hill Pioneer Village.

*Pride of the Murray* was built up from the barge C24.

*Mundoo* was built at Goolwa in 1987.

she could make the journey in four hours. She was also used for evening excursions on Auckland Harbour during the summer.

During 1871 *Golden Crown* was purchased by the newly formed Auckland & Thames Steam Packet Co., remaining on her original service, but the gold discovery proved to be less than anticipated and the rush of prospectors soon subsided. On 8 May 1872 the Auckland & Thames Co. went into voluntary liquidation and *Golden Crown* passed into the ownership of the Auckland Steam Packet Co. Ltd, only to be offered for sale again in 1874.

Purchased in October 1874 by the Sorrento & Queenscliffe Co., *Golden Crown* crossed the Tasman under steam and on arrival in Port Phillip Bay was prepared for service as a full-time excursion boat. Her first trip departed Port Melbourne on 19 December 1874, which happened to be a Sunday, when no public transport was provided in Melbourne. A special train was organised to carry passengers from Melbourne to Port Melbourne, but to get it they had to walk from their suburban homes. *Golden Crown* departed the wharf at 9.15 a.m., with 220 passengers on board, and had a rough passage down the bay, arriving at Sorrento at midday. As no catering facilities were provided on board, the excursionists flocked ashore to the one hotel, seeking lunch. However, being Sunday, the dining room was open to residents only, though the excursionists were allowed to consume the leftovers, but at a high price. That afternoon the *Golden Crown* carried her passengers back to Port Melbourne and, despite the problems, the vessel was considered a success, with wide open decks and a comfortable interior.

There now began a period of intense rivalry between the *Golden Crown*, which became popularly known simply as 'The Crown', and the *Williams*. Both were about the same size, and fitted out in similar manner, but which was the faster? Although the two never engaged in a race, the *Golden Crown* covered the 20 nautical miles from the Gellibrand Lightship to the West Channel Lightship in 105 minutes, while the *Williams* took 111 minutes. The pair began operating a daily excursion schedule, with the *Williams* going to Queenscliff, Portsea and Sorrento, while the *Golden Crown* did not call at Portsea. Inevitably, the rivalry led to a price war, and many claims and counter-claims regarding the opposition. Extra ports were added to the itinerary of the *Williams* (Schnapper Point and Dromana), and the fact that the Deane boat left Port Melbourne at 9 a.m., 15 minutes ahead of her rival, resulted in the *Williams* being called the premier boat. In 1875 the following advertisements appeared in the Melbourne daily newspapers:

THE PEOPLES RECREATION STEAMER
'GOLDEN CROWN':
ALTERATIONS IN THE TIMETABLE TO
QUEENSCLIFF AND SORRENTO:
SPECIAL EXCURSIONS
The SORRENTO and QUEENSCLIFF STEAM NAVIGATION COMPANY, having destroyed an illiberal monopoly and enforced speed and civility for the comfort of the public, with a great reduction in the hitherto high fares in order that all classes may enjoy a trip to

Sorrento, to the most picturesque and convenient retreat in the Bay for picnic parties, beg to announce that by general request a slight alteration has been made in the hour of starting, which will have the effect of correcting a ridiculous announcement assuming 'Pride of Place', starting at 9 a.m. for Queenscliff and Sorrento. Tickets 7/6.

Three days later, the opposition replied with:

THE EXCURSIONISTS' STEAMER
(Par Excellence) 'WILLIAMS'
For Queenscliff and Sorrento. The undersigned, feeling satisfied that visitors to Queenscliff and Portsea, Schnapper Point and Dromana will not be satisfied to entrust their travelling arrangements to any company specially interested in advancing a rival township, have determined, consequent upon liberal patronage hitherto received from the public, to keep the steamer *Williams* permanently in the passenger trade at greatly reduced fares, which in no case will exceed the advertised rates charged by any other steamer. JAMES DEANE & Co. Fares 5/–.

As the fare reductions were matched by each side, the only real winners were the passengers. Back in the 1860s, when excursions were run by tugs, the fare to Queenscliff was 10*s*. one way, 15*s*. return. Thousands flocked to the two excursion steamers, taking advantage of the ridiculously cheap cost of a day's outing, but the situation could not last. Neither operator was making any money out of the operation of its excursion boats, and the inevitable happened. James Deane could support his excursion trade from profits gained by his other boats, but the *Golden Crown* was the only asset of the Sorrento & Queenscliff Co., and while they were able to remain in the trade for some years, by 1882 they were in deep financial trouble. Eventually the company had to be reorganised, and was renamed the Port Phillip Steamship & Hotel Co. Ltd, a major shareholder being James Deane.

Intent on improving his position in the Port Phillip Bay excursion trades, James Deane went to Scotland to order a new paddle-steamer, whose construction he would oversee. The Clyde River paddle-steamers were the finest excursion boats in the world, and were built in great number. Between 1889 and 1914 there were 75 excursion boats on the Clyde, and only five were not paddle-steamers. James Deane wanted a boat that would be the equal of any, and placed his order with R. Steele & Co., at Greenock, for a vessel with a steel hull, 200 feet (60.9 m) long, to be powered by a pair of two-cylinder surface-condensing compound engines. The construction of the vessel was badly delayed, and by the time it was launched at the end of 1882 Deane was aware that he had not produced the type of boat he wanted. Named *Lonsdale*, the vessel ran trials in Scotland, but was not able to attain the hoped-for speed.

Rigged as a three-masted schooner, *Lonsdale* made the delivery voyage to Australia under sail, arriving in Port Phillip Bay in April 1883, too late for the excursion season. In a desperate effort to improve her speed, Deane had the *Lonsdale* cut in two, and an extra section inserted aft of the paddleboxes, increasing her measurements to 228 feet (69.5 m) length, and 551 gross tons. It was also thought

The unfortunate *Lonsdale* had a very short career on Port Phillip Bay. (PN)

that the paddlewheels were biting too deeply into the water, so they were raised, but none of the modifications made any difference to her speed. Totally disillusioned with the vessel, James Deane was pleased to sell her to the Port Phillip Steamship & Hotel Co., in which he retained a financial interest.

Unlike the *Williams* and the *Golden Crown*, *Lonsdale* was not equipped with a permanent awning to cover her top deck, in typical Clyde steamer fashion, which was a drawback in Australia, especially on hot or wet days. However, her saloons and lounges were very comfortably furnished. Such was the demand for excursions on Port Phillip Bay that *Lonsdale* was able to hold her own with the *Golden Crown* and the *Williams*, and for a few years was actually quite popular, as speed was not essential for excursion steamers.

James Dean's discomfort over the total failure of the *Lonsdale* to meet his expectations can only have been heightened by a disaster that befell another of his boats, the *Black Eagle*. Although primarily engaged in towing duties around Port Phillip Bay, the *Black Eagle* continued to operate short excursions during holiday periods, having a licence to carry 190 passengers. On Boxing Day, 1884, *Black Eagle* was operating excursions between St Kilda and Brighton, but during the afternoon she sprang a leak and water poured in. The captain ordered full speed and managed to reach the St Kilda wharf, where all passengers safely disembarked, but then the *Black Eagle* settled on the bottom and broke her back. Considered a total loss, the wreck was sold at auction on 31 December to John Clark for just £10, though her value at the time of the sinking was quoted as £3,000. Clark quickly organised the removal of the wreck from the St Kilda pier.

That was not the end of the matter, as an enquiry was held into the sinking on 3 January 1885 by the Steam Navigation Board. It was concluded that the reason for the sudden inrush of water could not be determined, and exonerated the owner and the master. This produced an outcry in the press, with the *Argus* claiming:

> the *Black Eagle* was a leaky old tub thirty-two years old, making water heavily always. How came such a craft as that to have the Board's certificate to carry 190 passengers anywhere in Port Phillip? And if the Board licensed the antiquated tub, how came it that she was plying with only two life-buoys, and one boat capable of holding twelve persons? . . . Had the vessel been in mid-channel there would have been a tragedy first and a verdict of manslaughter afterwards.

Of course this was in the days when vessels did not have to carry sufficient lifesaving equipment for all on board, a regulation that would only come into effect after the sinking of the *Titanic* in 1912.

James Deane's situation could easily have been even worse, and he must have come to the conclusion that the name Lonsdale was a jinx for him. On 4 July 1883 his pride and joy, the *Williams*, was engaged in her winter tug duties, towing the barque *George Roper* outside Port Phillip Heads, when a dense fog descended. The *Williams* suddenly found itself running towards a reef off Point Lonsdale on the western side of Port Phillip Heads, and in trying to evade the rocks, struck heavily, doing some damage to her bottom. The tow line had to be dropped hurriedly and the *Williams* headed off for repairs, but the *George Roper* ended up on the reef and became a total loss. While attempting to refloat the *George Roper* on 8 July, the propeller-powered tug *Black Boy*, also owned by James Deane, ran aground on the reef at Lonsdale Point too, and became a total loss.

The *Lonsdale* was a most unfortunate vessel throughout her short career, being involved in numerous incidents during her first four seasons of operation. These included running down a small boat and causing the deaths of two men in it, sinking another small boat, going aground at Portarlington, and colliding off Schnapper Point with a yacht, which lost its bowsprit. *Lonsdale* suffered no damage in any of these accidents, but when she once came in to berth at Queenscliff at too great a speed, and hit the pier bow-on, both vessel and pier were badly damaged. On 17 December 1886 *Lonsdale* came into collision with the trading schooner *Tyro* in the West Channel. Again the steamer was undamaged, but the *Tyro* was near to foundering and the *Lonsdale* towed it to Williamstown. The collision had its sequel in a court case, where the long list of incidents in which the *Lonsdale* and her master, Captain Richardson, had been involved was recited. As a result, the

*Lonsdale* was found to have been at fault and her owners had to pay considerable compensation for the collision. To add insult to injury, it was also decided that the cargo aboard the *Tyro* was damaged owing to negligence on the part of the *Lonsdale* when towing the sinking schooner to safety. The amount finally awarded to the owner of the *Tyro* was £827, which the Port Phillip Steamship & Hotel Co. Ltd could ill afford to pay.

On 18 December, the day after *Lonsdale* had her encounter with the *Tyro*, the vessel received another major setback. It was on that day that a new excursion boat, the *Ozone*, made its first trip on Port Phillip Bay. The *Ozone* was also built on the River Clyde, by Napier, Shanks & Bell at Glasgow, having a steel hull 260 feet (79.2 m) long. Her machinery, built by the Glasgow firm of Rankin & Blackmore, comprised a pair of two-cylinder direct-acting diagonal compound engines, and her paddlewheels were larger than usual, being almost 22 feet (6.7 m) in diameter. *Ozone* was owned by Bay Excursions Co. Ltd, which had been formed specially to finance the construction of the new vessel.

On 25 August 1886 *Ozone* departed Glasgow on her delivery voyage, the first call being Waterford in southern Ireland. From there *Ozone* went to Gibraltar, then Malta and through the Suez Canal, to arrive in Aden on 19 September. As the engines were giving trouble, *Ozone* did not depart Aden until 4 October, taking 10 days to reach Colombo. Leaving there on 15 October, stormy weather was encountered as *Ozone* steamed to Batavia, where she berthed on 23 October. Next call was Thursday Island, then down the Queensland coast to Sydney, leaving on 23 November on the last leg of the voyage.

As *Ozone* entered Victorian waters for the first time, the weather began to worsen, and off Wilsons Promontory the steamer was bucking into a full gale. It was a very relieved master who finally brought his vessel safely through Port Phillip Heads on 25 November 1886, never to venture outside them again.

For the delivery voyage, *Ozone* carried two masts, but the main was removed once she arrived. At the same time, the main saloon was enlarged and an iron roof fitted along the entire length of the promenade deck. This roofing added some 50 tons in weight to the tophamper of the vessel, but did not seem to affect her speed. On trials in the Bay, *Ozone* made four runs over a 15-mile course and averaged 18¼ knots.

On 18 December 1886 *Ozone* made her first excursion, from Port Melbourne to Queenscliff and Sorrento. Despite inclement weather, some 300 passengers were aboard, but on the outward journey the engines overheated, causing speed to be reduced. In order to cool the bearings, cold water was played on them, and eventually *Ozone* was able to build up to full speed again. It had been hoped that *Ozone* would overtake her main rival, the *Lonsdale*, on the outward journey, but this did not occur. Coming in to berth at Queenscliff, the captain misjudged his approach and *Ozone* came into heavy contact with the pier, causing some minor damage. No passengers on *Ozone* were injured, but two holes were punched through plating forward of the paddleboxes. On the return trip to Port Melbourne, *Ozone* did manage to pass *Lonsdale*, and was considered to be the fastest vessel on the Bay.

On 16 January 1888 another new vessel joined the Port Phillip Bay excursion trade, the propeller-driven *Courier*, owned by Huddart Parker & Co. *Courier* was placed on the regular passenger and cargo service from Port Melbourne to Portarlington and Geelong, and her owners claimed she was the fastest ship on Port Phillip Bay, having averaged 17½ knots on trials. This claim was disputed by the owners of the *Ozone*, and one day they decided to prove the superiority of their paddle-steamer.

In February 1888 *Ozone* entered dry dock to have her bottom scraped and polished and the machinery overhauled. All temporary awnings and other fittings were removed, and on Saturday 18 February she was ready for the big, though unofficial, event. On a Saturday, *Courier* used to depart at 10 a.m. for Portarlington and Geelong, while *Ozone* would not leave until 2 p.m. for Sorrento. On this day, though,

*Ozone* was a very popular excursion vessel for many years. (RWB)

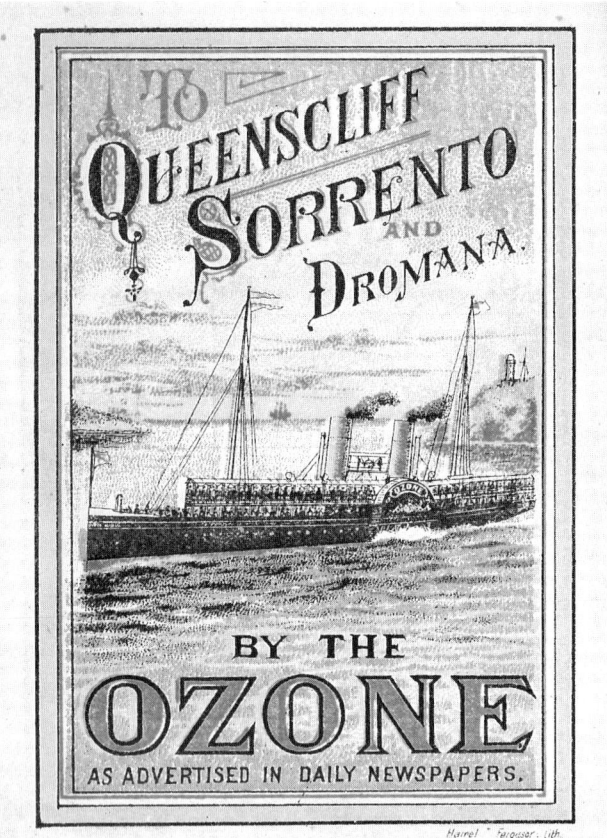

*Ozone* promotional poster from 1886. (RWB)

*Ozone* was bunkered with just enough coal to get her to Portarlington and return, and carried just 25 invited guests. *Courier*, whose bottom had not been cleaned since her arrival, took aboard 450 passengers and a full cargo, and left her wharf in the Yarra River at 10 a.m. as usual.

As *Courier* left the river and entered Port Phillip Bay, *Ozone* was lying in wait off St Kilda, and built up speed to close the *Courier* off the Gellibrand Lightship. Black smoke poured from the twin smokestacks of both ships as the stokers poured on the coal. Racing down the channel, the pair were neck and neck, then gradually the paddler began to move ahead. As Portarlington loomed, *Ozone* had opened a lead of three lengths, and in triumph swept across the bow of *Courier*, then turned back to Port Melbourne. As the vessels passed, a flag featuring a crowing rooster rose to the masthead of *Ozone*. It was later reported that *Ozone* averaged 18½ knots on the journey from Gellibrand Lightship to Portarlington.

The captain of the *Courier* claimed the race was not a race at all, as he had a full load aboard. But Huddart Parker was not prepared to accept the result of the race, and laid its own plans for a rematch, but on its own terms.

Just on a year after the first race, Huddart Parker issued an official challenge to Bay Excursions for a race between *Courier* and *Ozone*, which was declined. Huddart Parker put *Courier* into dry dock for hull cleaning, and on 16 February 1889 she was ready to take on *Ozone*. This time it was the Huddart Parker vessel that carried few passengers, only 70 invited guests, while *Ozone* took on board almost 900 daytrippers.

*Courier* cancelled her trip to Geelong, instead leaving her wharf at 1 p.m. and waiting near the Gellibrand Lightship. *Ozone* left on schedule at 2 p.m., though her captain was under orders not to engage in a race. As the two vessels drew level, *Courier* came up to speed, and for a short while the two boats travelled abreast, with passengers on both ships hurling insults across the intervening waters. Then *Courier* increased to full speed and began to pull ahead. It was at this point that the paddles of *Ozone* stopped, much to the disappointment of those aboard. As *Courier* disappeared into the distance behind a screen of black smoke, *Ozone* started off again and changed course for the shallow Coles Channel, which *Courier* could not use. Instead, *Courier* turned east and headed off towards Mornington, those aboard satisfied they had proved which was the faster vessel. In fact, neither contest proved anything, but they enlivened the Port Phillip Bay excursion trade.

The advent of the *Ozone* had a major effect on other vessels engaged in the excursion trade. The *Williams*, by now totally outclassed and only called upon to operate in peak holiday periods, spent the rest of her time on towing duties. The *Golden Crown*, with her outmoded wooden hull showing signs of wear and tear, was also used very sparingly. It was left to the *Lonsdale* to try to compete with the *Ozone*, but the new steamer was superior in every way. The public flocked to travel on the *Ozone* and only turned to the other steamers as a last resort. In January 1888 the Port Phillip Steamship & Hotel Co. Ltd announced it was in liquidation. *Golden Crown* was laid up, while the *Lonsdale* was offered for charter at greatly reduced rates. The vessel ran occasional trips during the year, but early in 1889 ownership of the *Golden Crown* and the *Lonsdale* passed to the major creditor, the Colonial Bank of Australasia. The *Lonsdale* then joined the *Golden Crown* in lay up in 'Rotten Row', an area of Hobsons Bay filled with derelict or unwanted ships.

The *Lonsdale* was lying in 'Rotten Row', with her former mate on board as caretaker, when a gale swept through Port Phillip Bay on 14 June 1889. *Lonsdale* broke free of her moorings and was blown across Hobsons Bay, ending up hard aground on the beach close to the old Port Melbourne swimming baths. She defied all attempts at salvage until a channel was dredged from the beach.

On 23 January 1891 the *Lonsdale* was finally pulled off the beach and anchored again in 'Rotten Row', but by the end of the year had been broken up, ending a short, unhappy career of just nine years. The *Golden Crown* remained on Rotten Row until 1892, then she too was sold to shipbreakers.

In 1889 another notable paddle-steamer made a brief appearance on the waters of Port Phillip Bay. The *Newcastle* was a 1,251-gross-ton steel-hulled steamer which had been built in 1884 for the Newcastle Steamship Co. to operate between Sydney and Newcastle. The completion of the railway line between these two cities in 1889 resulted in a huge drop in patronage on the steamers, and the Newcastle Steamship Co. was quite keen to sell its largest vessel. In August 1889 Huddart Parker Limited decided to enter the trade between Melbourne and Launceston, in Tasmania, but did not have a suitable vessel immediately available,

*Ozone* looked very smart when painted white. (RWB)

so it charted the *Newcastle* in October 1889, with an option to buy. The *Newcastle* was a powerful-looking ship, with three funnels, two forward of the paddleboxes and one aft, a rather unusual arrangement. Twice a week, the *Newcastle* would race down Port Phillip Bay on her way to the Heads, and on into Bass Strait, returning two days later. The Newcastle Steamship Co. was very hopeful that Huddart Parker would be sufficiently impressed with the *Newcastle* to exercise the option to buy, but unfortunately she was a very expensive vessel to operate, with a healthy appetite for coal. In April 1890, when the Huddart Parker propeller steamer *Coogee* had completed refitting for the Tasmania trade, the *Newcastle* was returned to her owners.

Mention should be made here of another small paddle-steamer, the *Bellarine*, which operated on Port Phillip Bay for some years, though is now almost totally forgotten. The *Bellarine* was built in 1877 at Milang, on the Murray River in South Australia, and was originally named *Dispatch*. She had a composite hull, wooden planks over an iron frame, with a square stern, straight bow, and was 117 gross tons. *Dispatch* was built for A.H. Landseer, and was christened by his daughter. Unfortunately, the launching did not go as planned, due to lack of water, and the paddle-steamer *Jane Eliza* had to be called upon to haul the *Dispatch* off the slip.

*Dispatch* was built for the Royal Mail service across Lake Alexandrina between Milang, where the railway line from Melbourne ended, and Meningie, a major link in the overland service between Adelaide and Melbourne before the railway went right through. She could carry 60 passengers and had a saloon with berths for 12 men and 8 women, these being used by travellers between the two cities. *Dispatch* remained on Lake Alexandrina until November 1888, when she was bought by Howard Smith & Sons Ltd.

Renamed *Bellarine*, the vessel passed out through the Murray Mouth, bound for Port Phillip Bay, but encountered bad weather and was forced to shelter at Robe for several days. Once the seas calmed down, *Bellarine* continued her voyage and reached Melbourne safely. The vessel had been bought to operate a very short service, from Geelong to the California Tea Gardens at Point Henry.

Point Henry had been the landing place for hundreds of early immigrants to the Geelong area, before the main port was opened up. It was later considered to be the ideal site for a pleasure resort, and on 1 October 1849 the California Tea Gardens opened there. The resort operated with mixed success until it was purchased by Howard Smith & Sons, who expanded and developed its accommodation and entertainment facilities. The *Bellarine* was bought to provide direct access to the resort from Geelong, from where the bulk of the day excursion trade to the resort emanated, the return fare being 6d. At that time, Howard Smiths was running the steamer *Edina* on a service from Melbourne to Portarlington and Geelong, and added a call at the California Tea Gardens to her itinerary. As the *Edina* was too big to come right into the dock, the hulk of the former sailing ship *City of Melbourne* was moored near the channel in October 1889, and Melbourne passengers were transferred across the hulk from the *Edina* to the *Bellarine*, which conveyed them to the Gardens. Unfortunately, the hulk sank on 31 January 1890.

It was said of the *Bellarine* that she leaked very badly, and a former boiler attendant on the vessel recalled one night trip when the water rose so high in the stokehold he was sure the vessel was going to sink. However, she was safely run aground on Eastern Beach, and after repairs resumed her trade. The popularity of the California Tea Gardens declined towards the end of the century, and in 1898 they were sold for grazing purposes. Today the same spot is the site of the huge Alcoa complex. *Bellarine* was subsequently used to carry cargo between the Werribee River and Melbourne until she was wrecked near the mouth of the river in 1908, and broken up in 1913.

The major operator on the route between Melbourne and Geelong was Huddart Parker & Co., which had built a series of fine propeller steamers to operate the route. The company had also expanded into the Australian coastal trades, and also to New Zealand. It therefore came as something of a surprise when it decided to enter the excursion trade from Melbourne to Sorrento and Queenscliff, but in 1890 it took delivery of a new vessel, the *Hygeia*, which was the first paddle-steamer to be built for the company, being designed for the Port Phillip Bay excursion trade. Built in Scotland by Napier, Shanks & Bell, *Hygeia* was similar to the latest Clyde River excursion paddle-steamers, and far larger than previous Port Phillip excursion boats, 987 gross tons and 300 feet (91.4 m) long. She was fitted with a pair of four-cylinder triple-expansion reciprocating steam-engines, built by Rankin & Blackmore, and during trials on 2 August 1890 topped 20 knots. The construction of *Hygeia* marked the start of the golden age of the Port Phillip Bay excursion steamers. The three permanent excursion boats were paddlers, *Hygeia*, *Ozone* and *Williams*, while another five propeller-powered vessels operated occasional excursions, these being *Courier*, *Coogee*, *Excelsior* and *Alert*, all owned by Huddart Parker, and the *Edina* of Howard Smith Ltd. All these vessels were regularly employed on other Bay and short coastal trades.

In preparation for her delivery voyage, the light hull was strengthened with timber braces, and boards were fitted over all windows and along the entire length of the lower deck. *Hygeia* left Glasgow on 21 August 1890, under the command of Captain Stewart Patrick but soon ran into heavy weather and was forced to shelter in the harbour at Lamlash, on the Isle of Arran. The voyage continued the following day, going to Wicklow in Ireland. Shortly after leaving there, more bad weather forced *Hygeia* to turn back and seek shelter in Kingstown Harbour, near Dublin. Two days later the storm had blown itself out, so *Hygeia* was able to proceed, making a comfortable 9 knots across the Bay of Biscay and through the Straits of Gibraltar. After a refueling call at Malta, *Hygeia* passed through the Suez Canal, then stopped at Aden, Colombo, Batavia and Thursday Island. A call was made at Brisbane, and then Sydney, before *Hygeia* passed through Port Phillip Heads on 18 November.

In general appearance, *Hygeia* was similar to *Ozone*, but she had an attractive light blue hull and yellow funnels, which were elliptical in shape and had tops parallel to the decks. The top deck was covered by a full-length permanent awning, with the open bridge amidships between the funnels. The interior was fitted out in the most sumptuous style, with comfortable lounges and saloons.

*Hygeia* entered service on 6 December 1890, operating from Railway Pier at Port Melbourne to Queenscliff and Sorrento. *Hygeia* was not only the fastest vessel on Port Phillip Bay, but also in Australia, and probably the fastest paddle-steamer ever built in the world. In 1894 it was claimed that she averaged almost 22 knots on a passage down the West Channel. However, she had to operate to a schedule, and usually ran at an economical 16 knots.

On 25 December 1894 *Hygeia* was involved in a collision with the tug *Sprightly* when leaving her pier on a Christmas Day excursion. On leaving her berth, *Hygeia* began making a leisurely turn in the direction of St Kilda Pier as the small tug approached. *Sprightly* was affected by the wash from *Hygeia* and collided with the paddler on the port quarter. *Hygeia* suffered a few damaged plates, while the bow of the tug was pushed back by the impact, but both vessels were able to continue on their way.

*Hygeia* was licensed to carry a maximum of 1,600

*Hygeia* speeds across Port Phillip Bay. (RWB)

passengers, but on occasions, especially public holidays, more than this number would swarm onto Railway Pier at Port Melbourne and try to get aboard. On these days, crew members would be stationed at each entrance port, counting the passengers coming on board. As soon as 1,600 was reached, the gangways would be swiftly pulled in and the lines dropped, leaving the latecomers screaming and cursing. Sometimes families would be split up, with some on board and others still on the wharf. Sometimes the *Hygeia* would be chartered for a day by a trade group or organisation, who would be instructed to sell no more than 1,600 tickets. In some cases, they would sell 2,000 or more and there would be howls of rage when the vessel suddenly pulled away from the wharf, having reached her limit. Occasional special trips would be run from Geelong to the Mornington Peninsular.

The first master of the *Hygeia* was Captain Stewart Patrick, a cheery man who was well known around Melbourne. In summer he and his officers would be dressed in white linen uniforms, with gold braid trimmings, while in winter it was blue serge and brass buttons. Once the bustle and responsibility of getting *Hygeia* away from the wharf were over and the boat was settled into her steady, rapid stride down the Bay, Captain Patrick used to invite selected passengers to join him on the bridge. This had to include any dignitaries making the trip, but the captain had a good eye for attractive young ladies, and two or three would find themselves on the bridge for the trip to Queenscliff, which would take about two hours.

*Hygeia* immediately became the most popular excursion boat on the bay, but *Ozone* still had a band of faithful followers and was able to continue a profitable service. The *Williams* was now used very rarely for excursions, and in November 1894 she was sold to shipbreakers, ending a varied career that had lasted 40 years. There were now very few paddle-steamers operating on Port Phillip Bay—just the two large excursion boats and a few tugs, including the *Albatross* owned by James Paterson, which served on the Bay until 1917.

One other service that still employed paddleboats was the ferry between Port Melbourne and Williamstown, on which the *Gem* had been plying since 1868. In 1900 another paddler was added to this service, but far from being a new vessel, the *Queen* was 16 years old and had already had a varied career. Built in 1884 in Sydney, she had originally been named *Natone* and was owned by the Tasmanian Steam Navigation Co. as a tender at Launceston. Within a year, the vessel had moved to Brisbane, and spent many years on ferry services there before coming south again, when purchased for the Hobsons Bay ferry trade. The *Queen* was quite a smart-looking vessel, with a covered lower deck containing saloons for passengers, and an open top deck. She was double-ended, and had two wheelhouses, either side of the single funnel. Following the pattern set by the *Gem*, the *Queen* was given a white hull and a red funnel with black top.

In 1907 another paddler was added to the ferry service between Port Melbourne and Williamstown, the *Bald Rock*, again purchased second-hand. Also built in 1884, she had

a wooden hull, and when completed was named *Bald Rock*. She operated on the ferry service between Balmain and Sydney until September 1900, then was renamed *Vaucluse* for a new service from Sydney to the Eastern Suburbs, reverting to *Bald Rock* in September 1905, when she returned to the Balmain trade. When sold to Melbourne, her name was amended to *Baldrock* and she was repainted white with a red funnel and black top. Also double-ended, *Baldrock* had open wheelhouses on either side of the funnel, and offered limited covered accommodation for passengers. *Baldrock* was not a good purchase, as she suffered continual engine and boiler problems, and the lack of covered accommodation was not popular with passengers.

The use of these three paddlers, *Gem*, *Queen* and *Baldrock*, on the ferry service between Port Melbourne and Williamstown, came to an end in 1911. The *Gem* was then used for pumping silt into hopper barges on the Yarra River, then towed to Adelaide, where she became a floating bridge, with funnels and wheelhouses removed. The *Queen* was converted into a hulk and served in this capacity at Townsville in Queensland for many years. *Baldrock* was used for towing duties until 1922, then was converted into an explosives lighter, being finally broken up in 1928.

When the various states combined to form the Commonwealth of Australia on 1 January 1901, Melbourne was the largest city in the country, so it was there that the first Federal parliament met. The Duke and Duchess of York travelled to Australia to represent Queen Victoria at the opening of the first parliament, voyaging on the chartered Orient liner *Ophir*. When the royal couple, who later became King George V and Queen Mary, arrived in Port Phillip Bay on 6 May 1901, the *Hygeia* was selected to convey them from the *Ophir* to St Kilda pier, where the official welcoming party waited at the end of a red carpet.

Huddart Parker Ltd now virtually controlled the excursion business on Port Phillip Bay, with a mixed fleet comprising propeller-powered and paddle-steamers. The company had bought a major interest in Bay Excursions Co. Ltd, so the operation of the *Ozone* was tied in with that of the *Hygeia*. As the first decade of the twentieth century drew to a close, the enormous sucess of the *Hygeia* and *Ozone*, and the booming excursion trade on Port Phillip Bay, encouraged Huddart Parker Ltd to place an order in 1909 for the construction of another vessel, similar to the *Hygeia*, only larger. Considering that by that time the day of the paddle-steamers was considered to be well and truly over, it was a brave move, but the people of Melbourne had shown they preferred to travel on paddleboats on the bay. The order went to another Glasgow firm, A. & J. Inglis, and the design was again based on the latest paddle excursion boats being built for the Clyde River trade.

The new vessel, the *Weeroona*, was completed in August 1910. At 1,412 gross tons, with a length of 310 feet (94.4 m) and a beam of 36 feet (11 m), she was one of the largest paddle excursion boats ever built, certainly bigger than any boat that operated on the River Clyde. The machinery comprised a three-cylinder compound steam-engine, with six coal-fired boilers. A new feature was the installation of a three-crank system, whereas *Hygeia* and *Ozone* had only two. The new system provided a more even distribution of power to the paddleshafts, overcoming a surging problem that afflicted the earlier vessels. On trials down the Skelmorlie measured mile, *Weeroona* recorded 18 knots.

For her delivery voyage, *Weeroona* had her main deck boarded up and strengthening added to the hull, as had *Hygeia*. The bunkers were only designed for short runs, so coal had to be carried on the main deck and in the saloons. The extra weight made her sit very low, the paddleboxes almost touching the water. Coal trimmers had the unenviable task of shovelling the coal into wheelbarrows and trundling them along the main deck to the scuttles leading to the stokehold below. Her main deck never really recovered from this treatment. In command was Captain Stewart Patrick, transferred from the *Hygeia*.

The route followed was similar to that taken by the *Hygeia*. Departing Glasgow on 18 September, *Weeroona* crossed the Bay of Biscay to Gibraltar, where more coal was taken on. Next stop was Malta, then Port Said for more coal. Here the crew had to be very watchful, as the natives wanted to carry away anything that was movable. The passage through the Suez Canal was made at night, followed by a hot run down the Red Sea to Aden, for more coal and water. Across the Indian Ocean went *Weeroona* to Colombo, where bumboatmen proved troublesome. Being low in the water, it was easy for them to get onto the deck to try to sell their curios.

Continuing her voyage, *Weeroona* passed Sumatra on her way to Sourabaya, where more coal and water were taken on. Next stop was Thursday Island, then down the east coast of Australia, with a brief call at Townsville before arriving in Sydney, berthing at Garden Island. The roughest weather of the entire trip was encountered on the final leg to Melbourne, but on Sunday, 27 November 1910, 10 weeks after leaving Scotland, *Weeroona* passed through Port Phillip Heads and made her way proudly up the bay for the first time. It was a major event in Melbourne, and thousands turned out to welcome the new steamer.

Being larger and higher powered than *Hygeia*, it was assumed that *Weeroona* would be a faster boat than her predecessor, but in the matter of speed, *Weeroona* was a disappointment. Prior to entering service, trials were run on Port Phillip Bay, but no official times were ever released. It was claimed by some experts that the problem lay in the paddleboxes, which they said were too close to the paddlewheels, resulting in a less than efficient action. In an attempt to improve her performance, an expensive alteration was made to the paddleboxes, but the improvement was negligible. However, speed was not essential, as the vessel ran to a timetable and a speed of 16 knots was sufficient to meet these requirements.

*Weeroona* made her first excursion on Port Phillip Bay on 19 December 1910, just in time for the peak holiday period, going to Sorrento and Queenscliff, which would be her regular route. With a capacity of 2,000 passengers, she was able to cater for the huge crowds that turned up each day to sample the luxury now being offered, but there were still some days when people were left on the wharf, due to the ship being full. With *Hygeia* and *Weeroona* in service, and their interest in *Ozone*, Huddart Parker completely dominated the Bay excursion trade as 1910 came to a close.

From a distance it was difficult to differentiate between *Weeroona* and *Hygeia*, but there were some notable differences. The promenade deck of *Weeroona* extended the full length of the hull, and only a section at the bow was not covered. In addition, *Weeroona* had a central upper promenade deck, about 100 feet (30 m) long, with open deck space. One feature had not changed from *Hygeia*, an open

*Weeroona* in service on Port Phillip Bay. (RWB)

bridge sited between the funnels, with only a canvas awning to provide some protection from the elements. Internally, the saloons and lounges were sumptuously furnished, and new features included a hairdressing salon and a bookshop.

There was a great deal of friendly rivalry between *Hygeia* and *Weeroona*, though they never indulged in races, *Hygeia* being clearly the faster ship. Both ships developed their own followings, but *Hygeia* seemed to be the more popular and is the best remembered of all the bay excursion boats. As to which was the more attractive, that is a matter of opinion. Both were beautiful creations, whose classic lines were emphasised by the colour scheme they so proudly wore. The crews took great pride in their ships, which were maintained in spotless manner and run with immaculate efficiency. During the summer season they ran almost together, on a daily basis, which gradually reduced as the season drew to a close, with a final fling at Easter.

Both *Hygeia* and *Weeroona* were fitted with six coal-fired boilers, three forward of the engine room, and three aft, of a special design, to keep the centre of gravity low. This was important for the stability of the vessels, as the huge number of passengers on board liked to move around during the voyages. As the summer season was drawing to a close, the run back to Port Melbourne from Queenscliff could be quite chilly. Passengers had a tendency to gather along the port side, to enjoy the warmth of the waning sun, but if too many congregated on the one side, the port paddlewheel would become submerged, and choke, while the starboard wheel would be almost out of the water. When this situation arose, the captain would order the crew to lower and secure the canvas screens along the port side, and the sudden cold would induce the passengers to find a more pleasant spot elsewhere on the ship.

December 1911 was a black period in the career of *Hygeia*, as she became involved in two unfortunate incidents within a week. On 18 December she was backing out from Railway Pier on a regular morning excursion to Queenscliff and Sorrento when a small sailing boat was noticed close-by. The paddles were stopped and the master of *Hygeia*, Captain Maitland, watched helplessly as the boat, driven along by a southwesterly wind, came into contact with the paddle-box. Its mast became trapped in the paddlebox, causing the boat to capsize, throwing the nine occupants into the water. *Hygeia* quickly lowered a boat, which rescued those in the water.

It was later discovered that the sailing boat was from the naval training ship *John Murray*, and the crew was composed of the second officer and eight young trainees. Surprisingly, once *Hygeia* had retrieved her boat, she set off for Queenscliff, taking the survivors with her. It was not until *Hygeia* reached Queenscliff that it was ascertained that one boy was missing. His body was recovered later. A subsequent inquiry blamed the sailing boat for the tragedy, but also censured Captain Maitland for his actions in leaving the scene without checking that anyone was missing.

Just four days later, on 22 December, Captain Maitland and the *Hygeia* were again in bother. This time the problem occurred at Sorrento, where *Hygeia* was berthed, as was the brand-new *Weeroona*. Both paddlers were scheduled to depart for Queenscliff, with *Weeroona* leaving first. When *Hygeia* made her departure, she reversed away from the pier as usual, then began turning. Just at that moment, when the vessel was most vulnerable, a sudden wind storm blew up. With no headway on, *Hygeia* was blown broadside and ran hard aground on a sandbank close to the Sorrento Pier. With much vibration and thrashing of water, the paddles were brought up to full revolutions astern, but *Hygeia* remained held firm.

In command of *Weeroona* was Captain Stewart Patrick, who had noticed that his previous command had not followed him across the Bay, so he collected his passengers at Queenscliff, then headed back to Sorrento. By the time she arrived, another small cargo and passenger boat, the *Charlotte Fenwick*, had a line to *Hygeia* and was trying to pull her free. When this failed, *Weeroona* also passed a line to the stranded ship, but the combined power of all three ships was not sufficient to free *Hygeia*.

Eventually *Weeroona* gave up the effort and pulled alongside *Hygeia* to take on her passengers and carry them to Melbourne. Huddart Parker dispatched their newest and most powerful tug, *Nyora*, to Sorrento, and on the high tide that night she managed to pull *Hygeia* free. The paddler had suffered no damage in the incident, was able to return to Melbourne under her own steam, and left on schedule at 10.30 a.m. for her next excursion.

For the young boys travelling aboard *Weeroona*, the engine-room was an endless source of delight. It was brightly lit, and there were spots from where they could watch the enormous crankshafts of the paddle mechanism rising, reaching and plunging. The greaser was considered the most daring of men, as he darted around the machinery squirting his enormous oil can at moving parts as they rushed at him, but never being caught by them.

The engineers of the boats had an unusual way of deciding the right moment to stop feeding the furnaces when they were homeward bound. Approaching Port Melbourne, a check would be kept on the positions of the tall brick chimney at the Newport Railway Workshops and a large elevated water tank in the same area. When the two structures came into line the firemen would be told to stop firing, as there was enough heat in the furnaces to get the vessel back to the wharf, with a final burst of 'Full Astern' as she came alongside.

On 1 January 1912 Huddart Parker was reorganised as a public company and in April a subsidiary company was formed, Bay Steamers Ltd, to which both *Hygeia* and *Weeroona* were transferred. This change did not affect their operation in any way. In November 1917 *Ozone* was also added to the fleet of Bay Steamers, so all three vessels were operating under the same banner.

The war years brought some reduction in patronage, but *Ozone*, *Hygeia* and *Weeroona* continued to plough their way down Port Phillip Bay during the summer months. With the return of peace, it was hoped that the excursion trade would once again enjoy some fruitful years, but the golden days were gone, and the motor car was becoming king. Instead of taking a relaxing trip to the Mornington Peninsula on a luxury boat, many opted for the journey over rough

*Ozone* aground and partly dismantled at Indented Head. (RWB)

roads by car. As the 1920s proceeded, so the patronage on the excursion boats declined. In 1921, when the Prince of Wales, who later became King Edward VIII, then the Duke of Windsor, arrived in Melbourne, he was transferred to the shore on the *Hygeia*, the second time she carried members of the royal family.

In March 1925 the *Ozone* was withdrawn from service and offered for sale. A local shipbreaker, Mr J. Hill, bought the vessel and removed all the deckhouses and machinery, then offered the hull for sale, complete with paddlewheels. It was purchased by Captain W.G. Forbes, who had retired to Indented Head, a short distance from St Leonards. Forbes beached the hull of the *Ozone* in shallow water off Indented Head, to form a breakwater. Over subsequent years the hull was gradually pounded to pieces by the seas, but for a long time the huge paddlewheels remained almost intact. Some remnants of the *Ozone* are still visible at low tide.

Following the withdrawal of *Ozone*, *Hygeia* and *Weeroona* continued to operate the summer excursions, but the effects of the Depression were being felt and patronage declined each year. At the end of the 1931 season *Hygeia* was also withdrawn from service, having completed more than 9,000 excursions down the bay over a period of 40 years. On 15 June 1931 the magnificent old vessel was sold to a local shipbreaker, Mr H.W. Morris.

Morris intended to remove all items of value and sell them, following which he proposed to tow the hulk to Brighton Beach, where it would be sunk as a breakwater, similar to the fate of *Ozone*. The Victorian minister of works refused permission for this and Morris was told the vessel would have to be towed outside Port Philip Heads and scuttled. Morris stripped *Hygeia* bare, and there were buyers for everything he offered for sale. Apart from the usual deck fittings, lanterns and lifebuoys, the cutlery and crockery were very popular. Even the tall mast and the funnels were sold,

*Hygeia* being towed by tug *Eagle* to the "ship's graveyard", August 1931. (RWB)

while the engine ended up in Bendigo and was used in a goldmine for many years. In just two months the beautiful *Hygeia* was reduced to a lifeless hull, ready for her final trip. On the afternoon of 25 August 1931 the tug *Eagle* took the old paddler in tow, bound for the 'Ships' Graveyard', an area just outside Port Phillip Heads. On board were two men, both former members of her crew, and a considerable amount of gelignite which would be used to sink her. As the tow proceeded down the bay into the night, a storm swept in from the south-west, and off St Leonards the towline broke.

*Hygeia* was swept broadside eastwards across the bay, nearly turning over several times as she bounced on the shallow bottom around Mud Island. For the two men on board it must have been a terrifying trip, in the dark on a floating bomb. *Hygeia* with her load of gelignite was buffetted by the seas and struck the bottom on numerous occasions as she was swept over sandbanks. On one occasion *Hygeia* ran aground, but after a while she worked herself loose, continuing her erratic westward course and driving hard aground on the eastern shore between Sorrento and Rosebud. The two men on board were able to get ashore, and the gelignite was safely removed, but the hulk of *Hygeia* was firmly held.

The grounding of the *Hygeia* had a devastating effect on Morris, who had not made any money out of the venture, and in addition had lodged a £1,000 bond with the government, to be returned when the hulk was sunk. Morris became ill with worry and died soon after, leaving the fate of *Hygeia* in the hands of the State government. The navy came up with a proposal to refloat the vessel and use it for target practice, while residents in Rosebud wanted the hulk to remain where it was and become a tourist attraction, possibly housing a museum or refreshment stalls. However the government rejected all these proposals.

For many months *Hygeia* remained stuck firm, but in early June 1932 she was finally pulled free by tugs. Once again the hulk was prepared for sinking, this time with dynamite charges being placed around the hull. On the morning of 10 June 1932 the hulk was towed through the Heads by the *Rip*, of the Department of Ports and Harbours, followed by a few launches carrying members of the press and some very sad shiplovers. On reaching the Ships' Graveyard area, the tow was slipped and the dynamite charges detonated. *Hygeia* began to settle slowly by the stern, then stopped as though unprepared to meet her fate. Suddenly the stern disappeared, and her bow rose high into the air, until it was pointing straight up into the grey sky.

The *Hygeia* was gone, with only the disturbed surface and a few bits of flotsam to indicate where she had been.

The Port Phillip Bay service was now reduced to a single excursion vessel, though she was the largest ever built for the trade. Throughout the 1930s *Weeroona* continued to operate regularly throughout the summer season, being laid up for the winter. During this period one of her masters was Captain Wake-Kilpatrick, whose knowledge of Port Phillip Bay was second to none. Being such a huge harbour, the bay was subject to many weather conditions, including heavy fogs that could descend quite suddenly. On these occasions, Captain Wake-Kilpatrick would maintain his vessel at full speed, chalking calculations, which only he could understand, on the bridge decking. He was a cheery soul, very popular with passengers and crew, and never had a mishap.

The outbreak of war in 1939 did not effect the operation of the *Weeroona* at first, and for the next three summer seasons it was business as usual. On Sunday, 2 March 1942, *Weeroona* operated her final excursion for the season, but little did those passengers who left the vessel in the evening realise that they had been on the last such trip the *Weeroona* would ever make. Just a few weeks later, *Weeroona* was sold to the United States Navy for use as an accommodation and convalescent ship. In typical American style, the interior of the vessel was transformed at great expense in Melbourne. The social hall was converted into a huge freezer, three boilers removed, numerous structural alterations made and the open decks were wired over. In August 1943 *Weeroona* proceeded under her own power from Melbourne to Sydney, where she commenced her duties as an accommodation ship, anchored out in the harbour.

*Weeroona* backing out from the pier at Port Melbourne. (RWB)

Changed appearance of *Weeroona* in Sydney Harbour during the war. (RWB)

In May 1944 *Weeroona* was towed to Brisbane, where she stayed a further six months. With the Americans closing in on Japan, *Weeroona* left Brisbane under tow, bound for Milne Bay in New Guinea, on 3 November 1944, arriving there six days later. On 26 November, again under tow, she left Milne Bay for Hollandia, where she arrived on 30 November, then went on to Manila, where she was moored alongside one of the piers. On 11 October 1945 *Weeroona* was on the move again, being towed to Manus Island, in the Admiralties, arriving there on 27 October. However, the need to use the ship had now passed, so *Weeroona* was towed all the way back to Sydney again, entering the harbour on 14 November 1945.

*Weeroona* was almost unrecognisable. Gone were the classic lines, open decks, even the forward funnel. The Americans had no further use for the vessel, so they gave her to the Australian government. They offered to return the boat to Huddart Parker, but this was declined. *Weeroona* was then offered for sale by the Australian government, but for six years she lay idle in Sydney Harbour, slowly deteriorating. In 1947 reports appeared in the press of a sale to Chinese interests, but this fell through. In 1951 shipbreakers began dismantling the *Weeroona* where she lay in Kerosene Bay, and soon there was nothing left of the former pride of the Port Phillip Bay excursion boats.

Today the only reminders of *Hygeia* and *Weeroona* are superb models of them, which are housed in the Melbourne Science Museum.

*Weeroona* being broken up in Sydney Harbour. (RWB)

# 11 Tugs

Paddle-steamers were used for towing from the beginning of the steam era. In Australia, the first example of a steamer being used for towing was when the *Sophia Jane* towed the sailing ship *Lady Harewood* out of Sydney Harbour on 12 June 1831. All of the early paddle-steamers on the coast were used for towing sailing ships at some time in their careers. Later, tugs were specially built, and they tended to be moved from port to port, much as tugs are moved around today, seeking the most profitable employment. The three ports most in need of steam tugs were Adelaide, Melbourne and Newcastle, which had difficult approaches to their harbours. In Melbourne it was often necessary for tugs to tow sailing ships right across Port Phillip Bay, through the Rip and well out into Bass Strait, before they could raise their sails. Sydney, Hobart and Brisbane were not so badly placed, and the implementation of regular tug services was not as immediate. It is possible here to only give a very brief account of the operation of paddle tugs in Australia.

One of the first paddle-steamers to be referred to as a tug was the *Corsair*. This vessel was built in Scotland in 1827 and arrived in Adelaide on 3 March 1841, from London. Attempts to find suitable employment for the *Corsair* varied from operating a service between Adelaide and Melbourne to being the first excursion steamer on Port Phillip Bay, but all failed. In 1844 she was advertised for sale in Sydney as being suitable for service as a tug, but she went to Hong Kong at the end of 1845.

In 1845 the small steamer *Courier* was imported from Britain for service in Port Adelaide as a tug, becoming the first steamship to be registered there. The first owner of *Courier* sold the vessel to the South Australian government in December 1846, but she was not a success, so in 1847 the engine was removed and the vessel converted into a lightship. She was later reduced to a hulk and spent many years in this capacity around Port Adelaide.

To replace the *Courier*, the South Australian government had a new vessel built in Britain, which was named *Adelaide*. She served in the port for 10 years before being sold, and later was converted into a sailing ship.

The first vessel constructed in Australia as a tug was the *Diamond*. Built on the banks of the Yarra River in 1847, she was 56 gross tons and had the steam-engine that was formerly in the *Governor Arthur*. This was common practice in those days, as engines were hard to come by in the colony. The *Governor Arthur* had been burnt out and sunk in the Yarra on 23 December 1841, and was raised in February

1844. The engines were removed, overhauled and then placed in the *Diamond*.

The *Diamond* operated as a tug and general workboat around Port Phillip Bay, and was quite well known in the area. On 11 July 1853, while unloading a consignment of gold in the Yarra River, a quantity worth £10,000 was dropped, but later salvaged from the river bottom. In the early 1860s the *Diamond* was transferred to Brisbane, where she is generally considered to have been the first tug stationed there. In 1869 her engines were removed and *Diamond* finished her career as a trading schooner, being wrecked about 10 years later.

Another early paddle tug in Melbourne was the *Lioness*, imported from Britain and originally intended for service on the Murray River. Instead, *Lioness* spent 12 years on Port Phillip Bay from the time of her arrival in 1854, then was sold to New Zealand interests. A further imported tug on Port Phillip Bay at this time was the *Washington*, built in 1844, which arrived 10 years later. In April 1854 the *Washington* was serving as a tug at Geelong, but by 1861 she had been moved to Sydney, where she also operated excursions for up to 350 passengers. In 1862 the *Washington* was sent to Shanghai to be sold, and spent some years operating on the Yangtse River. The *Cobre*, built in Wales in 1849, was imported in 1853 for towing duties on Port Phillip Bay, but the following year transferred to Launceston, and later Hobart. In 1869 the *Cobre* came to Sydney, then in 1874 moved on to Newcastle, where she finished her career about 1917.

One of the best remembered tugs of this period in Tasmanian waters was the *Tamar*, which was imported in 1854 by the Launceston Marine Board for duties on the Tamar River as a tug. In 1890 she was purchased by the Mersey Marine Board and served at Devonport for three years, being discarded in 1893.

The influx of tugs to Port Phillip Bay continued, with the *Challenge* being imported in 1856, followed by the *Resolute* in 1858, both owned by James Deane, who later became a founder of the Melbourne Steam Ship Co. Another early tug owner in Melbourne was George Ward Cole, who owned the *Diamond*, along with *Vesta, Maitland, Prince Albert, Kangaroo, Lioness, Ada* and *Geelong*.

The first steamship to be registered at Newcastle was the *Doorebang*, a wooden-hulled tug built on the Hunter River at Morpeth in 1861 for J. & A. Brown, well-known colliery owners. The exporting of coal around the world in sailing ships made Newcastle the busiest port in the country, and tug services were of major importance to the port. The *Doorebang* was wrecked on Nobbys while trying to enter Newcastle in fog on 31 July 1873.

In 1862 an imported tug, the *Bungaree*, arrived in Newcastle. Built in Glasgow for the Australasian Steam Navigation Co., *Bungaree* was sunk in a collision in Newcastle Harbour on 2 October 1865 but was salvaged and returned to service. On 21 July 1866 she grounded on rocks near Nobbys, and sank, only to be raised again and repaired. Over the years the *Bungaree* passed through numerous owners in Newcastle, including J. & A. Brown, and she remained in active service until the 1920s, then was broken up.

One of the more interesting tugs of this era was the *Goolwa*, which was completed in Newcastle in England in January 1864. She started her career as a tug in Port Adelaide, then moved to Sydney in 1870, when sold to Captain Thomas Heselton, who operated the Manly ferry service at that time. The *Goolwa* was used as a tug in Sydney Harbour, but also operated as a ferry when required. In January 1874 *Goolwa* was transferred to Newcastle, and in 1876 was sold to the Newcastle Co-operative Steam Tug Co., which had been established in 1867. Other tugs owned by this organisation at various times included *Southland*, *Prince Alfred*, *Leo* and *Bungaree*. The *Goolwa* served in Newcastle until 1905, then was sold for scrapping. However, she remained laid up until 1919, then sank at her moorings. Salvaged, the vessel was run ashore on the river bank near Hexham, where her remains can still be seen.

A paddle tug worth mentioning is the *Francis Hixson*, built in Britain in 1876 for service on Sydney Harbour. Operated by J. & T. Fenwick, the *Francis Hixson* was named after a former Sydney harbour master and New South Wales lighthouse inspector. In common with other large tugs, the 156-gross-ton iron-hulled vessel was available for salvage work, which could be quite remunerative. When the steamer *Platypus* went aground in January 1883 near Ballina, at the entrance to the Richmond River in northern New South Wales, the *Francis Hixson* was dispatched to free her. Unfortunately, the tug grounded on rocks, was holed in the bow and quickly filled with water. Both the *Francis Hixson* and the *Platypus* were wrecked. In 1884 Fenwicks had a new tug built on the Richmond River, the *Protector*, into which the salvaged engines of the *Francis Hixson* were placed. The *Protector* also became a victim of the notorious Richmond River bar, being wrecked there on 1 July 1901.

The Richmond River bar also claimed another well-known paddle tug, the *Rescue*. This iron-hulled vessel, built in England in 1873, was first owned in Melbourne by James Paterson, a shipowner involved in the coal trade from Newcastle. In 1901 Paterson sold the *Rescue* to the Fenwick family and they placed the vessel in service along the river ports of northern New South Wales. The *Rescue* was wrecked on the bar at the entrance to the Richmond River on 9 April 1908.

One of the most famous of all the Australian paddle tugs arrived in Port Adelaide in 1877. The *Yatala* was quite large for the type, 287 gross tons, and 145 feet (44 m) long, being

The iron-hulled *Gannet* was typical of paddle tugs that worked in Australian ports. Built in 1884 in England, *Gannet* was first owned by the Melbourne Harbour Trust Commissioners, then moved to Fremantle in 1897. In 1914, *Gannet* went to Sydney when purchased by Fenwick & Co., being reduced to a hulk in the mid-20's, and broken up in 1941. (GA)

*Commodore*, the most famous Australian paddle tug, berthed in Newcastle. (GA)

fitted with two funnels, as well as two cargo holds. She was built to the order of the Adelaide Steam Tug Co. Ltd, by Blackwood & Gordon at Port Glasgow. For her delivery voyage, the *Yatala* was rigged as a brigantine, but also used her engines whenever possible. Crossing the Indian Ocean she ran out of coal and had to proceed under sail alone to Albany, but no coal was available there. Instead, 80 tons of wood were taken aboard and the vessel headed off for Adelaide. Slowed by strong headwinds, the wood was soon all consumed and the crew had to remove and burn the woodwork of the ship itself in order to reach Adelaide. *Yatala* was employed as a towing boat around South Australian waters for over 30 years, but in 1911 she was sold and converted into a sailing ship. Renamed *Thuraka* in 1920, the vessel was wrecked off the Tasmanian coast on 8 June 1929.

The 1870s were the heyday of paddle tugs in Australia,

as subsequently propeller-driven vessels were favoured. One of the finest, and most famous, paddle tugs to operate on Sydney Harbour came out in 1878, the *Commodore*. Built at South Shields, the *Commodore* was 187 gross tons and had twin funnels abreast. She was the first new vessel to be built for the Port Jackson Steam Boat Co., who became the Port Jackson Steam Ship Co. in 1881. *Commodore* served on Sydney Harbour as a tug during the week, but at weekends would be called into service as a ferry between Sydney and Manly. In September 1898 the *Commodore* was sold to J. & A. Brown, of Newcastle, and spent the next 20 years on towing duties in Newcastle Harbour. The last active paddle tug operating in Australian waters, *Commodore* was finally withdrawn from service in the late 1920s. Her hull was stripped of all useful components, then on 8 September 1931 the hulk was scuttled off Newcastle, a fitting end to a fine career.

# Part Two: The Murray River System

# 12 The Exploration of the Murray

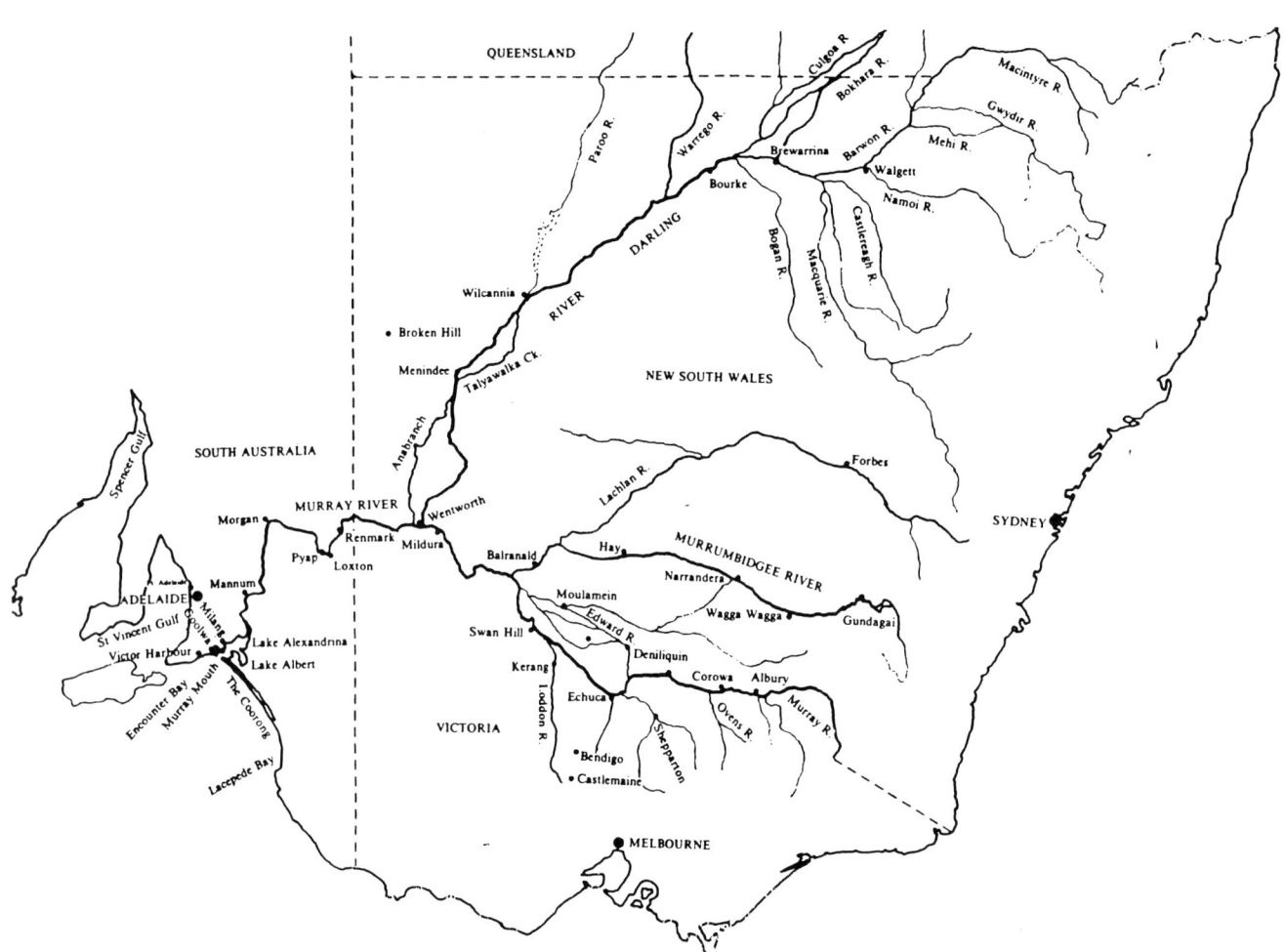

Map of Murray River System

The river we know today as the Murray was originally named the Hume, but before white man first laid eyes upon it various Aboriginal tribes gave the river a variety of names, including Goodwarra, Tongwillum, Ingalta, Parriang-ka-perre, Yoorlooarra and Moorundie.

It was in October 1824 that two men, William Hovell, a retired British sea captain, and Hamilton Hume,

Australian-born son of a convict, led a party out of Sydney to pioneer an overland route south. On 17 October they left Lake George, the last settled area, and headed into the unknown. They became the first white men to see the Australian Alps, then, on 16 November 1824, beheld a fast-flowing river 'no less than 80 yards in width and apparently of considerable depth'. Hume realised that the source of the

The former paddler *Decoy* is now a houseboat near Mannum. (LR)

*Lady of Barmah* was built along traditional lines.

*Impulse* is the largest houseboat on the Murray River.

The replica *William the Fourth* is based in Newcastle.

*Sydney Showboat* operates excursions on Sydney Harbour.

*Kookaburra Queen 2*, largest of the modern excursion boats.

*Enterprise*, restored at Echuca, is now on Lake Burley Griffin in Canberra.

*Cumberoona* operates excursions along the Murray from Albury.

river was in the mountains to the east, and that it flowed in a westerly direction. He named it the Hume River, in honour of his father, and marked a tree with the words 'Hume River' while Hovell marked another tree 'Hovell Novr 17/24'. Today the Hovell tree can still be seen, in Noreuil Park at Albury. Hume and Hovell explored the river in both directions for a suitable place to cross, eventually choosing a site close to where the Hume Weir stands today. The pair continued south, but a mistake in their navigation resulted in them reaching the western shore of Port Phillip Bay, instead of Western Port. They returned to Sydney in February 1825, reporting the discovery of fine pasture lands to the south, but the hoped-for rush of new settlers did not eventuate.

Meanwhile, others had been exploring the lands to the west of Sydney and in 1828 Charles Sturt, an Army captain who had arrived in the colony from Britain in 1826, followed the Macquarie River and discovered another into which it flowed. He named this river Darling, after the then governor of New South Wales. This discovery, along with other rivers in previous years, such as the Lachlan and Murrumbidgee, created a great mystery, as all flowed in a general west direction, and not south towards the sea. This led to the supposition that a huge inland sea existed in the heart of Australia. On 3 November 1829 Sturt led a party out of Sydney on a journey to find this sea. They headed south towards the station owned by Hamilton Hume, who declined an offer to join the expedition, then proceeded along the route pioneered by Hume and Hovell as far as the Murrumbidgee. Included in their supplies was a whaleboat broken down into sections, which was fitted together on the banks of the Murrumbidgee. A small skiff was then constructed from bush timber, to carry the supplies for the party. On 7 January 1830 Sturt and seven other men left the rest of the party and were pushed by the strong current down the Murrumbidgee. Several days later they passed the point where the Lachlan River joined the Murrumbidgee, but a short distance further on, the party ran into rocks across the river. Unable to stop their passage, the whaleboat was guided through safely, but the skiff overturned and sank, taking all their food. For two days Sturt and his men dived to the wreck to recover what they could, then continued on their way westward. The current was so strong they seldom had to use the oars, and each night they set up camp on the river bank.

On the afternoon of 14 January 1830 the boat was suddenly swept into a much larger river. Still the party continued their westward voyage, not sure where they were, and at times seeing Aboriginal groups. Sturt managed to befriend some of these tribesmen, who visited their camp on 17 January. Three days later the party came across a group of about 100 Aborigines, who made to attack the explorers, but suddenly three other Aborigines appeared and stopped the hostile actions. On pulling into the bank, Sturt discovered that the leader of the group he had befriended was the one who had interceded on his behalf and saved the party.

On 23 January Sturt reached the point where another river joined from the north and a short exploration of this led him to decide it was the bottom of the Darling, the upper reaches of which he had previously discovered. Sturt decided that it was time for him to give a name to the river on which his party had been travelling for over a week, so he called it the Murray, to honour Sir George Murray, the colonial secretary in the British government. Still the river drove them to the west, but then it took a dramatic turn to the south. The flat banks were replaced by towering cliffs for some distance, then the flatness returned. Suddenly the whaleboat drifted into a huge salt lake and from a nearby hilltop Sturt saw the sea in the distance. Following shallow channels, the party managed to reach the mouth of the mighty river, an opening so insignificant that it had not been sighted by explorers who had charted the coatline in previous years.

So the great mystery was solved. There was no inland sea, and all the rivers discovered up to that time eventually flowed into the Murray. Sturt and his party attempted to sail their boat through the narrow mouth of the river, but were thwarted by huge seas running over a sandbar. Eventually they had to admit defeat and face the prospect of rowing against the current back the entire distance they had come. It was a long, hard journey for the men, but when they finally reached the point on the Murrumbidgee from which they had started, they found the rest of their party had returned to Sydney. For a further 17 days the half-starved men rowed against the current, then Sturt sent the two fittest men overland for help. Just in time, a rescue party arrived, and the remaining five were brought back to Sydney. Sturt was totally exhausted and partially blind, but he had travelled over 3,000 kilometres and proved that no inland sea existed. There are several monuments to his momentous voyage to be found along the Murray, including a cairn in Mildura, and another at Mannum, topped by a model of the whaleboat that carried the party so far.

Between 1831 and 1836 Major Thomas Mitchell, surveyor-general of New South Wales, led several expeditions into the Murray basin area, discovering further rivers and also naming Swan Hill. He followed the Murray for much of its length and was the first to establish that the Hume and Murray rivers were the same waterway. This led to a series of disputes between Hume and Sturt, and the question of the correct name for the river remained unresolved. However, as settlements sprang up along the length of the river, it was usually referred to as the Murray and that name has continued in popular use. The upper reaches are still sometimes called the Hume or the 'Little River'.

# 13 Randell and Cadell

The Murray River is considered the home of the Australian paddlewheeler, but just who was the pioneer of Murray steam navigation? On the surface, this should be an easy question to answer, but it has been a source of contention for years. On a cairn erected in the Recreation Reserve at Mannum is a plaque, dedicated to 'William Richard Randell, the first steam navigator on the River Murray', while in the tiny township of Cadell, near Morgan, stands another cairn with a plaque that reads: 'A tribute to Captain Francis Cadell, after whom this town is named. He was the outstanding pioneer of Murray steam navigation'.

There is no doubt that both these men played a major role in the development of steam navigation on the Murray, but Randell was the first man to operate a paddleboat on the river. Born in Britain in 1824, he migrated to South Australia with his family in 1837, and several years later his father established a flour mill in the town of Gumeracha, in the hills between Adelaide and the Murray. The family also bought a property on the river, just north of Mannum, which was called Noa-No, and here William Randell lived, managing the family grazing interests. For reasons unknown, Randell decided to become the first man to put a steamboat on the river. This was a surprising decision, as he had no marine background, but with the help of his brothers Thomas and Elliott, William Randell designed and then built a 52-foot (16-m) paddleboat on the banks of the Murray, at Noa-No. He named it *Mary Ann*, after his mother, and it was launched on 19 February 1853. No-one had any experience of building a boiler for the steam engine, which was built in Adelaide, so it was built with flat sides.

Memorial cairn to *Mary Ann* at Mannum.

This boiler can still be seen in the Recreation Reserve at Mannum, and is a lasting memento of this famous vessel. The first time it was fired up the engineer was so unsure of the structure he hid in nearby trees, waiting for it to blow up. That fact that it did not was due more to luck than to good design, but it became evident that special precautions were necessary, as the sides had expanded to such an extent the boiler was the shape of a Rugby football. Special strengthening struts were added along each side, and just to make sure, chains were wrapped around the entire structure.

In March 1853 Randell loaded a cargo consisting of 20 tons of flour and groceries, to be taken upstream, but first he had to clear South Australian customs. This was refused in Mannum, so Randell took *Mary Ann* down the river to Goolwa to complete the necessary formalities. While returning across Lake Alexandrina, a storm blew up and *Mary Ann* was almost wrecked, but she made it back into the river. On 25 March 1853, with William Randell in charge, *Mary Ann* steamed out of Mannum, bound for Swan Hill. This was the first ever voyage along the river by a steamer for commercial purposes, but it was not a success. The river level was very low and Randell only got as far as Penn's Reach, near Lake Bonney, before being forced to turn back.

Boiler of *Mary Ann* at Mannum.

Memorial cairn to Francis Cadell and *Lady Augusta* at Cadell, near Morgan.

Unbeknown to Randell, another man, Captain Francis Cadell, had decided to commence a steamer service on the Murray. Born in Scotland in 1822, the son of a shipbuilder, Cadell came to Australia in 1849 and joined the coastal trade in command of his own ship. He heard about an offer being made by the South Australian government of £4,000 to be paid to the 'first two iron steamers of not less than 40 horsepower, and not exceeding two feet draft of water when loaded', to navigate the Murray from Goolwa at least as far as the junction with the Darling, a distance of 551 miles (887 km). Cadell designed a paddle vessel 105 feet (32 m) long, which was built in Sydney by T. Chowne & Co., at Pyrmont, and launched on 23 March 1853. She was named *Lady Augusta*, after the wife of the governor of South Australia, Henry Fox Young. The vessel was rigged as a ketch for its delivery voyage, leaving Sydney on 1 June for Melbourne, from where she departed on 27 July, arriving in Port Elliot on August 6.

On 16 August *Lady Augusta* safely negotiated the dangerous bar across the mouth of the Murray and berthed in Goolwa. Here the finishing touches were made to the ship and Cadell took delivery of the barge *Eureka*, which had been built in Goolwa for him. *Lady Augusta* was a far more impressive looking vessel than *Mary Ann*, having two decks and two funnels, and also provided accommodation for 16 first-class and 8 second-class passengers. The crew was extremely cosmopolitan, and included three Aborigines, two Indians, two South Sea islanders and a Chinaman. On 25 August 1853 *Lady Augusta* left Goolwa, towing the *Eureka* barge loaded with cargo, and having on board a group of notables, including Governor Young and his wife.

Meanwhile, Randell had left Mannum again on 15 August in a second attempt to reach Swan Hill. He was totally unaware of the existence of the *Lady Augusta*, and was not interested in the prize being offered by the South Australian government, as his vessel had a wooden hull and was too small to qualify. On 14 September the men on *Mary Ann* heard a strange commotion coming from astern of them and were shocked to see *Lady Augusta* charging up the river towards them. This started a race between the two boats, with the lead changing several times over the next two days. *Lady Augusta* arrived in Swan Hill three hours ahead of *Mary Ann* on 17 September. Two days later, Randell left to go further upsteam, and on September 24 reached Maidens Punt, which today is known as Moama, opposite Echuca. Cadell gathered a cargo of wool and returned to Goolwa, where he claimed his prize from the government. Randell, on the other hand, made no such claim, but the pair had proved that the Murray River was navigable to steamers.

# 14 Opening Up the Rivers

Over the next nine years, Cadell and Randell were instrumental in extending the limits of navigation on the Murray, and also several of its tributary rivers. However, most of the voyages by these men were undertaken in a spirit of intense rivalry. Cadell in particular saw the commercial possibilities that trade on the river presented, and in December 1853 was granted a charter by the South Australian government to raise capital with a view to forming The River Murray Navigation Co., though sufficient capital was not raised until 1856. In the meantime, though, Cadell introduced several new paddle-steamers on the river under his ownership. He also had numerous alterations made to *Lady Augusta* to make it more suitable for the river trade.

In August 1854 Cadell purchased the iron-hulled paddle-steamer *Melbourne*, built in Glasgow in 1852, which had arrived in Melbourne under sail in March 1853. *Melbourne*

was used briefly in the trade to Geelong, but when purchased by Cadell it was loaded with cargo and brought around the coast to the Murray Mouth, which she passed through on 19 August. The *Melbourne* proceeded up the Murray to the Beechworth and Ovens goldfields, where the cargo was sold. *Melbourne* then returned to the Murray Mouth, passing out on 28 August bound for Adelaide. *Melbourne* did not make any further trips up the river, but ran between Adelaide and Goolwa until being wrecked while entering the Murray Mouth on 16 November 1859.

Cadell took the *Lady Augusta* up the Murray again in August 1854, reaching Gooramadda, above Echuca. He felt he was the only person who should be allowed to operate steamers on the river, and wrote to William Randell, offering to transport his flour. Cadell also added that if Randell should 'impute this letter to any fear of rivalry on my part, you will do wrong as I am fully prepared (if

*Albury* was the first steamer to reach Albury, in 1855. (FT)

requisite) to carry on a vigorous opposition, and from the reiterated assurance I have from every settler on the river whose support is worth having, I may add a successful opposition'. Cadell had ordered two iron-hulled steamers to be built in Glasgow by Napier & Co., and shipped in sections to Port Elliot. They duly arrived on the brig *Lady Emma* in January 1855 and were transferred to the shore, using the boilers as floats. When assembled, these 139-gross-ton vessels were named *Albury* and *Gundagai*. Reporting on the trial trip of the *Gundagai* on 1 September, the *Observer* newspaper stated that a 'speed of 10½ knots was estimated. The engine is on the oscillating principal, and fitted with locomotive starting gear, and can develop up to 38 revolutions per minute. The draught is 18 inches, and there are sleeping berths for 22 people.' Both these vessels were intended to operate on the Murray as far as Albury. The *Albury* was the first of the pair to enter service, departing Goolwa on 26 August 1855 towing the barge *Wakool* and proceeding up the river to Albury, where she arrived at 4 p.m. on 2 October.

Although the overall journey took 37 days, the vessel was steaming for only 270 hours, being tied up at night, and stopping at other settlements along the way. The arrival of the *Albury* in her namesake town was a major event. News of her coming had preceeded the vessel and people had waited at bends in the river and other vantage points to catch a glimpse of the steamer. As there were no wharf facilities at Albury at that time, a wharf not being built until 1871, the cargo had to be swung onto the river bank. To show their appreciation, the people of Albury presented Captain Johnston with a purse of £100 and an inscribed cup. Four days after her arrival, the *Albury* took 300 people on an excursion further up the river, during which a German band played on board. The vessel reached a point near where the Hume Dam is located today. With regard to the return journey, the instructions Johnston received from Cadell were quite specific:

> At the different stations which you pass you will sweep off all the wool you can get hold of. Should there not be sufficient wool to load your vessel regulate your departure so as to ensure a full barge of say 300 to 350 bales for the steamer; at any rate do all you can to clean the wool off so as to leave Randell nothing.

The *Gundagai* left Goolwa on 7 September 1855 on her first voyage up the river to Albury, with a party of passengers, including Sir Thomas Elder. He wrote of the vessel:

> The saloon is raised above the deck with windows on both sides, a large airey space, used as a dining room and a sitting room during the day, and as a sleeping apartment for gentlemen at night, curtains extending from the roof ensuring the requisite privacy. Several state cabins at the stern are reserved for the ladies and children. One of the first things passengers do on coming aboard is to select the place they propose to sit at table, which is kept during the voyage. Considering the small sum charged for passage money from Goolwa to Albury, a distance of 2,000 miles, namely £15, including provisions, we had good reason to be satisfied with our fare and steward's attendance.

Both the *Albury* and the *Gundagai* continued to operate regularly along the river, and in October 1856 the *Gundagai* arrived at Albury from Goolwa in just 22 days.

William Randell had also improved his boat, the *Mary Ann*, which was lengthened and had a new boiler installed. On 21 August 1854 he set off from Mannum again to head up the Murray to Albury, though he did not get that far. Randell decided that the *Mary Ann* was not suitable for the river trades and designed a new craft. The hull of the *Mary Ann* was retained and a new hull of similar dimensions built. The two hulls were then joined together with decking, on which was built a deckhouse, with a promenade on top. The boiler was left in the former *Mary Ann* hull, while a new engine was placed in the other hull, to balance the vessel. A paddlewheel was inserted between the hulls, and Randell named the vessel *Gemini*. She left on her first trip up the river from Mannum in August 1855. The *Gemini* proved to be difficult to handle and was involved in numerous incidents. On 8 January 1856 she was snagged and sunk, not being raised until 7 March.

Having opened up the Murray River to navigation, both Randell and Cadell turned their attention to the main tributary rivers. In August 1858 Randell took the *Gemini* up the Murrumbidgee River as far as Illillwa, just beyond Hay. In the same month, Cadell in the *Albury* went up the Murrumbidgee as far as Gundagai, arriving there on 16 August, 1,300 kilometres by river from the junction with the Murray. Both men then turned their attention to the Darling River, which was more difficult to navigate, being narrow and prone to very low water levels. In January 1859 Cadell took the *Albury* as far as Mount Murchison, but on 2 February 1859 Randell in the *Gemini* left Wentworth, reached Bourke, and then went further up the river to Brewarrina, arriving on 23 February. The last of the great pioneering voyages was made by Randell, who departed Goolwa in the *Gemini* on 1 November 1861. Taking advantage of flood conditions, he journeyed past Brewarrina to Walgett, 1,760 kilometres from Wentworth and the Murray Junction. It is said that, on his return voyage, he carried as a passenger the notorious bushranger Frank Gardiner, who was disguised as a clergyman.

Randell and Cadell had kindled in others an interest in the possibilities of the river trade. John Acraman and James Cooke, of Adelaide, imported two iron-hulled paddle-steamers in sections from England. They were built by John Laird of Birkenhead, who specialized in building shallow-draft steamers that could be shipped overseas in pieces and assembled by unskilled labour. When the two vessels arrived in Adelaide, Acraman and Cooke decided to assemble only one at first, and if it was unsuccessful, the other could be resold more easily in pieces. This vessel, named *Leichardt*, was 156 gross tons, could carry 200 tons of cargo and had space for 50 passengers. Entering service in May 1855, *Leichardt* initially ran from Adelaide to St Vincents Gulf, but in June 1856 she made her first trip up the Murray River.

In Port Adelaide, the *Leichardt* took on board 319 Chinese, recently disembarked from the sailing ship *Jamestown*. They were carried to Port Elliot, then put ashore to walk the 11 kilometres to Goolwa, while *Leichardt* steamed through the Murray Mouth. At Goolwa the Chinese reboarded and were carried up the river to Echuca, from where they dispersed to the goldfields. With *Leichardt* proving a success, the second steamer was assembled and named *Sturt* when launched on 29 September 1856. On 14 November *Sturt* left Port Adelaide for Goolwa, but grounded while entering the Murray Mouth, though refloated safely. *Leichardt* worked on the Murray until 1859, then was sold overseas. *Sturt* operated between Port Adelaide and Goolwa until 1863, then was sold to New Zealand.

Another newcomer was the paddle-steamer *Moolgewanke*, which had also been imported in sections in 1856 by Adelaide businessmen R. Napier and W. Webb, and began working on the Murray River in May 1856. *Moolgewanke* became the first steamer to journey up the Edwards River, reaching Deniliquin on 13 July 1860. However, trade on the smaller rivers would be minor, as they tended to be very narrow and twisty.

The first paddleboats built to trade along the Murray River and its tributaries were not greatly successful, as they were not designed specifically for the rivers on which they operated. Most were altered several times during their careers, but all had been side-wheelers. It was only a matter of time before a stern-wheel vessel was built for the Murray River, as these types of boats were particularly successful on the major American rivers. Between 1861 and 1863, three stern-wheelers were built, with mixed results. Of the two men behind the construction of these vessels, one was a former American citizen, Peleg Whitford Jackson, who had arrived in Australia in 1853 and taken out British citizenship in 1859. His partner, Captain Alexander Sinclair Murray, was a Scot. It appears neither man had any previous association with American steamboats.

Jackson and Murray placed an order with Mr H.C. Fletcher of Port Adelaide, to construct a vessel out of timber specially imported from Oregon, with the machinery being built in Sydney. The hull was launched on 22 June 1861 and taken to Goolwa to have the superstructure added. Named *Settler*, she had a length of 143.5 feet (43.8 m), or 167 feet (50.8 m) including the stern-wheel, the longest vessel to be built for service on the Murray River until the advent of modern cruise boats in the 1970s. Newspapers compared her superstructure to a two-storey house, containing cabins lined with cedar. Two 100-horsepower steam engines were fitted, and four rudders, located forward of the stern-wheel. *Settler* departed Milang on 18 October 1861 on her first river trip, managing to reach Echuca, leaving there on 31 October for the return trip. The vessel soon proved to be too long to be able to easily navigate the

*Lady Daly* at the Echuca wharf circa 1864. (FT)

river, especially the section above Mildura. In August 1862 *Settler* struck a snag and sank below Paringa, and after being raised she left the Murray River for good. Fitted out in Adelaide for a voyage to New Zealand, she eventually ended up in Brisbane, where she worked for a number of years.

On 25 June 1862 the second stern-wheeler built for Jackson and Murray was launched at Fletcher's slip and named *Lady Daly*. This vessel was shorter and proved to be much more adept at handling the river, remaining in service until the 1890s. The last built of this trio, *Lady Darling*, was also the smallest. Launched on 2 September 1864 she entered service in January 1865 but had a short career, being destroyed by fire on 23 August 1867. The operation of these three vessels proved that side-wheels were the best form of propulsion for the Murray River, though a few more stern-wheelers were built over the years.

As the river trade developed, so the number of companies formed to operate boats increased. Some came about through local dissatisfaction with the service being offered by existing organisations, such as the Albury Steam Navigation Co., which commenced operations in 1866, the Wagga Wagga Steam Navigation Co., formed in 1869, and the Hay Steam Navigation Co., of 1874. In later years commercial firms developed quite large fleets of steamers and barges to operate along the river, the best known of these being Arnold's Line of River Steamers Ltd, the Gem Navigation Co. Ltd, A.H. Landseer Ltd, the McCulloch Carrying Co. Ltd, and Permewan, Wright & Co. Ltd. In 1919, as the river trade declined, several of these companies merged their fleets to form Murray Shipping Ltd, which survived until 1952.

# 15 Cargo Boats and Towboats

The majority of paddle-steamers built to operate on the Murray River system were either cargo boats or towboats. Cargo boats were capable of carrying quite large loads, while towboats were designed to pull one or two barges, in which all types of merchandise and produce could be loaded.

Cargo boats were built to a simple design, being fitted with a hold forward, sometimes another aft, and could also carry a considerable amount of deck cargo. The steam machinery would be set on the deck amidships, and above would be a superstructure, sometimes containing a few passenger cabins. The galley was set aft of the engine and, if there were passengers, a dining saloon would take up the space otherwise occupied by the second hold. They were owned by the major river shipping companies, such as the Gem Navigation Co., whose fleet included the cargo boats *Corowa, Tarella, Wm Davies, Murrumbidgee, Lancashire Lass, Decoy* and *Princess Royal*. Permewan Wright & Co., which were based at Echuca, owned two of the largest cargo boats, the *Pevensey* and the *Ulonga*, each of which could carry 800 bales of wool. Sometimes a cargo boat would also tow a barge, to more than double its cargo capacity, especially when transporting wool.

Towboats tended to be smaller than cargo boats and were more simply laid out, with a steam-engine amidships surrounded by a small superstructure containing quarters for the crew and little else. They were the real workhorses

*Ulonga* and barge, both loaded with wool, at Echuca wharf. (FT)

of the river, sometimes towing an empty barge to one location, then going off to collect a full barge and deliver it to a main town before returning to tow the first barge, now full, to its destination. Towboats often worked with the same one or two barges, though in larger companies they would be allocated any barge that was available.

*Lady Augusta*, one of the first two vessels to steam along the Murray, towed a barge, the *Eureka*, built at Goolwa, as it was realised from the start that this was a good way to transport bulk goods. The Murray barges were all built along the banks of the river, and many had red-gum hulls, while some were composite, with iron frames covered by red gum, and a few had steel hulls. They were all built to the same general design; a big empty hull with several large holds separated by bulkheads. The actual shape of the barges did vary, depending on the rivers they were to run on and the purpose for which they were built. The original timber barges were quite narrow, with curved sides and rounded bottoms. This could, and sometimes did, cause a badly loaded barge to capsize when taking a bend in the river. As the design developed over the years, the later steel barges were built with square sides and bottom. Along each side was a narrow deck, with a hatch coming around each hold to prevent water coming in.

On the outward journey from a port like Echuca, Morgan, Mildura or Wentworth, the barge would be loaded with a wide variety of merchandise, some to be sold to stations along the way, while others would be orders from shops or businesses in the various town springing up along the rivers. The most frequent return cargo carried in barges was bales of wool, up to 2,000 or more, stacked in the hull, and several tiers high above the deck. Smaller barges, like the *Hartley* and *Uranus*, could carry about 950 bales, but the largest barge built for the Murray, the 151-foot (46-m) *Crowie* built in 1911, could carry 2,600 bales. To prevent overloading, the deck cargo could not be higher than the equivalent of two-thirds of the width of the barge, the maximum being six tiers. There were also different types of wool, and it was essential that oily wool be stowed under other types.

Loading the barge with wool was an art, and much depended on the actual barge itself. Some of the wooden barges were 'hog-backed', or curved up in the middle, while 'sway-backed' barges curved down. To load a 'hog-backed' barge, it was essential to start in the middle and build the tiers out to the ends, while a sway-backed barge was loaded from the ends to the middle. If a barge was loaded straight through from end to end, this would sometimes cause the seams between the planks to open up and the barge would leak like a sieve. The more modern steel-hulled barges presented no such problems.

Once the holds were full, the deck cargo would then be loaded in a pyramid shape. As each tier was added, the next one would be stepped in by one foot all round, with a single row of bales, known as a 'rider', on top. If all the bales beneath had been stowed properly and the barge was riding on an even keel, then the rider would be secured so that it ran along the centreline of the barge. If a list to one side was evident, the rider row could be offset, to bring the barge back to an even keel. Each tier would be securely tied by running a 'ring rope' around it. The maximum possible pressure was put on the ring rope so that it bit tightly into the bales, this being done by a block and tackle, known as a 'handy Billy'. Once the barge was loaded to capacity, the cargo was secured with up and down lashings, pulled taut by the handy Billy. To keep rain out, a tarpaulin could be placed over the entire cargo, tied together over the rider bales, which acted as a ridge to allow water to run overboard.

When barges first carried wool on the river the upper ties would be lashed firmly to the deck, but if the barge took on a list at any time it was liable to capsize. In 1870 the barge *Hume* did just that when rounding a bend, and only the quick action of the skipper of the towboat *Kennedy* saved the situation. He jumped aboard the barge and cut the deck lashings, allowing 150 bales to fall into the river, following which the barge came back on an even keel. Subsequently, the upper tiers of wool just rested on the tiers in the hull, and if the barge developed a list the rider tier would slide overboard and prevent a capsize.

Of course, all the loading work had to be done manually by the crew of the barge and the towboat, and often in less than satisfactory conditions. Most stations did not have a wharf, so the towboat would pull up at the river bank and the barge would be tied up to suitable trees. The wool would be transported from the station sheds to the river bank by horse and cart, then each bale was carried on board and placed in position. When the river was low, the banks might be quite high and a shute would be constructed, down which the bales would be rolled to the side of the barge, and then carried across a wooden plank for loading. The main discharge ports, Echuca and Morgan, had steam-powered cranes which would unload the wool in much quicker time.

Steering a barge was also a tricky business. Once the last tier of wool was secured on the barge, a board would be run across it near the stern and the wheel set up. Sometimes the barge would pick up wool at several locations along the river, so as each successive tier was added, the wheel chains would be released from the rudder and eased along the deck, and the wheel stage lifted onto the next tier. Once the towboat started pulling, it was essential for the man at the wheel to concentrate on his job, as it was too easy for a barge to swing wildly, especially when rounding a bend.

The steersman was in a very exposed position, so as the wool was loaded, a recess would be left under each end of the plank on which he stood. Whenever overhanging branches or other impediments loomed into view, the steersman would abandon his position and jump down into this recess, leaving the wheel-stage to be knocked flat by the branches.

The crew of a barge usually consisted of the bargemaster and one or two men, who took turns in steering. On some barges there were very basic quarters provided for the crew in the forecastle, which were extremely uncomfortable. On other barges the crew would be changed at regular intervals by running up to the towboat and changing places. Meals also varied, some being cooked on the towboat and passed across, while other barges had to make do for themselves.

If the steersman saw that the cargo was about to slip, or some other problem had arisen, he would pull a string that ran to the forecastle, where it was connected to a tin filled with pebbles. The rattling of the tin would alert the men in the forecastle that something was amiss and they would come on deck immediately. This caused a tragedy once, when the *Willandra* barge, with a full load of wool, hit a cross-current and began to list. The two crewmen in the forecastle began to climb out, but as the first emerged a bale of wool slid across the hatch, catching him by the foot. He pulled himself free, but in so doing the wool blocked the hatch completely and moments later the barge rolled over, drowning the man still in the forecastle.

Of course the barges had no motive power of their own, and were totally dependent on the towboat to keep them moving. However, when going downstream, the flow of the current under a fully laden barge could cause it to develop a momentum of its own, with a dramatic increase of speed. There was many a towboat captain who looked out of his wheelhouse to see the barge he was towing going past him. Then there would be a frantic rush to drop the towline, and the bargemaster would seek out a suitable piece of riverbank on which to run his barge aground and wait for the towboat to come up and reconnect the line.

Barges were as prone to being sunk by snags as were the steamers. In some cases, being deeper in the water, barges were in more danger, and it was not unknown for a steamer to pass over a snag, only to have the barge behind hit it and sink. Trying to raise a barge fully laden with wool was not a pleasant business. If the wool stayed in place it would have to be removed from the sunken barge, and each bale opened up to dry on the river bank. Sometimes the bales would break loose, despite the lashings, and these would have to be chased down the river. Once a barge was refloated and repaired on the site, the wool cargo would then be reloaded and the journey continue.

Not all barges were used in the general trades, some being designed to carry logs from forests to timber mills. These came in two types, insiders and outriggers. Outrigger barges transported logs floating in the water alongside, suspended from beams set across the hull, and were used when travelling with the current, while insider barges, into which the logs were lifted, were used when running against the current, as outriggers could make little headway against a current.

For many years the *Adelaide* was used to tow outrigger barges from Echuca upriver to the nearby forests at Barmah,

Outrigger barge near Echuca, with *Adelaide* in backgound. (FT)

or insider barges downriver beyond Perricoota. On arrival at the cutting site in the Barmah Forest, *Adelaide* would drop her tow, usually two barges, and then return alone to Echuca. The barges would be loaded by the cutters and then set adrift to ride the current on their own back to Echuca, a journey that usually took them about three days. It was found quite early that dragging a length of chain behind a barge kept it running smoothly with the current and eased the burden on the helmsman. The barges would be guided into the sawmill wharf, unloaded, then towed back upriver again by the *Adelaide*. When working downstream, the *Adelaide* would tow the insider barges in both directions.

Most of the barges were quite well known, usually being towed by the same steamer all the time. An unusual naming system was adopted by Murray River Saw Mills, which built a barge in 1911, which they named *A11*. When a second barge was added in 1922 it was named *B22*, then came *C24* and finally *D26*. A small number of barges still survive, including the *Ada* at Echuca, which used to be towed by the *Pevensey*. The outrigger barge *D26* was restored at Echuca in 1990 and operates with the *Adelaide* in demonstration runs once a month. At the Swan Hill Pioneer Settlement, the *Vega* has been fitted out as a display of a typical wool-carrying barge. Barges continued to be built on the river until the mid-1920s, among the last to enter service being the *Kulnine* in 1923 and the *Cowirra* in 1924. Sometimes barges were rebuilt into paddle-steamers, which was a relatively simple operation. The hull shapes of both barges and steamers were almost identical, so all that was necessary was the installation of a power plant, and wheels hung on either side. Two examples of this are still to be seen at Echuca, where the *Pevensey* was originally built as the barge *Mascotte*, while the excursion boat *Pride of the Murray* was built up from the barge *C24*.

Unlike the conventional tug that one sees around a seaport, the river towboats did not attach a line to their stern, but to a towpost. This was a strengthened mast set high up on the superstructure, almost amidships. In this way the line was kept clear of the water at all times, so avoiding becoming entangled in snags. It was also necessary because of the many bends to be negotiated, some very sharp. At times the towing boat would be on one side of a bend, while the barge could be on the other side, even facing in the opposite direction, and the rope would be stretched high between them over the intervening spit of land. It was at times like this that both the steamer skipper and the barge steersman had to be very alert, as a wrong move could cause the barge to sheer wildly towards the bank, or even capsize.

Cargo boats usually worked with only one barge, but the towboats would pull several. If the river was narrow, the barges would be towed in tandem, with sheer legs erected on the front one to act as a towpost. Where the river was wider, barges would be lashed alongside the towboat, and if three barges were being worked, one would be lashed on either side and the third towed behind. Some of the highest powered towboats could pull four barges.

As the river trade developed, certain rules of the road were established by mutual consent between the various skippers. One of the most important concerned passing, to make things easier and safer for a steamer travelling downstream. If two steamers met on a bend, the one going upstream, which was easier to control, would pull in to the side of the river to allow the barge of the other boat a free run around the bend. By adhering to this rule, very few collisions occurred on the river, despite the huge amount of traffic it carried at its peak. When a steamer and her barge travelling downstream came to a bridge, the steamer had to round up or turn around and face upstream, allowing the barge to drop behind. Once boat and barge were lined up in the centre of the river, the pair would drop slowly stern-first through the opening. A similar procedure was adopted when coming in to berth. Again, a boat and tow coming downstream would have to round up, and they would then slowly come into the wharf stern-first, always berthing with the bow facing upstream.

Life aboard a towboat was not easy, and the following extracts from the log kept between September and December 1906 on the *Rothbury* are typical. The *Rothbury* was built in 1881 and passed through several hands, being owned in

*Goldsborough* with barges lashed on either side. (FT)

1906 by William Wilson. It is still in service as an excursion boat at Mildura.

The skipper of the *Rothbury* was Captain William Bailey, known as 'Wild Bill Bailey', who kept the log, though his command of English was not totally accurate. To be a riverboat skipper, a man had to be the master of all trades, as these excerpts clearly show. The *Rothbury* had returned to Echuca from a 10-day voyage to the Murrumbidgee, and after a two-day stay, left Echuca again, towing the barge *Namoi*. Two days later they reached Murrumbidgee Junction at 3.15 a.m. and Bailey wrote:

> ran dead slow for a few bends and tied up. Did not like the way they was stearing [*sic*] the barge at 4am. Started at 5.15am—was booming along when arse over head went the wheel stage in a straight reach. Stopped the boat and called out to Mira [the bargemaster] to keep clear from the stem and sit down. Barge making between two trees inland. Just tightened tow line and brought broadside in against a tree. Mira would not take advice and concussion knocked him off his equilibrium into the river. Then there was hell to pay, what with steam and Dusting yelling out you could hear nothing. Mira in the meantime was swimming alongside the barge and got hold of the line thrown to him. Went alongside and straightened up wheel-stage and mended it. Got away 6.40am.

The voyage continued to Hay, which was reached at 6 p.m. on the Friday night. Twelve hours later the crew began discharging cargo, then took on fresh cargo, being ready to depart at 10 a.m. However, the engineer had taken a part ashore for mending and it was 2 p.m. before the *Rothbury* pulled out. At 6 p.m. they reached Illilliwa, landed cargo and left for Elli Elwah, where more cargo was landed. Arriving at Gree Gree at 8 p.m., more cargo was worked, then the crew knocked off for the night. Next day they continued to Carathool to discharge more cargo, and continued up the river until 7.45 p.m. On the Monday morning, 444 bales of wool were loaded at Togenmain, then the *Rothbury* and *Namoi* returned to Carathool to load a further 344 bales, leaving at 4.45 p.m. The voyage continued down the river until 7 p.m., when the captain decided to pull in for the night. Bailey wrote in the log:

> in pulling up the current set the boat into the trees, running across the bend at a terrible pace. Had to let go barge after giving her a check. Bargeman got line out and in checking up barge bumped up against a knot on a tree stoving a plank above water, springing another also stringer and cracking iron frame. Tied up alongside and found all safe and making no water so left her till morning.

The next day, Bailey 'started at 5 a.m. to cut plank out and put new one in, caulked, bolted and finished at 12.20. Had dinner and started at 1 p.m. arriving Burrabogie at 3.50pm.'

Back in Hay on Saturday, the crew loaded skins and other cargo, also several passengers joined for the trip to Echuca. At Miles woodpile, the *Namoi* was let go while the *Rothbury* was pulled in and 'took on 18 tons of wood, knee deep in water, steamed up to the barge and camped for the night at 11pm. On the voyage down carried away Pevensey

*Rothbury* towing the *Echuca* barge towards Echuca. (FT)

[ a sheep station] telephone lines.' Sunday was spent at rest, but on the Monday they

> started at 5.15am, when in a straight reach a few bends above the Lachlan Junction, the crank shaft broke. Rounded up in the bend, called out to Boco to steer barge in for a clear place. Got line out and made all secure and no damage done. Saw everything secure, started hands to get a bit of wood and laid down, downhearted and disgusted with the whole turnout. Only laid down a few minutes, got up and started taking broken shaft out. Got it out and swung the spare one round and placed it in position and finished for the night at 9pm.

Next morning, Bailey

> commenced work at 5am to put pinions on, all hands helping. Williams cutting keyway for eccentric sheaves, had a stiff job to get port one on. Went on putting plumber [*sic*] blocks and brasses in. Mended water heater pipe, screwed up and oiled towing gear, cleaned out smoke box, covered up barge and finished for night at 7pm. Hurricane blowing, lightening [*sic*], thundering, and raining heavily.

The remainder of the voyage was uneventful and the *Rothbury* finally arrived back at Echuca after a trip lasting 22 days. After a mere two days in port, the *Rothbury* was ready to depart for the Murrumbidgee again.

The short time in port often caused problem in securing a crew for each voyage. For Wednesday, 31 October, Bailey wrote in the log: 'left Echuca at 8pm after a lot of trouble with the hands. Had to run about from pub to pub looking for them after working all day. Run down to just below Torrumbarry headworks and tied up at midnight.' This voyage also took the *Rothbury* up the Murrumbidgee past Hay to Carathool, loading wool for the return trip.

On Wednesday, 14 November, the *Rothbury*

> made a start at 5.20am. On getting away Mira let the barge sag down into the limb of a tree, he cleared away and left the wheel and she run into the bank and swing around. Sung out to J. Gray to jump ashore and take a turn. The other three fools stood with their mouths open, as luck would have it no damage done. Towed them upstream to

a clear place and sent Roco on board and he soon regulated things. Swung her around and away we went at 6.20am.

Three days later Bailey wrote the boat was 'stopped at 5.30am, paddle wheel going all to pieces knocking top off paddle box. Set to work to mend it, finished at 12.30 and started.' The final entry shows: 'arrived at Echuca 5.50am Sunday morning with 120 bales of wool'.

These trips were made when there was ample water in the rivers. The river trading season lasted from five to seven months, depending on the river water levels, but sometimes boats would get caught on a falling river. There were numerous reefs along the rivers, which had to be negotiated very carefully when the river level was low. A particularly notorious reef, near Swan Hill, was known as the Bitch and Pups, and in very low water there was a 60-centimetre waterfall over the main reef. Another reef was known as Kelpie's Leap, because the steamer *Kelpie* went over the top of it at full speed on a low river to avoid being trapped.

Falling river levels were something a riverboat skipper dreaded. If he was caught on a falling river, the skipper would go as fast as possible for as long as possible every day. If the steamer ran aground on a sandbank, a line would be run out to a suitable tree and hooked around the drive shaft of the paddles. Full power would be applied and the steamer would drag itself over the sandbank.

Sometimes the river levels fell so quickly that steamers and their barges would be trapped in pools, occasionally for months at a time. When this happened, the crew would be brought back to their home town by other means and a caretaker left aboard the stranded vessel. When the water began flowing again, a new crew would be sent out to bring the steamer home. The Darling River was particularly notorious for sudden drops in water levels and vessels were frequently stranded.

Captain Charles Payne, who worked between Bourke and Wilcannia around the turn of the century, had a reputation for sinking more boats and barges than any other skipper on the Darling. On one trip, he left Bourke with a steamer towing two barges. The first barge was holed and sunk on Nulty Nulty Reef, the second went down on Curranyalpa Reef, then the steam boat had her bottom torn out on Murtee Reef. Captain Payne and his crew arrived at Wilcannia in a dinghy.

One of the most famous river stories of all concerns the paddle-steamer *Jane Eliza* and a trip she made up the Darling. In May 1883 the *Jane Eliza*, under Captain William Robert Porter, left Morgan for Bourke, towing the barges *Wangaratta* and *Isabel*. Most of the cargo in them consisted of wood for a new hotel to be built in Bourke, in readiness for the coming railway line from Sydney. The steamer and its barges were deep in the water and only managed to reach Avoca Cutting, 52 kilometres above Wentworth, when the water level dropped and they had to stop. Shallower vessels were able to come and go, but the *Jane Eliza* remained stuck and in April the following year Captain Porter was relieved by Abe Dusting. On 3 August 1884 came news of water coming down the river and on 2 September the *Jane Eliza* and her two barges headed upstream once again, but the next day the log shows: '*Success* passed down; struck boat's port paddle-box and also struck both barges with the *Nonpareil* barge. We were at the bank. Stopped below Barrowclough's woodpile, no damage done.'

Four days later the log reads: '*Wangaratta* making water fast. Got all pumps to work. Found a plank stove in on the port bow. Made a bag, filled it with mud, and stopped the leak.' Three days later the rush of water was subsiding rapidly, and when the barges began to thump on the bottom, Dusting was forced to tie up 58 kilometres below Wilcannia, still 640 kilometres short of Bourke. 'Got into a deep hole and camped till river rises again. *Burrabogie* and *Saddler* [both steamers] camped also, drawing six inches less than me.' Six days later another steamer, the *Freetrader*, and her barge joined the group.

*Jane Eliza* remained holed up until 5 November 1884, when it was thought there was sufficient water to continue but the barges kept 'sticking continually round Culpaulin Island'. Dusting was forced to work them past the island one at a time, then set off again, only to have both barges break their lashing and run onto the bank. After refloating them, the *Isabel* ran aground again, then the next day it was the turn of *Jane Eliza*: '11am. Stuck at Ten Mile Point, hove through and stuck on a snag at 5pm. Hove till 10pm and knocked off for the night.' Still the bad luck continued with the 'barge dragging continuously . . . *Isabel* stuck on sandspit. Got stuck opposite Mud Island.'

The next day the *Jane Eliza* came to a very shallow section and could not get past. The steamer *Ellen* helped out by pulling one barge through, then went on to Wilcannia, and next day the *Albury* arrived to help. The two steamers working together could not move the second barge, so some of its cargo was transferred to the *Shamrock*, a shallow-draught vessel, and it was then able to be moved. Dusting steamed on until he found a deep hole and settled down to wait for the next rise in the river. It was a long wait, 17 months, then a flood came down the Darling. Dusting set off for Bourke, but now he had trouble following the river, as the whole countryside was covered in water. In June 1866 the *Jane Eliza* finally reached Bourke, having taken 37 months for the journey. Unfortunately, a hotel had already been built with materials brought from Sydney on the railway line completed 10 months previously, and the man who had ordered the *Jane Eliza*'s materials had left town. The consignor at Morgan refused to pay the outstanding freight charge, so Hugh King, who owned the *Jane Eliza*, ordered Captain Dusting to sell it, except the lime and cement, which had gone hard. When the wood began bringing in high prices, the consignor suddenly decided to pay the freight bill and sold the materials himself to a contractor. It is said the timber was taken by camel to Broken Hill and used to build a bank. The *Jane Eliza* made a quick trip back down the Darling, towing three barges containing Broken Hill ore and 2,600 bales of wool, and was back in Morgan in December 1866.

Once the river trade had become established on the Murray, the boats were usually built along the river. One vessel to be imported from Scotland was the *Decoy*, which was completed in 1878. *Decoy* was designed along the lines

*Decoy* was imported from Scotland, and had an iron hull. (FT)

of contemporary British steam tugs of the 1870s and was brought to Australia as a speculative venture, probably for use as a tug in one of the major ports. Assembled in Melbourne, she was purchased by Herbert Hughes, who owned several properties along the Darling River. He already owned a barge, the *Reliance*, specially designed to transport live sheep. *Decoy* was brought into the river in July 1878.

Unlike the locally built boats with their red-gum or composite hulls, *Decoy* had an iron hull and was completely decked over, with the engine below and hatches fore and aft. She was one of the very few riverboats to have portholes in the hull. The boiler had been designed to burn coal and had to be modified for wood-firing. However, the hatchways were quite small, and when taking on wood, it was difficult to pass the standard 5-foot (1.5 m) logs through the opening. There was no ventilation below decks, and when steaming along the interior became very hot, acceptable in British waters but a living hell in Australia, especially in the summer.

Despite her faults, *Decoy* proved to be quite successful on the rivers, both as a towboat and a cargo boat. She was also called upon to refloat boats and barges on several occasions. From 1902 to 1909 *Decoy* left the river, going as far afield as Western Australia, but in March 1910 she was purchased by the Gem Navigation Co. and returned to the river as a towboat again. Today she is still afloat, though in the static capacity of houseboat near Mannum.

It was always the practice on the Murray and Darling rivers to tow barges, or have them lashed alongside the towboat. In America, where the rivers were wider, the practice was to push barges, as it still is today. In all the years that the Murray trade flourished, there was only one vessel that ever pushed barges, the *Captain Sturt*.

Imported from America in sections, the *Captain Sturt* was assembled near Mannum and completed at Blanchetown

*Captain Sturt* was imported in sections from America. (FT)

in 1916. She had twin, pontoon-like steel hulls, with the machinery located well forward, and twin smokestacks in front of the bridge. Owned by the River Murray Commission, *Captain Sturt* was obtained to assist in the enormous task of building the series of locks and weirs along the length of the river. As she was a pushing rather than towing boat, the barges for *Captain Sturt* had to be specially designed and built. Each could carry 150 tons of crushed granite and *Captain Sturt* could push up to six of them, fully laden, at a time. She became a familiar sight along the river from Blanchetown to Kulnine between 1917 and 1934. Old rivermen had a saying, 'the Murray hates steel', and this proved true for the *Captain Sturt*. In 1923 her original steel boiler had to be replaced, and by 1934 the hull was pitted with rust, cracks and small holes, which were patched up with concrete. *Captain Sturt* can still be seen at Goolwa, where she sits on the shallow bottom serving as a storehouse for Murray River Cruises.

By the time the *Captain Sturt* arrived on the river, the business of the towboats and cargo boats was rapidly disappearing, as the network of roads and railway lines grew. There were still some boats being built, most of which were quite large. When the *Arbuthnot* was destroyed by fire at Kyalite on the Wakool in October 1913, the remains were bought by J.G. Arnold and rebuilt at Mannum. Renamed *J. G. Arnold*, with a composite hull, the steamer was 104 gross tons, and 98 feet (29.8 m) long. In 1919 Arnold's fleet was combined with others to form the Murray Shipping Ltd and the *J. G. Arnold* operated on the Murray and Darling rivers. In 1930 the *J. G. Arnold* became the last commercial steamer to visit Bourke, and a few years later the vessel was laid up.

In 1919 J.G. Arnold built another large paddle-steamer at Mannum, the 366-gross-ton *Mannum*, which was 135 feet (37 m) long. The frames for the hull were made from recycled channel iron, which had been laid on the main road from Adelaide to Port Adelaide and was removed in 1916. Arnold bought the channel iron and had it shaped for use in the hull of the *Mannum*, which was planked with red-gum to the waterline, the topsides being steel.

The *Mannum* was gutted by fire and sunk at Mannum on 22 May 1921, not being raised until the following year. When rebuilt, she was given a much smaller deckhouse. *Mannum* survived into the 1950s, but as with so many of the river steamers, her final fate is obscure.

It is generally claimed that the last commercial steamer to be built for service on the Murray was the *Alexander Arbuthnot*, completed in 1923 at Koondrook. Her machinery reportedly came out of the paddle-steamer *Glimpse*, built in 1886 and sunk in 1914. *Alexander Arbuthnot* was built for the Arbuthnot Saw Mills and operated out of Echuca for many years, towing timber barges. In 1942 the vessel was running

*Alexander Arbuthnot* at Shepparton following restoration. (GA)

between Echuca and Yeilima, 110 kilometres upstream, but by 1947 it had been abandoned at Yeilima and subsequently sank. Refloated in 1973, *Alexander Arbuthnot* spent some years at Shepparton, but is now at Echuca, fully restored, and operating excursions from the main wharf.

The decline of the river trade was accelerated during the 1930s, when there were only about 30 towboats and cargo boats still in service. In 1936 the only boats operating out of Echuca as wool-carriers from the Murrumbidgee were the *Ulonga* and *Invincible*. The *Ulonga* was the last boat to operate on this trade, as the *Argus* on 11 June 1937 reported: 'the last cargo vessel on the Murray/Murrumbidgee run has been sold to Capt Reed of Renmark and will be used to cart firewood. She was to leave Echuca immediately.' The

The crew of *Invincible* pose for their picture to be taken. (FT)

*Oscar W* and *Avoca* with their barges at Mildura wharf. (FT)

*Ulonga* served on the lower reaches of the Murray until 1948, when she went to Port Adelaide and was rebuilt as a schooner.

A handful of boats survived until the 1950s, but the opportunity for commercial trade was almost non-existent. The Collins family were operating the *Excelsior* between Mannum and Mildura, but in 1947 she was withdrawn and converted into a houseboat. In 1949 Jack Searles began a regular cargo service between Mildura and Morgan, using the *Wanera*, and things looked promising when he was able to obtain a full load of wool to be taken downstream. On the next trip, 100 bales of wool were carried, plus a load of empty 44-gallon drums. Searles had been promised a load of full drums at Morgan but the oil company then reneged on the arrangements. Instead, *Wanera* loaded a small cargo, which proved to be the last to be taken from the once-bustling wharf at Morgan. This was the end of *Wanera*'s career as a cargo boat and she subsequently became a cruise boat on the river.

In August and September 1956 the Murray region was inundated by major flooding, and stations found they could not ship their wool by usual methods. The paddle-steamer *Success*, which had been lying derelict near Morgan, was reactivated and made several voyages along the Murray and Darling. While towing the *Vega*, loaded with 876 bales of wool, to Mildura, the *Success* suffered engine trouble and both boat and barge were swept away by the strong current. The *Vega* smashed into a huge gum tree, which was hauled out by the roots and disappeared in the raging waters. Attempts to tie the *Success* up to a tree failed as they continued to be pulled out, but eventually the *Success* and

*Kelvin* with live sheep on the foredeck. (FT)

*Vega* became trapped in a stand of flooded trees. A few minutes later the engine on the *Success* came into operation again and the voyage to Mildura was completed without further incident.

Another paddle-steamer brought in to help during the 1956 flood was the *Etona*, which had been lying idle since 1944 on the banks of the Murrumbidgee River. Her wheelhouse had been removed and used as a chickenhouse, and her general condition was poor, but Archie Connor managed to reactivate his old fishing boat and she became the heroine of the Balranald region, operating a number

*Dispatch* carried passengers and mail across Lake Alexandrina. (FT)

of mercy missions. In some places the river was up to 95 kilometres wide, and many stations were complete isolated. *Etona* carried supplies to homesteads, transported shearers to Murrum Downs station and collected the wool clip a few weeks later.

In the Swan Hill region, the paddler *Hero* was also called upon to assist, being used to transport 85 head of flood-bound cattle to dry ground. *Hero* was still in use by Chislett Bros sawmill at Boundary Bend, but in January 1957 the vessel was totally destroyed by fire at the sawmill. Also still active as a timber barge towboat was the *Edwards*, working out of Evans Bros Sawmill at Echuca, but she sank there early in 1958. Not raised until 1981, the remains of this

steamer were moved to a paddock outside Echuca, but she is now in a derelict condition. At Mildura, the *Rothbury* remained active towing timber barges into the 1960s, and today operates as an excursion boat.

The *Adelaide* continued to tow barges until 1958. It was estimated that she had brought at least 200 million super feet of timber to Echuca over the previous 70 years. After 20 years as a static display in a rose garden, *Adelaide* was returned to the river and is now a major attraction at the Port of Echuca.

By the end of the 1960s it was all over. There were no towboats or cargo boats operating on the rivers. Road and rail had completely taken over.

# 16 Snagging Boats

From the very first voyages along the Murray by Randell and Cadell in 1852, there had been a problem with 'snags', or obstructions in the river. Snags came in two forms: huge trees that had fallen into the river, and rocks that lay on the river bottom. Both could cause enormous damage to a boat or barge, often enough to sink it. Randell once described the number of trees blocking some stretches of the river as 'like a regiment of soldiers', while Cadell referred to those on the Upper Murray as a forest. If navigation of the Murray was to be successfully promoted, it was essential that these obstructions be removed. On his first voyage in the *Lady Augusta*, Cadell wrote in his log of coming up against 'a huge tree, blocking up nearly the entire stream; this we broke through by sheer force of steam, but not without almost sweeping the deck of passengers, who with difficulty avoided the branches as they passed over the vessel. The after bulkhead was also stove in.'

Cadell in particular was determined to rid the river of snags, and began petitioning the South Australian government to allocate funds for this purpose. He even made a survey of the Murray in a small boat, and determined that the bed of the river was strewn with trees that had fallen over many centuries. The same was true of the Murrumbidgee, but in the Darling the major problem was huge rocks forming reefs across the river at numerous points. The South Australian government supported Cadell and suggested to the New South Wales and Victorian governments that they should combine their resources to clear the rivers. New South Wales made a grant of £2,000, but Governor Hotham of Victoria refused to cooperate, stating that clearing the river would merely help South Australian steamboats divert to Adelaide the 'legitimate commerce of Melbourne'.

Using the grants from South Australia and New South Wales, Cadell began clearing the river, though some of his methods did not meet with universal approval. He would send his boat out in the summer months, when the river was at its lowest level, and have them cut off protruding branches at water level. These were then hauled onto the river bank to a height above the usual winter flood. While this method was satisfactory when the river was running high, steamers and barges continued to run foul of snags on a falling river, skippers often reporting they had struck a snag that had been cut 'Cadell-style'. The only effective solution to the problem was the total removal of the entire tree from the river bed. In some cases this was made possible by using bullock teams, which hauled trees out of the river, but in places where it was impossible for a bullock team to go, a special type of vessel would be required.

*Grappler* was the first snagging steamer on the Murray. (FT)

The first snagging steamer was designed by Cadell and built by John M. Webb at Echuca, under Cadell's supervision, and named *Grappler*. A wooden-hulled paddle-steamer, 80 feet (24.4 m) long, her beam was 26 feet (7.9 m), necessary for stability. Construction of the *Grappler* was financed by the South Australian government and she was launched on 1 February 1858, running trials on 10 April. The main task of the *Grappler* would be the removal of snags in the Upper Murray, concentrating on the stretch between Echuca and Albury. Cadell had promised the people of Albury that he would send his steamers to their town, but initial attempts had been prevented by the number of snags in the river. The *Grappler* went to work and was able to clear sufficient snags for the *Albury* to reach her namesake town in October 1858.

The method of tree-removal used on the *Grappler* was basic in the extreme, using a grapple, or length of chain attached to the boom on the foredeck. Among the crew were two South Sea islanders, specially brought in by Cadell, who would fix the grapples to the trees. Each of these men would dive overboard, holding the ends of the grappling chains, and secure them around the snag. This required them staying underwater for 30 seconds or longer, considered an amazing feat by the rivermen, many of whom could not even swim. By 1862 diving suits were being used in place of the divers. Once the grapple was secure, the steam-engine would be used to bring the log to the surface, and then it

*Madam Jade* roves the river as a floating shop.

The privately owned *James Maiden* has journeyed from Echuca to Goolwa.

The small excursion boat *Lady Joan* has operated from several Murray towns.

would be carried ashore and pulled high up on the bank. When a particularly large tree was being worked, it would be cut into sections, using a saw also driven by the engine. Rocks were removed by either the use of explosives, or hauling them onto the bank in similar fashion to the trees.

In practice, *Grappler* turned out to be something of a disappointment, being clumsy to operate, slow to work, and having a deeper draught than had been expected. The South Australian government often kept her laid up at times when she could have been working, and she became known as 'the White Elephant' along the river. Withdrawn from service in 1866, after some years of idleness, *Grappler* was fitted out as a police station and towed to Morgan; she was later converted into a dredge.

With the completion of a railway line between Melbourne and Echuca, the attitude of the Victorian government towards snagging changed dramatically. Echuca developed rapidly into the second busiest port in the state, and was described as the 'Chicago of the south'. With six trains or more a day operating between Echuca and Melbourne, it became increasingly necessary to have a clear river, so the wool clips could be brought quickly and safely to Echuca, for on-shipment to Melbourne. To this end, the Victorian government had several snagging boats built at Echuca over subsequent years.

The first of these boats, built from sections imported from Britain and launched on 8 April 1865, was the 60-foot (18.3-m) *Melbourne*, which worked along the Upper Murray both upstream and downstream from Echuca. The *Melbourne* was an unusual-looking craft, an iron-hulled stern-wheeler with a single deck structure only. Officially described as a snagging punt, she worked in the early years with the barge *Wardell*, which was later fitted with engines to also work as a snagging punt. For many years the superintendent of the Victorian government snagging operations was Mr Shelley, and the vessels were known locally as 'Mr Shelley's pleasure boats'.

Work on a snagging boat was anything but a pleasure, and at times it was incredibly difficult. The boats would stay out for weeks at a time clearing entire stretches of river. Sometimes it would take a day or more to remove a single, tree, and months would be spent on the same stretch of water until it was completely clear. However, within a few weeks more trees could fall into the river, and the job would have to be started all over again.

The removal of the trees from the river brought employment for another group of men essential to the river trade, the woodcutters. These men would live in total isolation for months, even years, at a time, sometimes accompanied by their families. They survived by fishing and buying their supplies from passing steamers who stopped to buy wood from them. Instead of cutting down trees, the woodcutters would chop up the trees hauled onto the bank by snagging boats, so they were not wasted.

The first *Melbourne* was built in 1865 at Echuca. (FT)

The New South Wales government also took an interest in clearing the rivers of snags. In 1874 they purchased the *Enterprise*, built at Moama in 1868. The *Enterprise* worked on the upper reaches of the Murray for some years, and may also have operated on the Murrumbidgee, which mainly runs through New South Wales. As the government vessel was not registered, it is difficult to locate much information on the *Enterprise*, which was sold and renamed *Rita*, though the date is unknown.

In 1912 the Victorian government built a new snagging steamer, which replaced the original *Melbourne* and was also named *Melbourne*. Unlike the original vessel, the second *Melbourne* was a side-wheeler and fitted with a powerful winch on the bow. By the time *Melbourne* entered service, the river trade was in decline and her services were not required as extensively as had been anticipated. After a few years work *Melbourne* was often laid up, though she was also used for other duties along the river, even occasional excursions from Echuca. In 1940 the *Melbourne* was sold and became a towboat for timber barges at Echuca. Today she is an excursion boat at Mildura, still powered by her original steam-engine.

The South Australian government had maintained a snagging boat on the lower reaches of the river for some years. In 1887 it purchased the paddle-steamer *Industry*, which had been built as a barge in 1876 and converted to a steamer in 1878. Obviously there was sufficient work to keep the vessel occupied, as in 1911 a new snagging boat was built at Goolwa and also named *Industry*. The second *Industry* was a very smart-looking vessel, with a large superstructure and a long boom on the foredeck. She was based at Renmark, and operated from there as far down the river as Goolwa, remaining in active service until 1970, when she was withdrawn. Subsequently presented to the town of Renmark, *Industry* is still to be seen there, having recently been reactivated after many years berthed in a specially constructed basin.

# 17 Hawking Boats

When the river trades first opened up, the main purpose of the riverboats was to deliver goods from the major centres to the developing towns and settlements along the river, returning with produce for sale in the capital cities or for export. However, beginning with Randell and Cadell, the boats' owners were not averse to trading with anyone along the river, be they private citizen or shop owner. This attitude tended to irritate the shop owners, who accused the riverboats of taking away their business. Realising where their greater business potential lay, the boat owners tended to trade only with shop owners. From this evolved a special type of river steamers, fitted out as travelling shops, which became known as hawking boats. They would sell groceries, hardware, haberdashery, clothes, timber, millinery and anything else the people along the river needed.

Hawking boats were operated with great success along the rivers for many years. They were based in the larger, established towns, such as Murray Bridge, Morgan, Wentworth and Mildura, and usually ran to a set schedule that enabled those along the river to know when they would be coming. Carrying all the goods the average settler would need for daily life, from toiletry items to garbage bins, the hawking boats concentrated on the more isolated homesteads and timber cutters' camps. Some hawking steamers were even operated by shop owners, to bring their goods to settlers unable to visit their stores.

One problem that affected the hawking trade was interstate taxes. Boats working along the lower Murray could safely trade as far as Renmark, but not much further, as they would then have to pay Victorian or New South Wales taxes on their goods. Similarly, businesses in Wentworth could trade along the Darling, which was entirely within New South Wales, but if they went along the Murray they could only stop on the north bank, as the south bank was Victoria. One Wentworth-based steamer had to go to Mildura, in Victoria, for repairs, and while there Victorian Customs sealed the shop and stores to prevent the sale of any goods on which tax had not been paid. This problem ended with Federation in 1901, but by then the hawking trade was in decline.

Just when the hawking trade began is uncertain, though it is generally accepted that the first such vessel on the Murray was the *Prince Alfred*, built at Goolwa in 1867 for Charles Oliver and Edward Walker. The Oliver family would be associated with the hawking trade for many years and operated two of the best known hawking boats on the river, the *Queen* and the *Pyap*.

The *Queen* had been built in Goolwa in 1865 and was a unique stern-wheeler, as the wheel was located under the hull. This arrangement proved unsuccessful and in 1872 the *Queen* broke down completely and had to be towed back to Goolwa, where she was converted to standard side-wheels. The Oliver family owned the *Queen*, sometimes in partnership, from 1868 to 1920, during which period she operated exclusively as a hawking boat. The vessel was fitted with a unique whistle, making a very odd sound. This was blown loud and long when approaching a stop, so that everyone would be aware that the *Queen* was arriving.

The *Queen* had new machinery installed at least twice, and was rebuilt several times over the years, twice due to serious accidents. The first of these occurred on 18 January 1874, when she caught fire and had to be scuttled to prevent total destruction. Rebuilt and returned to service, on 29 July 1876 the *Queen* was in collision with the *Jane Eliza* above Mannum and run aground in a sinking condition. Badly damaged, the *Queen* was raised two weeks later and returned to service after refitting. Sold out of the Oliver family in 1920, the *Queen* was totally destroyed by fire at Mypolonga on 13 September 1928.

Visitors to the Pioneer Village at Swan Hill can take an excursion trip on the *Pyap*, which spent the early part of her career as a hawking boat. Built for Charles Oliver, the *Pyap* was based at Murray Bridge, from where she would depart every Monday upriver. The *Pyap* retained the appearance of a regular Murray steamer, but the *Queen* had a much larger deck structure, which extended almost the full length of the hull.

One of the major operators of hawking boats at one time on the Murray River between Goolwa and Wentworth was Fuller, Tonkin and Martin, which owned a fleet of these vessels, though they suffered some calamities. In September 1873 they purchased the *Moolgewanke*, dating from 1856, and converted her into a hawking boat. On 21 June 1874 a boiler explosion killed three men and the vessel was subsequently reduced to a barge. Her engine was removed and installed in the *Paringa*, built in 1878 as a hawking boat. Unfortunately, the *Paringa* had a very short career, as on the night of 2 February 1890 she caught fire while berthed at Renmark. Her crew were asleep at the time, but all got ashore. Hawking boats carried a wide variety of cargo, and amongst that on the *Paringa* were some explosives which went up with such force it drew people from miles around. In less than an hour the *Paringa* was totally destroyed.

Another short-lived hawking boat owned by Fuller, Tonkin and Martin was the *Britannia*, completed in 1883 at Goolwa. It is recorded that the *Britannia* was fitted with

*Queen* and *Bourke* barge. Note banner promoting the dentist in board. (FT)

a shop 19 feet (5.8 m) by 22 feet (6.7 m), and she was 186 gross tons. Her machinery was formerly in the *Queen*. Following an extensive overhaul, the *Britannia* was carrying 20 passengers and 180 tons of general cargo on a regular service from Goolwa to Wentworth when she caught fire at Craigie Creek, above Morgan, on 23 July 1888. As the fire started at 5 a.m., all the passengers were asleep, but no lives were lost, though the vessel was totally destroyed within eight minutes. A more successful boat owned by Tonkin, Fuller and Martin was the tiny *Mayflower*, just 17 gross tons, which is still in existence as a houseboat.

About 1875 Charles Oliver sold the *Prince Alfred* to John Egge, of Wentworth, who was one of the notable characters of the river. Of Chinese descent, Egge was taken on as a cabin boy by Francis Cadell when he was trading in the China Seas in the 1840s. When Cadell came to Australia, he brought Egge with him. After leaving Cadell's employ, Egge became a river skipper, shop owner in Wentworth, and eventually boat owner, being known as the 'white Chinaman'. Egge operated the *Prince Alfred* from Wentworth along the Darling River for several years. In 1886 he purchased the *Murrumbidgee* and operated her as a hawking boat on the Darling for some years too.

Another Wentworth shop owner who went into the hawking trade was William Bowring, who originally came from Jersey, in the Channel Islands. Bowring purchased a business at Wentworth in 1874 and subsequently expanded into the river trade. He also owned the *Prince Alfred* at one time, and set up an establishment in Mildura, so he was able to trade on both the Darling and the upper Murray, using a mixed fleet of steamers and barges. One of Bowring's earliest vessels was the *Emily Jane*, built in 1881,

which he purchased in November 1888. *Emily Jane* spent the next 10 years on the Darling as a hawking steamer, but on 24 December 1899 she was burnt to the waterline near Wentworth.

To replace the *Emily Jane*, Bowring purchased a steamer recently completed at Milang. The *Marion* was built as a pleasure boat for Mr G.S. Fowler, but he died before it was completed and Bowring was able to purchase the boat from his estate. Fitted out as a hawking steamer, the *Marion* traded on the Darling for several years, but in July 1908 was sold and converted into a passenger boat. She is still afloat, at Mannum.

In August 1908 William Bowring purchased the *Florence Annie* to replace the *Marion*, but she cannot have been very successful in this role, as just two years later the vessel was reduced to a barge. She was one of the worst handling barges ever on the rivers, and it is said of one voyage down the Darling when only half-loaded that the *Florence Annie* hit every tree along the river bank.

Just as it seemed the era of the hawking boat was coming to a close, the Diener family entered the trade. In the 1890s Jack Diener bought a small, hand-operated stern-wheeler, a type known along the rivers as a 'rag boat', which he ran on the Darling, selling small items of haberdashery and clothing. In 1893 Diener built himself a small paddle-steamer at Morgan, the *Eva Millicent* of just 17 gross tons, which he used on the Darling River. Business must have been good, as in 1904 he was able to build a large paddle-steamer, which he named *Merle* after his daughter.

Jack Diener built the *Merle* himself at Morgan, and she was a most peculiar looking craft, with a very tall smokestack close to the bow, and a stern-wheel. She was 86 gross tons,

*Merle* was a most unusual looking craft. (FT)

*Emily Jane*, one of the hawking steamers operated by Wm. Bowring & Co. (FT)

with a length of 83 feet (25.3 m). There were two decks on a very low hull, the lower one containing the shop while the upper one was accommodation. Diener also designed the engine, which was built for him by May Bros at Gawler. The *Merle* was the first steamer to be actually designed as a floating shop, and for the first time employed assistants to serve behind the counter. There was also accommodation for 19 passengers, as the vessel worked to a regular schedule along the Darling River. The *Eva Millicent* was converted into a barge to carry extra stock and renamed *Eva*. As his business grew, Diener had a larger barge built for him in 1911 at Goolwa, named the *Flo D*, which was 100 feet (30.5 m) long. Originally intended to carry stock, Diener fitted her out as a shop too, and it was claimed she had the longest counter on the rivers, 65 feet (19.8 m).

In 1912 the Darling River was so low it was impossible for a steamer to move along it, so Jack Diener transferred the *Merle* down the Murray and began working from Morgan to Mildura. Some time later he moved his operation to the lower end of the Murray, including Goolwa, which required a crossing of Lake Alexandrina. In March 1917, while the *Merle* was crossing the lake, a sudden storm came up, during which the *Merle* was swamped and sank. It was fortunate that Lake Alexandrina is quite shallow, so the Diener family and the crew were able to scramble onto the top of the upper deck, as all the boats were in the barge. One of the barge crew attempted to reach the *Merle* in a boat but was prevented by the bad weather. Eventually, Captain Diener floated a line to the boat, which was pulled in to the *Merle*, and all aboard were safely transferred to the barge. They remained there all night, being rescued next day by a boat from Milang.

The *Merle* was raised, but her career as a hawking steamer was over. Her engine and boiler were removed and she was sold for service as a barge. The *Flo D* was then lengthed to 141 feet (43 m) and the engine and boiler from the *Merle* were installed, driving a peculiar stern-wheel arrangement in which twin wheels were placed at the stern, either side of the engine. The boiler was placed well forward, to give balance, with a tall smokestack. The vessel was renamed *Kookaburra* and enabled the Diener family to continue their hawking trade. When Jack Diener had to retire, his son Tom took over the boat, but in 1928 the *Kookaburra* was sold. The vessel survived until the 1960s, then was sunk near Nyah, where her remains can still be seen.

# 18 Fishing Boats

Many visitors to the Port of Echuca take the opportunity to have a short trip along the river on the paddle excursion boat *Canberra*. Now powered by diesels, this vessel was originally a steamer and her original plant is still in place. With two decks for passengers, the *Canberra* provides all the comforts one expects of an excursion vessel, yet she was originally built in 1912 as a fishing boat.

It might come as a surprise to those not familiar with the Murray River to learn that it once supported a thriving professional fishing industry. Some of the craft used by these men were extremely basic rowing boats, but others had paddle-steamers. Professional fisherman would be found along almost the entire length of the Murray River and its tributaries, and for many years they made a comfortable living.

The most popular catch along the river was the Murray cod, which was delicious to eat. Murray cod were plentiful in the early days, and also tasted better than the few cod that can be found today, which are rather short, fat fish. In early days they were longer and leaner, the result of having to battle the current. The construction of a system of locks and weirs changed the flow of the river, as the current was much slower.

Each professional fisherman had to obtain a fishing licence, and was then able to claim a 'fishing reach', a two-mile (3-kilometre) stretch of river. This was clearly marked by signposts bearing the name and licence number of the owner. Sometimes one man would own a number of these reaches. During certain seasons it was allowable to use nets, though the size of the mesh was strictly regulated, so that small fish could get through. At other times nets were banned and the fishermen had to resort to rod and reel, again being compelled to throw back fish below a certain size.

The fishing steamers were quite small, and most were of a very simple design. Many were built by the fishermen themselves on the banks of the river, yet they were surprisingly sound vessels, with a wide beam for stability. Often the entire family would live on the boats, or base themselves at an encampment along the river. Very few of the fishing boats were registered, so details of them are scarce.

The fishing steamers would operate during the times the river was flowing well, but would be laid up when the river was low. At such times the fishermen would have to find alternative employment, usually in one of the river towns. Some maintained woodpiles as an alternative means of earning an income, and spent the low-water periods cutting timber.

A less popular group of fishing men were known as 'Murray whalers'. They were itinerants, who drifted along the river from town to town in small boats, doing odd jobs as well as fishing, and not being averse to lifting anything that happened to be handy. One Murray whaler was well-known for towing a boat filled with dirt in which he grew vegetables. Most of these men travelled on their own, had no family and very few friends.

One problem facing the fisherman was getting his catch to market in a good condition. To keep the fish fresh, most fishing boats towed a second boat that was kept flooded, and as fish were caught they would be put in there alive, and kept until a passing cargo steamer could be stopped. The fish would then be killed, cleaned and packed in wooden crates. Between each layer of fish they would put a layer of willow leaves. These crates would then be taken to either Echuca or Morgan and sent on by rail to Melbourne or Adelaide. At other times the fishermen would sell their catches directly to the cook of a passing steamer, in particular the passenger boats, where fresh fish were always popular on the menu.

A few men were able to build up a fleet of fishing boats, and established sizeable businesses. Probably the best-known was Archie Connor, who owned a number of boats, including the *Nelson, Patsy, Ranger* and *Viola*. In 1912 he bought the former mission steamer *Etona* from the Church of England, and she became one of the largest of the fishing boats to operate along the rivers. Connor owned a great many fishing reaches along the Murray, Murrumbidgee, Darling and Lachlan rivers, which kept his boats occupied.

A few of those former fishing boats still survive, though none is used in its original capacity. Apart from the *Etona* and *Canberra*, already mentioned, at Echuca, work is underway restoring the *Ranger* on the river near the main wharf. Built in 1909 by Charles Felshaw at Echuca, and used as a fishing boat until the 1920s, *Ranger* was then purchased by Barham Saw Mills, renamed *Barham* and used to tow timber barges. In 1926 the *Barham* was sold to Permewan, Wright & Co. and continued to tow barges for some years. She had been lying derelict in the river for many years when Bill Collins began work on restoration, but he died before it was completed.

Another small paddler used for fishing at various times is the *Roy*, which today sits high and dry in the Wilabalangaloo Flora and Fauna Reserve, between Renmark and Berri. Sometimes described as the smallest paddle-steamer built for the Murray, which is not correct, the *Roy* was built in 1908 at Mildura and went through a number of owners over the years. In the 1930s she was stripped of all useful

*Viola* and *Ranger* were typical of Murray River fishing boats. (FT)

equipment and abandoned near Euston. Bill Collins and his brother Norm rescued the derelict vessel from the river bank in 1936 and rebuilt it, using timber from various other river steamboats. The Collins brothers also obtained a steam-engine and boiler, said to have been built in 1880. The rebuilt vessel was then sold several times, and used for fishing again by Frank Beveridge, who also used her as a houseboat. On his death, the *Roy* was abandoned near Berri and allowed to decay again, but in 1977 restoration work started and the *Roy* was active once more in 1978. After twice sinking at her moorings at Berri, the *Roy* was run aground, and several years later taken out of the water to become a static site at Wilabalangaloo. Numerous schemes to return the vessel to the river have come to nought, and the longer she sits out of the water, the more her hull will decay.

Visitors to Echuca who take a stroll along 'Rotten Row' upstream from the wharf will come across a tiny paddle-steamer bearing the proud name *Murray Queen*. This is a replica of a typical fishing boat, built in Melbourne and launched at Echuca in January 1973 by Peter McLeod. Powered by a horizontal single-cylinder steam-engine, this 30-foot (9.1-m) vessel is used purely for pleasure trips by the owner, but is a very accurate representation of an original fishing vessel.

The fishermen were a breed apart from other rivermen. They operated by their own rules and kept pretty much to themselves. In his book *Paddlewheels and Mudbank Sailors*, Paddy Hogg tells the following story about Archie Connor. He was called on to act as helmsman when the passenger boat *Gem* was towed from Mildura to Swan Hill in 1962. At the time, Connor was nearly 80 years old and had spent

*Roy* was one of the smallest of the fishing boats. (FT)

his entire life on the river, running his own boats. Having safely delivered the *Gem*, towed by the *Oscar W*, Connor said to the others, 'Well I think I'll put in an application for me Skipper's Ticket'. The others, all rivermen of repute, were amazed that the veteran skipper had never bothered to get himself a ticket, which he should have done years ago to operate his vessels. The authorities tried testing Connor on his river knowledge, but soon realised that he knew more than they did, so they gave up on the examination and wrote him a ticket. At last he could rightfully be referred to as Captain Archie Connor.

# 19 Mission Boats

The evolution of settlements along the river into villages, then towns, and in some cases, cities, was quite slow. The opening up of the Murray to trade by steamboats certainly speeded up the development of some areas. This was especially so along the reaches of the Murray within South Australia, where the State government developed a scheme to help the unemployed, who were sent out to establish what were called 'village settlements' at various places, such as Holder, Waikerie, Moorook and Kingston-on-Murray, Pyap and Lyrup.

In his book, *Riverboats and Rivermen*, retired Murray steamboat skipper William Drage recounted the following story of his parents' move to the river. His father, a Londoner who had run away to sea at the age of 10, then jumped ship in Port Adelaide some years later, was one of the many to take up the government offer. As Drage wrote:

> My father, mother and eldest brother were one of twenty-eight families who were sent up to Morgan by train, and then towed forty miles in a barge behind the *Queen*. On 22 February 1894, they stepped ashore at Waikerie, where each family was given five sheets of corrugated iron and a bolt of hessian. The families joined into pairs, and each built a shack with a framework of bush timber, a roof of their ten sheets of corrugated iron, and hessian for the outer walls and a central partition. While the settlers were clearing their blocks they lived on government rations of tea, sugar, flour and meat, served out at Morgan. If you didn't go to Morgan you got no rations, so two men rowed the eighty miles there and back once a week. There was plenty of fish in the river, and the catches were shared out among all the families.

William Drage goes on to tell how his father fell out with the other settlers and moved his family on to Renmark, which was 'slightly more civilised than Waikerie. It had been settled since 1887, but the township was still no more than a straggle of wood and iron shacks along dusty streets.'

This was the kind of world into which William Drage was born in 1901. The settlements and townships had only the most basic of facilities, and none had a church. They relied entirely on travelling ministers to bring them spiritual comfort and perform weddings and christenings. It was only by coincidence that a minister would be on the spot to take a funeral service. The roads connecting the various populated centres were either very poor, or nonexistent, so it was natural that the men of the cloth should turn to the natural source of transport, the river.

William Drage wrote that his father, Sydney Drage, worked at one time as the engineer-deckhand-cook on a

*Etona* during her career as a mission boat. (FT)

mission boat, the *Glad Tidings*. This was a propeller-powered steamer built about 1898 and operated by the Wesleyan church, on which the Rev. Butters would attend his congregation scattered along the river from Renmark to Mildura. The *Glad Tidings* was destroyed by fire at Renmark, though the actual date is unknown.

In 1883 Bishop G.W. Kennion of Adelaide formed the Bishop's Home Mission Society of the diocese of South Australia, to bring religious sustenance to those who lived in isolated areas. Bishop Kennion was an old Etonian, and with the assistance of other old Etonians, he later raised funds to purchase a small launch, the *Patroller*, which was renamed *Etona*. This vessel was used to provide a mission service to settlers along the South Australian stretches of the Murray River. Many of these people were totally isolated from bigger centres, and at the time there were only four churches in the whole area.

Eventually the *Etona* became too small to provide an adequate service over 680 kilometres of river, and in 1898 the Home Mission Society decided to build a larger steamer. Once again Bishop Kennion turned to his fellow old Etonians, and boys at the school also contributed towards the cost of £1,000 for the new steamer, which was designed by Mr J. McLellan and built at Milang. The engine, built by Ransome, Simms & Jeffries in England, arrived in May 1899.

The new steamer was also named *Etona* and entered service in mid-1899. A small chapel, complete with an altar and organ, was installed in the after cabin, and could hold about 20 people at most. If a larger congregation gathered,

The restored *Etona* can be seen at Echuca.

then the service would be held ashore, under a tree or in a convenient building. Forward there were quarters for the ministers and guests. *Etona* also carried a small free lending library, often the only access riverfolk had to reading material. *Etona* looked very smart, being painted all white, with a white-painted cross set atop the wheelhouse.

The first minister to work from the *Etona* was Archdeacon Bussell, assisted by the Rev. F.H. King. Once a year the Bishop of Adelaide would accompany them on a round trip, to conduct confirmation services. The chapel was used for all regular church services, and there is a story told of a wedding held on board on a very hot summer day, following which some of the men, including the minister and the bridegroom, dived into the river to cool off.

Based at Morgan, the *Etona* worked to a regular six-weekly schedule which took her up the river as far as Renmark. The Rev. F.H. King, who took over from Archdeacon Bussell, recalled how on one six-week trip he conducted 47 services at 32 different places, and this was typical of the manner in which the *Etona* was operated.

A later minister on the *Etona* was the Rev. H.F. Severn, who during his time on the boat was once described in *The Bulletin* as 'a saint who lives on a raft on the Murray and boils eggs in his hat'. The last minister to work from the *Etona* was the Rev. F.W. Wilkinson. All these gentlemen of the cloth had to learn the ways of the river, as they were required to assist in the operation of the boat.

From time to time *Etona* would carry invited guests for a voyage. One such traveller in the early 1900s was Bernard

Law Montgomery, the son of the then Bishop of Tasmania, who assisted by playing the organ during the services on *Etona*. This young man later went into the British army and achieved eternal fame as Viscount Montgomery of Alamein.

For many years *Etona* was an integral part of the lives of many people who lived along the banks of the Murray River in South Australia. Her visits brought not only religious sustenance, but also advice and comfort, sometimes first aid, and at times even assistance in delivering babies. The arrival of *Etona* and the announcement of a church service gave people the opportunity to dress up in their best clothes for a change, and join with others in praise and the singing of hymns.

As the various settlements developed into townships and built their own churches, the necessity to rely on the *Etona* declined. The steamer kept operating as a mission boat until 1912, but by then she was no longer required. Her religious artifacts were removed and some found their way into new churches being built along the river. The organ that Bernard Montgomery had played was sold to the North Adelaide Baptist Church and remained there until the 1970s, when it was donated to the Murray Bridge Museum, where it can still be seen.

The *Etona* was sold to Archie Connor and converted into a fishing boat. Amazingly, she survived many years of neglect, to be salvaged by a syndicate from Echuca. They restored the old vessel to her original appearance, and she can still be seen, usually berthed just downstream from the wharf at Echuca.

# 20 Passenger Boats

The largest and finest of the steamers to be built for service on the Murray during the golden age of the river were the passenger boats. There were only a few of these boats, and fortunately three of them have been preserved. From the beginning of steam operation along the river, the transportation of passengers was a major business.

William Randell built his *Mary Ann* purely as a cargo boat, but with the *Lady Augusta*, Francis Cadell incorporated passenger accommodation. On his first trip along the Murray, Cadell was accompanied by a number of passengers. Many of the early cargo boats were fitted with some passenger accommodation, as were a few of the towboats. Hawking steamers, which usually ran to a regular schedule, were also sometimes fitted with cabins for passengers. In the early years there was not much demand for passenger accommodation, as settlements were few and far between. However, the development of these settlements into townships was the spur to the conversion, and later the construction, of boats aimed primarily at the passenger trade.

Typical of the vessels that carried cargo and some passengers was the *Shannon*, built in 1887, which had an extra deck added in 1881 with some accommodation. On 17 October 1885 the *Shannon* caught fire at Morgan and was scuttled to prevent her total destruction. Following repairs, she resumed her passenger and cargo trade, eventually being placed on a regular schedule between Mildura and Swan Hill. On 28 June 1901 the *Shannon* was holed by a snag at McFarlanes Reef, a short distance upstream from Mildura, and sank in 10 minutes. At the time she had 20 passengers on board, who were safely transferred to the shore, where they spent the night on the bank and were taken to Mildura next day. After being raised and repaired, the *Shannon* worked out of Echuca for a short while and was then sold to Tasmanian interests.

The establishment of passenger services along the Murray was hindered by the seasonal variations in river levels and the narrowness of the upper reaches above Mildura. When the railway line between Adelaide and Morgan was completed, that town became a natural terminus for the river trade and a large wharf was built there. Echuca offered the major rail connection to Melbourne, but it was not until Wentworth and Mildura began to develop that a viable passenger service could be started, using large boats.

The first major passenger vessel to be placed in service on the Murray was the *Gem*, which was converted for this purpose in 1882. She was launched in 1876 at Moama as a barge, but the following year machinery was installed and

the vessel operated as a cargo boat. Her original owner was Captain Elliott Randell, brother of pioneer William Randell, but he sold her in 1878. In 1879 the *Gem* changed hands again, when purchased by Captain Hugh King, who continued to operate her as a cargo boat, with himself as master.

On 11 February 1882 *Gem* arrived at the Goolwa shipyard of W. Gordon & Son, to be rebuilt as a passenger boat. The vessel was cut in two just forward of the paddlewheels, and the halves pulled apart by a bullock team. A new 40-foot (12.2-m) section was then constructed and the three parts joined together, creating a vessel 133.6 feet (40.6 m) long of 228 gross tons. *Gem* now had three decks with accomodation for 100 passengers in what were described at the time as 'commodious cabins', though by modern standards they were extremely basic. There were also saloons and smoke rooms, a dining room seating 60, and space for about 100 tons of cargo.

When completed, the *Gem* was placed in a regular service between Morgan and Wentworth, but was only able to operate for about six months of the year, being laid up when the river was too low.

In November 1888 Hugh King joined in partnership with George and William Chaffey of Mildura to form the River Murray Navigation Co. They had recently purchased the *Ellen* for conversion into a passenger boat. Built at Goolwa by Shetliffe & Sons, who were also her first owners, the *Ellen* was completed in 1877, being one of the largest vessels on the river, 134 gross tons and 120 feet (36.5 m) long. She was intended for service as a cargo boat and also towed a barge, the *Vulcan*. In 1886 she managed to journey up the Darling River as far as Walgett. The following year the *Ellen* left the rivers and began operating from Port Adelaide to Ardrossan, but in October 1888 she returned to the river, when purchased by the Chaffey brothers.

The Chaffeys extensively refitted the *Ellen*, extending the upper deck, adding passenger cabins, a large saloon and a dining room seating about 30, which made her rather top-heavy. The added weight, combined with her rounded bottom, caused the *Ellen* to roll very badly when going round bends in the river, and it was said that the crew used to move barrels of water around the deck to keep the vessel on an even keel. Her master for many years, Captain Tinks, is said to have kept a cup in the wheelhouse, and when the vessel went round a bend he would lean out and scoop up a drink of water. The stewardesses and cooks on the *Ellen* also had a hard time of it, trying to prepare and serve meals under such conditions, and many a passenger had his meal

*Gem* shortly after being enlarged in the 1880s. (FT)

shoot off the tables as the *Ellen* rounded a bend at speed.

The *Ellen* and the *Gem* began operating a regular service between Morgan and Mildura. Another passenger boat to join the fleet of the River Murray Navigation Co. was the *Nellie*, completed at Moama in 1882. Intended for service on the upper reaches of the Murray, the *Nellie* was only 80 feet (24.3 m) long, and 66 gross tons. She was also primarily a cargo boat. In 1891, when sold to the Chaffey brothers' River Murray Navigation Co., the *Nellie* was altered to a passenger boat, though with less accommodation than the *Ellen*. These two boats were able to operate a longer season than the *Gem*, as they were not as deep.

Another passenger boat of this era was the *Pearl*, designed by George Chaffey in the American style, as a stern-wheeler. Built by R. Smith & Co. at Lytham in England, then broken down into sections for transportation to Australia, the *Pearl* was assembled at Mildura. She measured 110 feet (33.5 m) in length and was 213 gross tons, and ran trials on 22 September 1890. She was a very strange looking craft, with three decks, two covered for their entire length, and a tall smokestack right forward. It is reported that the two boilers fitted in the *Pearl* were of different sizes and could not use the standard lengths of wood cut along the river bank. In service, the *Pearl* proved to be top-heavy, rolling excessively when rounding bends. The smokestack was cut down to just a stump, but still the *Pearl* caused many problems, and was never a success.

In November 1892 it was reported that a new engine had been installed in the *Gem*, though it is more likely that the original one was compounded and a new boiler fitted. Since

*Nellie* was one of the smaller passenger boats. (FT)

her rebuilding, *Gem* always had a slight list to starboard, but the engines worked well. When attempts were made to correct the list, the engines began to run rough and could not be adjusted, so *Gem* kept her slight list throughout the remainder of her career.

In 1895 the River Murray Navigation Co. went into liquidation when the Chaffey brothers' irrigation venture in the Mildura region collapsed. Hugh King and George Chaffey then formed H. King & Co. to operate the *Gem*, but in 1896 George Chaffey was declared bankrupt and he left Australia for good in 1897. Despite these problems, the passenger boats continued to operate as before, on a combined schedule.

In 1903 the *Nellie* was withdrawn from service as a passenger boat and sold. She spent several years operating as a hawking boat, but then her new owner obtained the mail contract for a service between Morgan and Mannum, on which she again carried passengers.

Life for the crew aboard a passenger boat was hectic, though conditions were better than on cargo boats and towboats. The *Gem* carried a crew comprising a captain, mate, engineer, fireman, cook, cook's offsider, three stewardesses, six deckhands and a purser. The boat was worked in two six-hour watches, the captain, engineer and two deckhands being on duty from six to twelve, morning and evening; and the mate, fireman and two deckhands from twelve to six, afternoon and night. The two other deckhands were called upon as required.

The *Gem* ran a regular weekly schedule during the season, departing Morgan every Saturday. She would arrive there about 5 a.m., and immediately the crew would start unloading cargo. As soon as all inward cargo was on the wharf, outwards cargo would be stowed. Meanwhile, disembarking passengers would have been shepherded ashore to the railway station, and joining passengers would be transferred from the station to the boat. About 1 p.m. the *Gem* would cast off and head upstream, the first stop being Renmark.

From there, stops would be made at stations along the river to unload general cargo and take on produce or wool. Arrival at Wentworth would be at about 3 a.m. on Tuesday, with cargo being worked as quickly as possible. Usually several hundred bales of wool would be loaded, for delivery to Mildura, and onshipment by rail to Melbourne. From Wentworth, the *Gem* would go straight to Mildura, arriving about 5 p.m. on Tuesday. The cargo would be unloaded that night, and passengers disembark. The crew's day, which had started before 3 a.m., would usually not end until nearly midnight.

Next morning, work would start again at 5 a.m., loading cargo for downstream. The joining passengers would come aboard and the *Gem* would set off in the early afternoon for Wentworth, and so along the river back to Morgan. Cargo was an important source of revenue for the passenger boats and the *Gem* carried anything that could be lifted aboard. At Morgan the cargo was worked by a crane on the wharf, but at all other stops the deckhands were called upon to carry everything on their backs. There were also several stops in each direction at woodpiles, when all the crew, whether on duty or not, would be called upon to 'wood-up'. Despite the hard conditions, there was never a shortage of men keen to work on the passenger boats, but as their operation was seasonal, they had to find alternative employment for about half of each year. Rates of pay ranged from £6 a week for a captain to 5s. a day for the cook's offsider and only slightly more for the deckhands.

*Ruby* at Swan Hill. (FT)

*Marion*, last passenger boat to enter service. (FT)

The *Gem* was known as the 'Queen of the Murray', but she was too big to operate for at least half the year, due to her great depth. As a result, Captain Hugh King decided to order a new passenger boat, the only such vessel to be actually designed and built for the transportation of passengers along the Murray River. Completed at Morgan in 1907, the vessel was named *Ruby*, the fourth riverboat to bear that name. She was 205 gross tons, 130.9 feet (39.8 m) long, and had three decks of accommodation for about 50 passengers, with a dining room that could seat 30, as well as a saloon and smoke room. The *Ruby* was placed in service between Morgan and Mildura and was able to operate a much longer season thatn the *Gem*. Initially, the three big passenger boats, *Gem*, *Ruby* and *Ellen* were owned by separate companies though they operated a combined service.

In 1914 the last of the passenger boats, the *Marion*, was

placed in service. The *Marion* had been ordered as a pleasure boat by Mr G.S. Fowler of Adelaide, but he died before the vessel was completed in 1897. Sold to William Bowring, the *Marion* became a hawking steamer on the Darling River, then in 1908 she was sold to Ben Chaffey, the son of George Chaffey and owner of the Ben Chaffey Steamboat Co. In 1909 this company merged with one of Hugh King's interests, the Gem Line of Steamers and A.H. Landseer Ltd to form the Gem Navigation Co., which owned a sizeable fleet. However, Ben Chaffey did not transfer the *Marion* to the new company, or the *Pearl*. As the *Pearl* was such a failure on the rivers, it was laid up, and in 1914 much of her superstructure was removed and installed in the *Marion*. In her new guise, the *Marion* had accommodation for 40 passengers spread over three decks. Lounges were located on the top and middle decks, with the dining room seating 30 on the main deck. The *Marion* was placed in service between Morgan and Mildura, but as with some other boats, she proved to be somewhat top-heavy and rolled excessively when rounding bends.

By the time the *Marion* entered service the river trade was on the decline, though the passenger boats still retained considerable popularity. The roads between the various river towns were still unsealed and a trip along the river was much more comfortable. Commercial travellers, who moved from town to town with their samples, were frequent passengers. The boats had been regularly updated and offered electric light and running hot water in cabins. In 1914 the river level remained very low almost the entire year and the *Gem* hardly left her berth, while the other boats operated a very short season. The same happened in 1915, but in 1916 things improved on the river, though the war reduced the amount of business. The combination of war and low water levels had such a bad effect on the river trade that many companies went out of business. In 1919 there occurred a major amalgamation of five companies, including the Gem Navigation Co. Ltd, to form Murray Shipping Ltd. This brought all the passenger boats, *Gem, Ruby, Marion* and *Ellen*, as well as the *Nellie*, under the same ownership for the first time.

When the river was running high, it was possible for the smaller boats, particularly the *Ruby* and the *Marion*, to proceed above Mildura, usually as far as Swan Hill. In 1921 the river was exceptionally high and overflowing its banks in places, when the *Ruby* ran hard aground on a levee bank shortly after leaving Swan Hill. It took the combined efforts of six paddle-steamers to pull her back into the river 12 days later, during which time the river level had remained high. Had it fallen, then the boat could well have been stranded for years. The *Ruby* only once went as far as Echuca, again on a very high river, but her funnel had to be removed to allow her to pass under the Koondrook bridge.

Unfortunately, as road and rail links improved, the age of the Murray River passenger trade was drawing to a close. In 1923 a snag penetrated the stern of the *Ellen*, which had to be run aground. As she settled, she began to roll to one side, but her captain ran a wire rope around the funnel, secured it to a tree ashore and prevented the vessel rolling right over. The *Ellen* ended up with her stern under water

while the bow was on dry land. Several months later she was refloated and towed to Morgan. Considering the parlous state of the river trade, it was decided to lay her up. At high river, the *Ellen* was pulled ashore in a small depression below the punt at Morgan and cannibalised for doors, fittings and other spare parts needed for other boats. Several years later the *Nellie* was pulled ashore next to the *Ellen*, and on 22 January 1930 both vessels were destroyed by a fire, believed to have been lit by vandals.

The *Gem, Ruby* and *Marion* managed to maintain a passenger service through the 1920s and into the 1930s, though patronage declined steadily throughout these years. Some years the river levels were so low that a very abbreviated schedule was operated, but in times of high river it was possible to look at new routes. In the early 1930s the *Marion* ran from Morgan to Swan Hill for several seasons, then in July 1934 she inaugurated a new service from Mildura to Echuca. This enabled passengers to leave Melbourne by train for Echuca, travel on the *Marion* to Mildura, transfer to the *Gem* and continue to Morgan, then go by train to Adelaide, or vice versa.

The first season of these trips ended in November 1934, but the *Marion* returned to the Echuca trade from June to November 1935 and July to November in 1936. In 1937 the level of the river was too low for the *Marion* to operate to Echuca, and instead she replaced the *Gem* on the service between Morgan and Mildura, but made only 16 round trips. The steady falling away of patronage meant that the *Ruby* was used less and less during the 1930s. Eventually she was withdrawn from service altogether, leaving the *Gem* and the *Marion* as the only passenger boats.

As the river level remained so low they could not operate at all, 1938 was a disastrous year for the passenger boats. Good rains in 1939 enabled the *Gem* to return to the service from Morgan to Mildura, and the *Marion* to run on the upper river to Echuca, leaving there for the last time on 17 December. Low water throughout 1940 caused the *Gem* to remain idle for another year, though the *Marion* was able to operate for 18 weeks between Morgan and Mildura, and continued running in 1941. In April 1941 the *Marion* was laid up at Morgan with the *Gem*, and both remained idle for the remainder of the war.

When the war ended, Murray Shipping Co. tried to re-establish their passenger operation, and returned *Gem* and *Marion* to service. There was enough patronage to keep the two boats going for the first couple of seasons, but then disaster struck. On 6 November 1948 the *Gem* struck a snag downstream from Mildura and settled to the bottom, though most of the superstructure was above water. Refloated on 20 November, the *Gem* was towed to Mildura for repairs and did not resume service until September 1949. The loss of revenue, and cost of repairs, were a major financial blow to the Murray Shipping Co., but it struggled on until 1952, then went into liquidation. The *Gem* and the *Marion* both ceased operating at the same time, and the operation of old-style passenger boats along the Murray River came to a close, to be replaced some years later by the cruise boats of today.

*Gem* leaving Lock II at Mildura about 1948. (FT)

*Gem* sunk, October 1948. (FT)

# 21 Cruise Boats

The Murray River and its environs have become a popular holiday playground for Australians. Some rent a houseboat to meander along the river at their own pace, while others take advantage of the regular weekly cruises operated from several towns. It is generally thought that cruising along the Murray River is a relatively recent innovation, but in fact the first holiday trips along the river were organised a century ago.

In the 1890s, Thomas Cook's Melbourne office regularly advertised a 'Tourist Trip' to Mildura. Passengers would board a train in Melbourne and travel to either Echuca or Swan Hill, to join one of the river steamers running to Mildura. There the travellers would live aboard the boat while the cargo was worked, then return up the river and back to Melbourne by train. While this could not be considered a luxury trip in the modern sense, it did offer the opportunity to have a holiday trip along the Murray. It was also possible for passengers from Adelaide to travel by train to Morgan, then join the *Gem* or another of the large passenger boats for the week-long trip to Mildura and return. However, these holiday trips were not taken in great numbers and the shipping companies did not actively market the idea.

One of the first men to realise the tourist potential of the Murray was Harold Drew. In 1913 he acquired a large stake in the Gem Navigation Co., which owned the large passenger boat *Gem*, operating a regular weekly service from Morgan to Mildura. Drew took a party of friends on a trip abord the *Gem* to Mildura, and in an interview told the local press that, in his opinion, the future of shipping lay in the tourist trade. He went on to say he intended to make a film to show people the pleasures associated with a river trip between Morgan and Mildura, but this apparently was not made. Despite his enthusiasm, Drew was unable to develop his idea, and when the war came it was forgotten.

By the 1920s the river trade was in decline and seeking a method of survival. The formation of Murray Shipping Ltd brought together the last surviving companies into a single entity, but that was not enough to save the trade. One of the few areas to continue with some semblance of regularity was the passenger trade, comprising three boats, the *Gem, Marion* and *Ruby*. Murray Shipping began offering package deals, combining river trips with rail connections, with cost about £1 a day. Going into the 1930s, even the passenger boats were hurting, and the *Ruby* was taken out of service, leaving the *Gem* and *Marion* to maintain the trade on their own.

The first real cruise on the Murray was operated by the

*Gem* cruising through Lock 5 in 1940. (FT)

*Marion*. In December 1934 she left Morgan with 35 passengers on board. The trip went upstream as far as Renmark, then returned downstream to Goolwa and back to Morgan. This proved highly successful, so on 28 December 1935 both the *Gem* and the *Marion* departed Morgan on a cruise, following the same route as the previous year. The two boats made a similar cruise in December 1936, which again was a great success.

One of the directors of Murray Shipping Ltd was Captain Johann George Arnold, a Swede who had settled in Australia in the 1890s and once owned his own fleet of riverboats. Arnold thought along the same lines as Harold Drew, that the future of river shipping lay in the tourist trade. Encouraged by the success of the cruises operated by the *Marion* and *Gem*, he travelled overseas in the mid-1930s to inspect river cruise boats on the Nile and European rivers, especially the Rhine. On his return, Arnold contacted several local shipbuilders and obtained quotes for the construction of a modern cruise vessel. Arnold then tried to interest his fellow directors of Murray Shipping in the idea, emphasising the success of the cruises operated by the *Gem* and the *Marion*, but they were not prepared to outlay the money necessary to finance the building of a new boat, so Arnold had to admit defeat.

Arnold and Drew were not the only ones to see that the future of the river trade lay in the tourist market. In 1937 the River Murray Tourist Co. Ltd was formed, and announced plans for the construction of a vessel for the tourist trade. The vessel would be 179 feet (54.5 m) long and 28 feet (8.5 m) wide, provide accommodation for 84 passengers on three decks, have a modern diesel engine, and be named *Murray Queen*. Unfortunately, there were insufficient subscribers to the company for it to proceed and the scheme collapsed. Possibly the uncertainty of river levels was a factor in this, as even the existing boats were having a hard time in the late 1930s.

Low river levels in 1937 meant that the *Gem* could not operate and the Christmas cruise was run by the *Marion* on her own. The river was so low in 1938 that neither the *Marion* nor the *Gem* could operate, but in 1939 the *Marion* and the *Gem* again made a Christmas cruise together. This was the last such trip trip they would make, as in 1941 both vessels were laid up.

With the end of the war, Murray Shipping Ltd tried to re-establish its passenger services, which were now marketed more as tourist trips. Both the *Marion* and the *Gem* made trips between Morgan and Mildura, but the Christmas cruises were not repeated. However, at the top end of the river, the first purely cruise vessel was entering service and opening a new era in the Murray River trades.

It might come as a surprise to find that the first company to place a cruise boat in service on the Murray was not one of the established river companies, but Murray Valley Coaches. Established at Echuca in November 1934, they operated a regular road service from Sydney to Adelaide, with stops at major towns along the river. During 1946, Murray Valley Coaches purchased the veteran paddle

*Murrumbidgee* prior to rebuilding. (FT)

steamer *Murrumbidgee*, but as part of the deal also had to purchase her barge too, the *J. L. Roberts*, the pair costing £800. As they did not want the barge, it was abandoned on the river bank, while work began on the *Murrumbidgee* to convert her into a cruise boat.

The *Murrumbidgee* was the oldest surviving Murray River paddle-steamer, having been built at Echuca in 1865 as a cargo boat. She was 83 feet (25.3 m) long and 16 feet (4.9 m) wide, powered by a two-cylinder semi-portable steam-engine, built in England. Over the years the *Murrumbidgee* changed hands on numerous occasions, her various owners including the McCulloch Carrying Co.,

*Murrumbidgee* as a cruise boat.

John Egge, Captain J.G. Arnold, A.H. Landseer and Murray Shipping Ltd. When other steamers were being forced out of work by road transport, the *Murrumbidgee* kept on working, towing the *J. L. Roberts* loaded with sleepers for the expanding rail network. In August 1943 *Murrumbidgee* and the *J. L. Roberts* went up the Murrumbidgee to Hay to cart firewood to an Italian internment camp. Due to low river levels, they were stranded at Hay through 1944 and 1945 and did not return to Echuca until August 1946. Shortly afterwards, *Murrumbidgee* and *J. L. Roberts* were sold to Murray Valley Coaches and started a new career.

Under the guidance of Captain Paddy Hogg, the *Murrumbidgee* was transformed from a mundane work boat into a cruise vessel. The superstructure was extended both fore and aft, while the original steam machinery was retained. The conversion job was completed in a few months, and in April 1947 *Murrumbidgee* began operating day cruises and charter trips out of Echuca. Early in 1948, further alterations were made to the vessel, to provide accommodation for 17 passengers, so that she could make four-day cruises out of Echuca as well. These proved very popular from the start, with special charter trips, and some fishing trips, being included in the schedule. As 1948 drew to a close the future of the cruise operation appeared secure, with good bookings held six months ahead.

On 29 November 1948, while cruising upstream from the Goulburn Junction, a fire broke out in a cabin. Within minutes, the blaze had spread to envelop most of the deck structures and Paddy Hogg at the wheel steered for the bank and ran the boat ashore. Once all aboard were safely evacuated, Captain Hogg filled the boiler with cold water to prevent it exploding, then took to the hull with an axe. The idea was to chop a hole and sink the vessel, so that the hull at least would be saved. As Paddy Hogg tells it, the axe was not very sharp and it was hard work smashing through the three-inch (8-cm) thick red-gum planks. Eventually the hole was made and the *Murrumbidgee* was set adrift, but instead of sinking in the river she ran aground on a sandbar. The fire devoured the superstructure and sections of the hull that remained above the water. This was the end of the career of the *Murrumbidgee*, though thankfully without loss of life. The official inquiry concluded that a spark managed to elude the spark arrester on the funnel and started the fire, but the general belief is that it was caused by a passenger's cigarette.

The loss of the *Murrumbidgee* was a devastating blow to Murray Valley Coaches, as the cruise operation was proving a great success for them. Sadly, though, the oldest steamer on the river was gone. In May 1985 a volunteer group salvaged the bow of the *Murrumbidgee* and it is now displayed on the wharf at Echuca.

Murray Valley Coaches began looking for a replacement for the *Murrumbidgee* and a number of steamers laid up along the river were inspected with regard to their suitability for conversion into a cruise ship. The company wanted a modern, well-equipped vessel which could carry up to 55 passengers and crew and undertake five-day cruises. None of the boats inspected was considered to be suitable, so consideration was given to building the new cruise boat on

the hull of the barge *J. L. Roberts*. Following an inspection, the barge was found to be in good condition and plans were drawn up for it to be rebuilt. Named after a director of Permewan, Wright & Co., the barge had been built in 1894 at Echuca and was 110 feet (33.4 m) long. The rebuilding was done alongside the wharf at Echuca and created great interest in the town. One night vandals set the boat adrift, but it was recovered safely, and on another occasion a carelessly dropped cigarette started a fire, which was quickly extinguished. Instead of steam machinery, a modern diesel engine was installed, using the middle shaftings salvaged from the *Murrumbidgee*. Other shaftings, and the paddlewheels, came from another old steamer, the *Excelsior*. When the rebuilding was completed, the vessel provided accommodation for 44 passengers in 21 cabins, and needed a crew of 12.

While the rebuilding was under way, Murray Valley Coaches organised a competition to select a name for the boat and received over 10,000 entries. A panel chose *Coonawarra*, the Aboriginal name for the black swan, and the joint winners won a cash prize and a trip on the maiden voyage. Due to delays in completion, the *Coonawarra* was not handed over to Murray Valley Coaches until 9 October 1950, when she made a short cruise up the river with a crowd of dignitaries on board. On Thursday, 12 October 1950, *Coonawarra* departed Echuca on her first five-day cruise, to Barmah and back. Other trips went upsteam as far as Moira Lakes, then down to Torrumbarry Weir, depending on river levels.

*Coonawarra* operated out of Echuca for three years, but low river levels caused the cancellation of many cruises, especially in winter. Eventually Murray Valley Coaches decided that the vessel could not continue to be based in Echuca, so on 29 October 1953 she left there for Mildura. The repositioning trip was scheduled as a cruise, the first passenger trip between Echuca and Mildura since the *Marion* in December 1939. Arriving at Mildura on 10 November, *Coonawarra* began cruising on a regular basis to Renmark and Waikerie.

By the time *Coonawarra* arrived in Mildura, there was another cruise boat operating from the town, the *Wanera*. This vessel had also been built at Echuca as a barge for Permewan, Wright & Co., and named *T.P.* after Thomas Permewan. Completed in 1900, the *T.P.* was composite red-gum and steel, and had a length of 112 feet (34.1 m). In 1911 Permewan, Wright decided to convert the *T.P.* into a paddle-steamer, so a 7-horsepower Marshall steam-engine was installed and deckhouses built. A senior executive at Permewan, Wright was not convinced of the wisdom of this conversion, claiming that the paddle-steamer era was waning, so the boat was renamed *Wanera*, a contraction of 'waning era'. She measured 98 gross tons and could carry 500 bales of wool.

*Wanera* operated as a cargo and tow boat and remained in the Permewan, Wright fleet until they merged with other firms to form Murray Valley Shipping Ltd in 1919. She was one of the few steamers to remain in active service through the 1930s, but in 1937 she was bought by Captain Norm Collins, of Mildura, who removed her machinery but

*Wanera* cruised out of Mildura for many years.

then resold the boat to Jack Searles. He converted *Wanera* into a houseboat and later installed a steam-engine, built in 1881 and formerly in the *Maggie*. During the war years the *Wanera* was used to transport wood, then in the late 1940s a new diesel engine was installed. Searles began operating the *Wanera* as a cargo boat between Morgan and Mildura, but this was not a success, and in 1951 work began on converting the *Wanera* into a cruise boat. The work took over two years, during which the appearance of the boat was completely altered. A full-length superstructure was built, containing accommodation for 37 passengers.

The first cruise by the *Wanera* from Mildura was scheduled for 3 August 1953, but only four passengers were carried. Over the first six months the boat averaged just 11 passengers per trip, and during the next six months it rose to 18 a trip. Gradually the public became more aware of the *Wanera* and her passenger numbers rose until she was often operating at full capacity.

*Coonawarra* and *Wanera* continued to operate out of Mildura for several years. Their route took them through Lock 11 to Wentworth on the Darling River, and when the levels allowed, further up the Darling, before returning through Lock 11 to cruise upstream past Mildura and back again. They had to be laid up during the great floods of 1955 and 1956, and on 22 August 1957 *Coonawarra* struck a snag and had to be run aground to prevent her sinking. Three weeks later the boat was back in regular service. In December 1958 Murray Valley Coaches was wound up and ownership of the *Coonawarra* passed to Valley Investments Ltd. In August 1960 they sold *Coonawarra* to a newly formed South Australian company, Coonawarra Cruises Pty Ltd, and the boat left Mildura for Murray Bridge, from where she continued to operate regular cruises. In 1963 *Coonawarra*

returned to Mildura for slipping, during which a new diesel engine was installed.

*Wanera* continued to cruise out of Mildura until January 1972, at which time Jack Searles took her out of service, having made arrangements to sell the boat. Unfortunately the deal fell through and *Wanera* spent the next three years lying idle. This left *Coonawarra* as the only cruise boat operating on the Murray River, still based at Murray Bridge and operating five-day trips up the river to Morgan and return.

It was about this time that two men from Goolwa, Bill Green, a motel owner, and Keith Veenstra, who had established a small boatbuilding business, approached the South Australian Department of Tourism for financial assistance to build an excursion boat. They were persuaded to put forward plans for a much larger vessel, to cruise the Murray, something Veenstra had long dreamed of doing. An arrangement was completed for financial assistance and in December 1972 Keith Veenstra began constructing the boat, which he also designed. The building dock was an excavation at Narnu Bay, on Hindmarsh Island, where they did not even have a crane.

The boat was floated out of the building basin on 27 June 1973 and named *Murray River Queen*. Although based on the typical Murray River steamer, the appearance of the new boat was quite different from anything previously seen on the river. Fully air-conditioned, the vessel had 44 two-berth cabins, all fitted with private bathrooms, and a large lounge/dining room. Operating under the banner of Murray River Cruises, on 22 March 1974 *Murray River Queen* left Goolwa on her first cruise, a five-day trip to Morgan and return, with calls at Murray Bridge and Mannum. For several years Keith Veenstra was in command, but in 1978 he left the river to oversee the fortunes of his expanding business interests.

The arrival of *Murray River Queen* revitalised interest in cruising on the Murray River. In 1975 *Wanera* was purchased from Jack Searles by two Melbourne businessmen who formed the Wanera Shipping Line. After refitting, *Wanera* returned to regular cruise service out of Midura during 1976. Jack Searles served as her captain for a year, retiring in 1977, when he was 80 years old. *Coonawarra* continued to operate out of Murray Bridge, though her accommodation was considerably inferior to that of *Murray River Queen*. In March 1979 *Coonawarra* changed hands again, being purchased by Poinco Pty Ltd, and was given an extensive refit, during which her accommodation was upgraded. After a further brief spell of cruising out of Murray Bridge, *Coonawarra* returned to Mildura in April 1981 and resumed her cruising schedule from there.

In May 1979 Murray River Cruises placed a second cruise boat in service, *Murray Explorer*, but she was built along the lines of modern European river boats and had twin propellers. *Murray Explorer* was based at Renmark, so did not compete directly with any of the three paddle-driven cruise boats. In 1981 a small cruise boat was placed in service out of Murray Bridge, the *Proud Mary*. Although appearing to be a stern-wheeler, *Proud Mary* was also powered by twin propellers, with the stern-wheel being turned by the forward motion of the vessel.

Whilst the day of the true paddle-steamer seemed to be over, at Barham on the upper Murray, an eccentric Englishman built himself a river cruise boat and fitted a steam-engine. Designed by Warwick Hood, better known for his America's Cup yachts, the boat was constructed between 1980 and 1982 by Anthony Browell and friends, having a steel hull with wooden decking and superstructure. The machinery comprised a two-cylinder double-acting horizontal Marshall steam-engine built in 1906. It was found at a local sawmill, dismantled and restored, then mounted on a high-pressure boiler. Named *Emmy Lou*, the new boat provided air-cooled cabins for 20 passengers, along with a lounge and dining room. She began operating short cruises out of Echuca, and also was used in peak holiday periods for daily excursions. The itineraries of the cruises are dependent on river levels. *Emmy Lou* has changed hands several times, but she is a popular attraction at Echuca.

*Wanera* and *Coonawarra* continued to cruise successfully out of Mildura during the 1980s, but then disaster struck. On 20 January 1985 *Wanera* was upstream from Wentworth when a fire broke out in one of the cabins. The blaze rapidly took hold and passengers were hurriedly ushered to safety on the river bank. The superstructure was entirely destroyed, but the engine, which was protected by a fire-proof shield, survived, as did the hull. Shortly after the fire the hulk of *Wanera* was purchased by Ian Mansell, who towed it to his home at Colignan, near Mildura, hoping to be able to restore the vessel to river service one day.

In 1986 the largest vessel ever to ply the Murray River entered service, *Murray Princess*. Having built vessels along the lines of Australian and European riverboats, Keith Veenstra based his third cruise boat on the design of the Mississippi stern-wheelers of the last century. Construction had begun at Hindmarsh Island in February 1985 on the 1,700-gross ton vessel, built entirely of steel and costing $4.5 million. Completed in August 1986, *Murray Princess* was based at Renmark, taking over the cruise schedule

The "Great Paddleboat Race" of 1988 near its climax at Mannum.

previously operated by *Murray Explorer*. *Murray Princess* is fully air-conditioned, provides accommodation for 120 passengers, and includes six special cabins for disabled persons. The various decks are connected by lifts and the stern-wheel is as high as a three-storey building. Externally the vessel is typical Mississippi style, the wheelhouse is a dummy, the actual bridge being on a lower deck. The interior is decorated in Australian colonial style, and a feature is a two-deck lounge aft, looking out onto the stern-wheel. To enable the 220-foot (67-m) vessel to round some of the tight bends, bow thrusters are fitted.

*Murray Explorer* was transferred to Mildura, in competition with *Coonawarra*, but late in 1987 *Murray Explorer* left the Murray and went to Brisbane. *Coonawarra* underwent another refit, during which her accommodation was further upgraded, all cabins being panelled in wood, and some fitted with private facilities. Despite her age, *Coonawarra* is an extremely well equipped vessel, and retains her popularity.

A regular feature each year on the Murray River is the 'Great Paddleboat Race', pitting *Murray River Queen* against *Murray Princess*. This was first held in 1988, when the two boats made a cruise together from Mannum to Morgan, and on the last day, 27 May, raced the final few miles back to Mannum, with *Murray River Queen* begin victorious. On 11 June 1989 the second race at Mannum resulted in a victory for *Murray Princess*.

In 1988 Murray River Cruises was sold by Keith Veenstra to Fendwave Pty Ltd, owned by Captain Trevor Hawarth, who also owned Sydney-based Captain Cook Cruises. On 9 July 1989 *Murray River Queen* left Mannum for Mildura and began a new career offering six-day cruises from the Victorian port. As a result of this change, the 1990 Great Paddleboat Race was held at Renmark on 17 June, with *Murray River Queen* being victorious.

It is to be hoped that the beauty and tranquillity of the Murray River will enable a cruise trade to flourish for many more years. As these words are written, *Emmy Lou* is still based at Echuca offering short cruises, while at Mildura *Coonawarra* and *Murray River Queen* depart weekly on six-day trips, as does *Murray Princess* from Renmark.

*Murray Princess*, the largest vessel to operate on the Murray River.

# 22 Excursion Boats

Several Murray River towns have a thriving excursion boat trade, and some of these trips are operated by paddlewheelers. Today excursions are operated on a daily basis, but this has not always been the case along the river.

It is impossible to state just when the first excursion trip was made by a paddler on the river, but it would have been within a few years of the opening up of the river for steamboats. The river boats would work for six days of the week and be tied up for Sunday. Sometimes one of these boats would be chartered by a group for an excursion, and there are numerous instances of this occurring. At other times the boats would make an excursion with the wives and families of their crew on board, as a social outing for them. Some of the larger boats, which carried passengers on their normal service, were used more frequently for these excursions, which proved quite lucrative for the owners. There was no restriction on the numbers carried, and it is amazing that none of the boats ever turned over under the weight on the people who would crowd aboard at times.

In order to make the boat more acceptable to the passengers, awnings would be rigged to shade the decks,

tables laden with food would be laid out, and if space was available, chairs would be provided too. For night-time trips, Chinese lanterns would be strung along the decks. Usually the excursions would go along the river a certain distance, then stop so that the passengers could go ashore for a walk, a swim or to play games. Ladies dressed in their finest outfits for these outings, which were the highlight of the year for children.

Very few boats were converted for full-time excursion work in the old days. Mildura, where the equable climate favoured its development as a tourist resort, was the first town to support such a vessel. The cargo boat *Maggie*, built at Moama in 1881, was rebuilt in 1910, when two extra passenger decks were added. *Maggie* operated as a passenger boat along the river until 1920, when she was bought by Wm Mayne and Jas Stewart of Mildura, who placed her on the afternoon excursion trade in Mildura. She remained in this trade until the 1930s, then was withdrawn and abandoned on the river bank.

In 1949, Mr W.V. Pendle, owner of a bus company, purchased the large paddle-steamer *Renmark* and converted

*Maggie* at Morgan, with *Ruby* and *Jolly Miller* berthed astern. (FT)

her for excursion work out of Goolwa, mainly on Lake Alexandrina. To suit the vessel for this trade, the lower deck was extended fore and aft, with large windows on all sides. Unfortunately, on 2 February 1951 the *Renmark* was totally destroyed by a fire at her Goolwa wharf.

The longest surviving of all excursion boats to operate on the Murray River is the *Avoca*, which first joined the trade in 1934 at Mildura. *Avoca* was built in 1877 and for many years was a towboat on the river. In 1891 she left the river and worked in Port Adelaide for over 20 years. In 1922 she sank in shallow water after being abandoned several years previously, and this could have been the end for her. Fortunately, however, Captain Johann Arnold bought the *Avoca*, refloated her and brought her back to the Murray in September 1922. Following a refit at Mannum, *Avoca* towed barges with supplies for the locks being built along the river.

In 1928 the *Avoca* was purchased by Dan Treacy, of Mildura, who used her as a towboat for a few years, but in 1934 had *Avoca* rebuilt as a showboat. In this guise, the vessel had a greatly enlarged superstructure, and operated evening excursions mainly, with a dinner service and a band for dancing. As other paddleboats disappeared from the river, the *Avoca* kept going strongly right through the war years and in 1949 was sold to the Collins brothers, Norm and Bill, both well-known Mildura skippers.

The Collins retained *Avoca* as a showboat in Mildura until 1957, when she was sold to E. & G. Doecke, of Murray Bridge. *Avoca* moved down to South Australian waters and spent the next 20 years making excursions from Murray Bridge. In 1963 her steam-engine was removed and replaced by a pair of GM diesels, which produced electricity to drive motors, which came from old Adelaide tramcars, attached to each paddlewheel. In January 1976 a group of Mildura businessmen brought *Avoca* back to Mildura, where she has operated ever since. The old boat was extensively refitted and is now rather unattractive, with a very square superstructure. The interior is air-conditioned, though a small open deck was retained forward of the wheelhouse. *Avoca* runs occasional day excursions out of Mildura, but mostly runs evening showboat cruises.

When the *Avoca* left Mildura, Captain Albert Pointon purchased the small paddle-steamer *Mayflower*. Built in 1884, the *Mayflower* was only 47 feet (14.5 m) long and had an extremely varied career. After being purchased by Captain Pointon, *Mayflower* was rebuilt as an excursion boat and her original steam-engine was removed and replaced by a diesel. *Mayflower* served as an excursion boat at Mildura for 10 years, then was sold and converted into a houseboat.

The *Canberra*, built in 1912 as a fishing boat, was another vessel to be owned at one time by the Collins brothers, who bought her in 1945. After use as a cargo boat, and then as a houseboat, in 1960 the Collins brothers began rebuilding her as an excursion boat. Among the parts installed in the boat were the funnel from the *Goldsborough*, two doors from the *Pearl*, the helm from the *Excelsior* and the steam whistle from the *Pyap*. At the same time, the vessel was changed from steam to diesel power, but the old steam-engine was left in place and appears to be working when the boat is under way. Once the conversion was completed, *Canberra* was taken to Echuca, where she has operated regular excursions ever since.

An excursion boat that made the trip in the opposite direction is the *Melbourne*. Built at Echuca as a snagging steamer in 1912, and later used as a towboat, the *Melbourne* was abandoned on the river bank near the Echuca wharf. In 1964 Captain Albert Pointon of Mildura bought the *Melbourne* and took her from Echuca to Mildura. Pointon spent a lot of time, and money, in rebuilding the *Melbourne* into an excursion boat, with an extra deck being added. On completion, the boat had space for 300 passengers and was painted in very smart red, white and blue colours. *Melbourne* replaced the *Mayflower* on the Mildura excursion trade, which she still maintains. She is the only one of the older paddle-steamers to retain her original machinery, and when she passes the smell of burning wood is very evident. *Melbourne* usually operates two trips a day, which pass through Lock 11.

Another Mildura excursion boat owned by Captain Albert Pointon is the *Rothbury*, dating from 1881. A former towboat, the *Rothbury* worked in the Mildura area for many years, towing timber barges. Sold to Pointon in 1967, he converted her into an excursion boat. Unfortunately, the steam machinery was in poor condition and had to be replaced by a diesel. As with the *Melbourne*, the *Rothbury* was painted red, white and blue.

*Rothbury* operates excursions on several days each week from Mildura to the Golden River Fauna Park. The full-day trip takes the boat through Lock 11 and gives passengers several hours to explore the Fauna Park. When not in service, both *Melbourne* and *Rothbury* tie up in front of the Pointon house, just upriver from the Mildura road bridge.

At Swan Hill, visitors to the Pioneer Settlement have the opportunity to take an excursion on the *Pyap*. Completed in 1896 as a barge, she was rebuilt as a hawking steamer two years later and served in this capacity until 1932. During this time, her original steam-engine was removed and replaced with machinery taken from the steamer *Victor*. From 1932 until the early 1950s, the *Pyap* was used as a fishing boat, but on being purchased by the Collins brothers the engine and boiler were removed and *Pyap* became a houseboat. After almost 20 years of idleness, the *Pyap* was bought in 1970 by Tony Henson, from Swan Hill.

Henson took the *Pyap* to Swan Hill and rebuilt her for excursion work, installing a new diesel engine. *Pyap* commenced her excursion career in 1971, but on the evening of 27 September 1978 the boat was swept by fire. Fortunately the hull and engine were not damaged, so the boat was rebuilt and resumed her career as an excursion boat. In 1984 the *Pyap* was purchased by the Victorian government for the people of the state, and is now run by the Pioneer Settlement on daily excursions, each lasting an hour.

In 1972 Max Carrington purchased for $100 the hulk of the barge *C24*, which had been abandoned on the river bank opposite Echuca many years previously. The barge was dug out of the bank and floated down the river to the old Moama slipway, where it was placed on a special cradle for restoration and rebuilding. The *C24* had been built in 1924 for Murray River Sawmills as an outrigger barge, and was used to carry logs from the Barmah Forest to Echuca.

During the restoration work, several planks had to be renewed, but the red-gum hull was in surprisingly good condition. A diesel engine was installed, then two decks of accommodation built up. In 1976 the work was completed, at which time the vessel was named *Pride of the Murray*. Since then, she has operated regular daily excursions down the river from Echuca.

In recent years three new excursion boats have been built for service on the Murray River. The first of these boats has operated at a variety of towns, with varying degrees of success. Built in Adelaide in 1978 as the *Julie Fay*, this small vessel came into the Murray under her own power, and initially operated at Morgan, then moved to Mannum. In 1985 she was sold and moved to Echuca, being renamed *Lady Jane*, but within a year she had moved further up the river, to Tocumwal, and was renamed *Lady Joan*.

A more recent addition to the Murray excursion fleet is the *Cumberoona*. Built at Albury and designed by Warwick Hood along the general lines of the older steamers, *Cumberoona* was launched on 1 March 1986 and entered service a year later. Scheduled to operate two or three excursions daily, the operation of the *Cumberoona* has been rather uncertain, due to varying river levels.

Without doubt the finest of the new excursion boats is the paddle-steamer *Mundoo*, based at Goolwa. Owned by Goolwa Cruises, a subsidiary of Murray River Cruises, the *Mundoo* was built on Hindmarsh Island in 1987 and is designed along the lines of the traditional Murray steamer. It was decided to fit a genuine steam-engine, and an approach was made to the Collins brothers for the engine they removed from the *Pyap* in the 1950s, which had been sitting in a paddock for over 30 years. The Collins brothers agreed to part with the engine, which was extensively overhauled and reconditioned and placed in the *Mundoo*, being a focal point of interest for passengers.

On completion in July 1987, the *Mundoo* began operating excursions from the Goolwa wharf across Lake Alexandrina, and down to the Murray Mouth. In conjunction with the paddle-steamer, a veteran steam railway engine was also restored, and operates a service from Adelaide to Goolwa, enabling enthusiasts to have a full day out on a steam engine and a steam boat. The *Mundoo* carries about 200 passengers and provides a full meal service.

No visit to a Murray town is complete without a trip along the river. All these vessels provide the opportunity to experience the romance of travel on a paddlewheeler while sampling the delights of the Murray River. It is an experience not to be missed, and never forgotten.

The excursion steamer *Melbourne* is a familiar sight at Mildura.

# 23 Houseboats

Houseboat holidays on the Murray River have become increasingly popular in recent years. The modern holiday houseboat is usually rather unattractive, little more than a punt with a square structure on it, or sometimes even a caravan. Internally, these craft are fitted out very well, and can accommodate up to eight persons comfortably.

Houseboats have been used on the Murray for many years, and a large number of paddle-steamers ended their days in this capacity. Even the passenger boat *Ruby* served as a houseboat for some years, before being rescued by the Rotary Club of Wentworth and restored as a static exhibit in Fotherby Park. As the paddle-steamer era came to a close, many boats were abandoned along the river bank and some of these were used as homes, though only a handful are left today. Upstream from Mannum, in South Australia, there are two veteran steamers to be seen. Lying aground in the reeds on the eastern bank is the *Tarella*, which served as a static houseboat for many years but is now abandoned and rotting away. On the opposite side of the river, at Greenings Landing, is the *Decoy*, which has served as a houseboat since the 1940s. Originally berthed below the Paringa Bridge, near Renmark, the *Decoy* was bought by Dick Broomhead in 1984 and moved to her present location. Her green hull still bears the dents inflicted when she was an active steamer, but today, though still afloat, the *Decoy* is almost unrecognisable, with her paddles and machinery removed. However, Dick Broomhead is hopeful that one day the *Decoy* can be restored to active service on the river.

A short distance south of the Goolwa wharf is the former paddle-steamer *Federal*, which is now derelict after many years as a houseboat. Built in 1902 at Morgan, the *Federal* became a houseboat in the early 1950s and at one time was renamed *Ipana*. In 1953 the engine was removed and the boat was run aground near the Goolwa Barrage, being used to give disadvantaged youths a riverside holiday, but the scheme failed. The *Federal* served as a houseboat until the early 1980s, but is now abandoned and derelict. At Goolwa is the *Captain Sturt*, a large, American-style stern-wheeler, sitting on the bottom and serving as a storeboat for Murray River Cruises. Also at Goolwa is a new style of houseboat, the *Goolwa*. Built in 1982, the *Goolwa* is a representation of a stern-wheel steamer, but is just a block of units that floats.

One boat to serve as a houseboat, then be refurbished and returned to service in a different capacity, is the *Canberra*, now an excursion boat at Echuca. During the 1950s *Canberra* was reduced to a houseboat and spent almost 10 years in this capacity before being rebuilt for excursion work. The *Wanera* also served as a houseboat for some years before being restored to active service as a cargo boat, and then was rebuilt as a cruise boat. Unfortunately, the *Wanera* was destroyed by fire in 1985.

A few of the old boats kept their machinery when converted into houseboats, or had a new engine installed. The *Enterprise*, dating from 1878, spent many years as a houseboat, travelling along the river and even taking part in a race with the *Etona* at Echuca in 1973. The *Mayflower*, now located at Morgan, served in a variety of capacities before becoming a houseboat in 1978.

In recent years a number of new paddle-driven houseboats have appeared, some very small. Usually built by their owners, they can be seen from time to time in the river towns, particularly Echuca. One of the more interesting of these little vessels is the *Colonial Lass*, which was built out of ferro-concrete by Basil Bryce on his dairy farm near Echuca. Also built at Echuca in 1982 was the tiny *Emma*, which has now left the river for Queensland waters, and after being stretched is known as the *Gemma*. Another small boat to be seen at Echuca is the *Sundowner*, which was for sale in 1987 but sank in shallow water when no buyer was forthcoming. A slightly larger houseboat to be seen in the Echuca area is the quaintly named *Bullfrog*, which is painted a bright shade of yellowy-brown. All these boats are powered by modified Ferguson tractor engines, which seem to be well-suited to this purpose, when geared down. Another ferro-concrete boat is the *Florence Annie*, built at Mildura in 1975 and powered by a diesel engine.

One of the more recently completed houseboats is the *Canally*, built at Berri by Denis Wasley. Construction of this boat commenced in February 1980 and the hull was launched in 1982. Building and fitting-out the interior proceeded quite slowly and it was only completed in 1987. The *Canally* is 15 metres long, with a beam of 4 metres and a draught of just 40 centimetres. The paddlewheels are 3.04 metres in diameter. The hull, deck and cabin frames were constructed from steel, with colourbond cladding for the deckhouses. As with most other houseboats, the *Canally* is powered by a converted tractor engine, but is to be converted to steam.

There have also been some quite large houseboats built. Usually tied up near the bridge at Barmah is the *Lady of Barmah*, built and owned by Rowley McGraw, one of the last of the old-style riverboat skippers. Having spent his life working on the river, he could not bear the thought of leaving it when he retired, so he built *Lady of Barmah*, on which he lives. The boat has a wooden hull 13.7 metres long and 4 metres wide, and is always kept in immaculate condition. Another boat to be seen in the Barmah district is the *Wanganui*, which is of a totally different, modern style, being a deckhouse on a pontoon.

By far the most impressive houseboat to be seen on the Murray River is the *Impulse*, built and owned by the Mansell family of Colignan, upstream from Mildura. *Impulse* was designed in typical Murray River style and gives the appearance of a real veteran. Constructed by Ian Mansell, his sons Robert and Ken, and some friends, work began in June 1982. The hull was built in the traditional composite style, red-gum planks below the water, with steel topsides, and was launched on 10 August 1983. Building the wooden deckhouse and fitting out the interior took another three years. A Massey Ferguson 65 tractor engine was installed to drive the 3.6-metre diameter paddlewheels, each of which has 12 floats. The boat was completed in May 1986 and is 24.3 metres long, with a width of 5.1 metres.

I was fortunate enough to be shown over the *Impulse* by Ian Mansell just before the start of the 1987 'River Ramble'. Comfortable accommodation for up to 12 persons was installed in six two-berth cabins. Two bathrooms are provided, one for men called 'Oscar's WC', while that for ladies is labelled 'Emmy's Loo', both plays on names of well-known riverboats. On the upper deck is a very pleasant lounge and dining area. The *Impulse* is used solely for family trips, but is one of the best looking boats to be seen on the river.

# Part Three: Paddleboats Today

In recent years, there has been a resurgence of interest in paddleboats around Australia. Today, more than 40 major paddlers are either in active service or on static display, with several more boats undergoing restoration or being built.

The birthplace of Australian steam navigation, Sydney Harbour, has only one paddleboat parting its waters, the *Sydney Showboat*. Built in Singapore and styled after a Mississippi River stern-wheeler, *Sydney Showboat* operates regular excursions and dinner cruises, but is far removed from the many fine paddlers that once called Sydney home. The Lane Cove River, which empties into the Parramatta River, has a side-wheel paddler operating excursions, *Turrumburra*, while at Penrith, on the Nepean River, the *Nepean Belle* also runs regular excursions. Both these boats are quite modern, and styled after American riverboats.

The first ocean-going steamship to be built in Australia was *William the Fourth*, completed in 1831, and in 1988 a replica of this vessel was completed at Newcastle. A very attractive little boat, the replica *William the Fourth* has a steam-engine, but is fitted with telescoping masts and funnel to enable it to pass under low bridges that have been built over the rivers in more recent times. *William the Fourth* runs excursions along the Hunter River from Newcastle and also makes occasional visits to other areas, including Port Stephens, Port Macquarie and Sydney.

In Queensland there is only one old paddler preserved, the *Maid of Sker*, which now sits in a park on the banks of the Nerang River at Nerang. Unfortunately, there are no signs up to indicate the identity or importance of this vessel, which is kept in excellent condition, though the engine has been removed.

In recent times, several very fine new paddleboats have been built for excursion work in Queensland. In Brisbane in 1987, the side-wheeler *Kookaburra Queen* was completed, to operate excursions along the river during Expo 88. However, this boat was then chartered for duty as a floating restaurant during the six-month duration of Expo 88. As a result, a second boat was built, the magnificent stern-wheeler *Kookaburra Queen 2*. These wooden-hulled boats were styled after the American Mississippi River vessels but did not seem out of place on the Brisbane River. Once Expo 88 ended, *Kookaburra Queen* operated some excursions from Brisbane, but also spent a considerable time on the Gold Coast, running excursions on the Broadwater. Both these vessels were offered for sale in 1991, but no buyers were forthcoming.

In the far north of Queensland, in the port of Cairns, the paddler *Louisa* operates regular excursions around the harbour and up the river. Also built along the lines of the Mississippi riverboats, *Louisa* can carry 52 passengers.

Moving to the other end of the country, at Launceston in Tasmania there is also a paddler operating excursions. Completed in 1982, *Lady Stelfox* operates one-hour trips from the Penny Royal entertainment complex along the river and through Cataract Gorge. To passengers, the power for the side-wheels seems to come from a side-beam steam-engine, but in fact the boat has a diesel engine. There is also a propeller to assist the boat when moving against the strong tidal flow through Cataract Gorge.

In the far west, a replica of the paddle-steamer *Decoy* was built in 1987 to operate excursions on the Swan River. The original *Decoy* is still afloat, on the Murray River near Mannum, but in 1905 this boat made a voyage to Fremantle, carrying prospectors to the newly found goldfields. On arrival there, the *Decoy* was sold and converted into an excursion boat, serving in this capacity for four years, then returning to the Murray River. The replica *Decoy* is powered by a two-cylinder direct-acting steam-engine dating from 1905, and is the first paddle-steamer to have worked on the Swan River since 1927.

In Victoria the paddleboats have almost gone, apart from Lake Wendouree at Ballarat. The *Golden City* operated there for 80 years, then was sold for service elsewhere, only to be brought back to its home waters in June 1987. Presently undergoing an extensive restoration, *Golden City* will be back operating excursions on the lake within a few years. For some years the paddler *Sarah George* operated excursions, then was replaced by the *Boronia Princess*, which makes regular trips around the lake.

The nation's capital, Canberra, has no connection with paddleboat history whatsoever, but in 1988 the restored paddle-steamer *Enterprise* was launched into Lake Burley Griffin. Restored at Echuca to its original appearance, after many years as a houseboat, the *Enterprise* is now owned by the Australian National Museum. Unfortunately, the museum does not have a building yet and the *Enterprise* is quite wasted in its present environment. Mostly, the boat is idle in a backwater at the eastern end of the lake, making an occasional foray. However, the sight of the vintage steamer with the modern buildings all around is quite jarring, and it would have been far better had the museum left the boat on the Murray River, where it belongs.

It is along the Murray River that paddleboats have enjoyed the most significant reincarnation. At one time over 300 paddlers worked on the Murray, but as their trade was taken away by road and rail competition, so the boats were abandoned and left to rot. A handful survived into the 1950s, and fortunately, a few were rescued before they could be destroyed. Now, with extensive restoration work, they are once again to be seen along the river. In addition, a number of new boats have been built, of varying styles and size, and more are being planned every year.

At each end of the Murray, new excursion boats have entered service in recent years. At Albury, in the foothills of the Snowy Mountains, the *Cumberoona* was built as a Bicentennial Project, entering service in January 1987. Although not a replica of the previous vessel of this name, *Cumberoona* is fitted with a vintage Buffalo Pitts agricultural-type portable steam-engine, though the boiler is new. At Goolwa, near the mouth of the Murray, the *Mundoo* was commissioned in July 1987 to operate excursions on Lake Alexandrina. *Mundoo* is also powered by a steam-engine, built in 1892, which was originally in the paddle-steamer *Victor*.

In January 1988 the Signal Point Interpretive Centre was opened at Goolwa, and one of its features is the restored paddle-steamer *Oscar W*, dating from 1908. After a lifetime working on the river, *Oscar W* was taken out of the water for restoration in 1975, but languished on the slip until early in 1988. The restoration of *Oscar W* then became a Bicentennial Project and sufficient money was provided to restore the boat to working order. Also to be seen in Goolwa are the *Captain Sturt*, now a storehouse, and the *Federal*, though it is rapidly decaying.

The work of restoring *Oscar W* was carried out at Murray Bridge, and now on the same slipway is the hull of the *Colonel*. One of the finest of all the Murray River towboats, the *Colonel* was abandoned at Renmark in the 1940s, and 40 years of neglect almost finished the boat, but it is to be hoped that it will be restored and back on the river one day.

A short distance upriver from Murray Bridge is the historic town of Mannum, from where William Randell departed on the first steamer trip on the river. The old Randell Dock, in the centre of town, has been home to the former passenger boat *Marion* since 1963. Always maintained in good condition, the *Marion* is being restored for active service again. Further upriver, the *Tarella* is slowly rotting away, having been abandoned in the reeds, while on the opposite bank, the old *Decoy* now serves as a houseboat. The owner of the *Decoy* has recently converted the former propeller-powered steamer *Amphibious* into a paddler, though it is only used for private excursions.

A century ago, the town of Morgan was one of the busiest ports in South Australia. Today, the wharf is falling to pieces and only one paddler is to be seen regularly, the *Mayflower*. One of the smaller Murray boats, *Mayflower* had a colourful career before becoming a houseboat. In 1990 a new boat was completed at Morgan, *Madam Jade*, which is now roving the river as a floating store.

Renmark is home port to the huge stern-wheel cruise boat *Murray Princess*, which is the largest vessel ever built for service on the Murray. For 20 years, the former snagging steamer *Industry* floated in a special dock at Renmark as a static display, but now the engine has been restored and *Industry* is active again, being featured in the TV series *The River Kings*. At the nearby Wilabalangaloo Flora and Fauna Reserve, the tiny former fishing boat *Roy* sits high and dry as a display. Various projects to return this vessel to the river have come to nothing, but there is always the hope that one day it will be afloat again.

At the junction of the Murray and the Darling rivers lies the town of Wentworth, which also used to be important when the river trade was supreme. Today, one of the former passenger boats, the *Ruby*, sits high and dry in Fotherby Park, just outside the town, as a memorial to those great days. Also in the town is an excellent paddleboat museum, with an extensive display of photographs.

A short distance from Wentworth is Mildura. Now a popular holiday destination, it is one of the few places where it is possible to see a number of paddlers working on any day of the week, as there are three excursion boats based there, plus weekly cruise boats. By far the most interesting of the excursion boats is the *Melbourne*, a former snagging steamer that was abandoned at Echuca, then brought to Mildura for restoration in 1965. Still equipped with its wood-burning steam-engine, *Melbourne* makes excursions twice a day along the river, passing through Lock 11. Partnering *Melbourne* is the *Rothbury*, now fitted with a diesel engine which was rebuilt from a towboat.

The *Avoca* has been a showboat since the 1930s, but was built in 1877 as a towboat, although the hull is the only original part of the vessel left. *Avoca* operates regular daily excursions from Mildura, and evening trips on weekends. The cruise boat *Coonawarra* has been based at Mildura for some years, operating weekly cruises, while in recent years Mildura also became home port for the larger *Murray River Queen*, which berths below Lock 11. Often to be seen around the town is the very attractive houseboat *Impulse*, built and owned by the Mansell family. They also own the *T.P.* barge, which was formerly the cruise boat *Wanera*.

The largest of the old passenger boats, the *Gem*, is a major attraction at the Pioneer Village in Swan Hill. Forming the entry to the attraction, the *Gem* is still afloat, but in an enclosed pond. Excursions from the Pioneer Village are run regularly by the *Pyap*, a former hawking steamer now fitted with a diesel engine.

Echuca calls itself the 'Home of Riverboats', and this claim can certainly be justified. The Port of Echuca has undergone an extensive restoration, and today is a major tourist attraction. One morning in October 1990 I stood on the river bank opposite the Echuca wharf and could see no fewer than 11 paddleboats. On the wharf, the *Alexander Arbuthnot* was undergoing restoration, while below it on the river were the *James Maiden*, *Adelaide* and *Pevensey*. Further along the riverbanks were the *Etona*, then the *Ranger*, also undergoing restoration. The excursion boats *Canberra* and *Pride of the Murray* were preparing for their first trips of the day, as was the cruise boat *Emmy Lou*, which was also making short excursions at that time. In the distance, the replica fishing boat *Murray Queen* lay snuggled up to a tree, with next to it the modern houseboat *Rochester*. Just outside the main town, the *Australien* was sitting in a paddock, undergoing restoration for a return to the river, while nearby the remains of the *Edwards* sat forlornly just off the road.

*Adelaide* makes a demonstration tow of the D26 barge at Echuca.

A short drive out of Echuca I found the small excursion boat *Lady Joan* swinging at anchor, while nearby a new houseboat, the *Killawarra*, was nearing completion. A further half-hour drive brought me to Barmah, where three more paddle houseboats were to be seen, *Lady of Barmah*, *Bullfrog* and *Wanganui*. Nowhere else in Australia could so many paddleboats be seen in one day. As well as paddlers, there are a large number of barges to be seen at Echuca. Some are afloat, having been restored or awaiting their turn, while others have been placed in parks or still lie abandoned on the side of the river opposite the town.

Twenty years ago, Echuca was no different from any other river town, with a glorious past but very little to look forward to in the future. The remains of the old wharf were slowly rotting away and there were only a couple of boats to be seen along the river bank. A group of local citizens formed a preservation group, and on 28 March 1973 work began on the restoration of the wharf. Since then the town has gone ahead rapidly and is now a major tourist attraction. Regular excursions along the Murray are operated by the *Canberra* and *Pride of the Murray*, and also by the *Emmy Lou* at times, though she mainly runs short overnight cruises.

The Port of Echuca specialises in the restoration of paddleboats, and several examples of their work are on display. Pride of the fleet is the *Adelaide*, the second oldest active paddle-steamer in the world. Dating from 1866, she has been fully restored, but still retains her original steam-engine, and makes occasional outings. Sometimes the *Adelaide* will tow the barge *D26*, also restored by the

shipwrights at Echuca. Largest of the old boats still in active service is the *Pevensey*, which was rescued from obscurity in Mildura and brought to Echuca for restoration. *Pevensey* operates tourist excursions several days each month, usually at weekends. In 1989 the Port of Echuca purchased the *Alexander Arbuthnot* from the town of Shepparton, and it has also been fully restored.

Berthed close to the wharf is the *Etona*, dating from 1898. Now privately owned, this former mission boat was saved by a group of enthusiasts and makes occasional outings. The *Ranger* is a former fishing boat that was being restored in Mildura by Captain Bill Collins, but soon after his death it was bought by a group from Echuca and is being rebuilt. Among other interesting privately owned paddlers to be seen at Echuca is *Murray Queen*, a replica fishing boat built by Peter McLeod. He also built the *James Maiden*, a fascinating little craft completed in 1988 that has made the journey to Goolwa and return.

Echuca was the setting of the TV mini-series *All the Rivers Run*, and the sequel, in which the *Pevensey*, *Emmy Lou* and *Adelaide* featured. Within the next few years there will be more paddleboats to be seen at Echuca, as the *Australien* is undergoing restoration and other new boats are planned or under construction.

With increasing awareness of the importance of riverboats to our maritime history, efforts are being made to save as many of the surviving vessels as possible. At Strathmerton, work is underway to restore the *Hero*, while a group of enthusiasts at Mildura have hopes of removing the *Success* from the spot where it has lain for many years and bringing it back to life.

Paddleboats exude a unique aura of romance and nostalgia, a reminiscence of a bygone era when the pace of the world was slower. Such ambience is very attractive, and can be applied in many ways. The introduction in recent years of a number of paddleboats for various excursion trades around Australia is ample evidence of their commercial viability. However, amongst the genuine paddleboats, there have been some that are not quite what they appear to be. In fact, they can best be described as imposters. There are a number of examples of fake paddleboats in service around the country, though some are advertised as the genuine article.

On the western side of the northern pylon of the Sydney Harbour Bridge there used to be a funfair known as Luna Park, sitting on the edge of the harbour. Berthed there was a vessel that gave the appearance of being a paddlewheeler, complete with highly visible paddleboxes. On closer inspection, no paddlewheel could be found, as it was no more than a floating restaurant, built on a barge but designed to give the appearance of a large paddle-steamer. This was probably the first of the imitation paddlers to be built in Australia.

In Brisbane there is a vessel advertised as the *Brisbane Paddlewheeler*, which was particularly active during Expo 88. Originally operated in Port Macquarie, then tried on Sydney Harbour for a short period, this vessel is one of the more unsuccessful attempts to fashion an imitation paddleboat.

It is basically a standard excursion boat, with a stern-wheel attached. This does not help propel the vessel, but freewheels when it is moving. The overall effect is less than convincing, and extremely unattractive. South of Brisbane, in the Broadwater near Surfers Paradise, I saw a boat that, at first glance, appeared to be a replica of a Mississippi stern-wheeler. Named *Riviera Queen*, on closer inspection it turned out to be nothing more than a barge built up into a large houseboat, and it was fitted with a very small stern-wheel which rather ruined the overall effect. It also transpired that the vessel had no engine and remained permanently moored.

Between Brisbane and the Gold Coast is a popular leisure park, Dreamworld. Among the attractions there is a ride on the stern-wheeler *Captain Sturt*. This vessel is not a replica of the *Captain Sturt* that used to ply on the Murray River, but it is a representation of a Mississippi riverboat. Based on the *Mark Twain*, which operates at Disneyland in Los Angeles, the *Captain Sturt* takes visitors on a 40-minute trip along the 'Murrissippi', a circular man-made canal. The *Captain Sturt* is quite an attractive vessel, though the stern-wheel is quite small, but it does not provide the motive power to the vessel, which actually runs on rails under the water. Passengers can roam the two decks and are treated to a bushranger attack during the voyage.

Even the Murray River, considered by many to be the home of Australian paddleboats, is not immune from immitation craft. Many of the small houseboats that appear to be genuine paddlewheelers are powered by propellers,

Pseudo-paddler *Proud Lady* runs excursions at Port Adelaide.

but there are also a couple of larger craft that fall into the fake category. On Lake Mulwala there is an excursion boat named the *Paradise Queen*, that operates from Yarrawonga and is called a stern-wheeler, but is in fact a barge with two decks of accommodation, fitted with a propeller and a free-turning stern-wheel. The overall effect is less than alluring; in fact it is quite awful.

Another imitation paddlewheeler is the cruise boat *Proud Mary*, which was built in 1981 at Berri by Mr Ron Proud. The design is again loosely based on that of the Mississippi riverboats, with a large, squared-off superstructure and a stern-wheel. However, the actual motive power is supplied by a diesel engine driving twin propellers, and the stern-wheel turns freely as the boat moves along. *Proud Mary* was built entirely of steel and is 113 feet (34.4 m) long. The vessel provided air-conditioned accommodation for 28 passengers

in 14 cabins when completed, but the capacity was increased to 36 passengers in 18 cabins in 1986. *Proud Mary* operates regular weekly cruises from Murray Bridge, as well as occasional longer trips when river conditions permit.

In mid-1988 an excursion vessel was completed near Murray Bridge as the *Proud Lady*. This vessel was previously a houseboat on the river, but was gutted by fire following an LPG gas cylinder explosion in December 1985. The hull remained sound, so it was rebuilt by Ron Proud as a two-deck excursion boat, with dining facilities for 70 passengers. The design of *Proud Lady* was based on the Australian river steamers, but the vessel is driven by a propeller. The side-wheels are very obvious, but they only move when the vessel is proceeding at a reasonable speed. In 1989 *Proud Lady* left the Murray River and has since been based at Port Adelaide.

Cruise boat *Proud Mary* is powered by propellers, not the sternwheel.

# Bibliography

Graeme Andrews, *The Ferries of Sydney*, Reed, Sydney, 1975.

*Veteran Ships of Australia and New Zealand*, Reed, Sydney, 1976.

John Bach, *A Maritime History of Australia*, Nelson, Melbourne, 1977.

Russell Braddon, *River Journeys - The Murray*, BBC, London, 1984.

Helen Coulsen, *Paddle Steamer "Adelaide"*, McCabe, Wangaratta, 1985.

G.W. Cox, *Bass Strait Crossing*, Melanie Publications, Hobart, 1986.

Peter S. Davis, *Man and the Murray*, NSW University Press, Sydney, 1978.

W. Drage and M. Page, *Riverboats and Rivermen*, Rigby, Adelaide, 1982.

T.K. Fitchett, *Down the Bay*, Rigby, Adelaide, 1973.

Ross Gillett, *Australian Ships*, Child & Associates, Sydney, 1988.

H. Godson, *The "Marion" Story*, Investigator Press, Adelaide, 1973.

Dickson Gregory, *Australian Steamships Past and Present*, Richards, London, 1928.

R. Holden and J. Loney, *Early Shipping in the Port of Geelong*, Geelong, 1969.

Captain Paddy Hogg, *Paddlewheels and Mudbank Sailors*, Larena, Mildura, 1987.

Colin Jones, *Ferries on the Yarra*, Greenhouse, Melbourne, 1981.

John Larkins and Steve Parish, *Australia's Greatest River*, Rigby, Adelaide, 1982.

Will Lawson, *Pacific Steamers*, Brown, Glasgow, 1927.

A.T.A. and A.M. Learmonth, *Encyclopedia of Australia*, Warne, London, 1968.

N.L. McKellar, *From Derby Round to Burketown*, University of Queensland, Brisbane, 1977.

Tom Mead, *Manly Ferries of Sydney Harbour*, Child & Associates, Sydney, 1988.

Ian Mudie, *Riverboats*, Rigby, Adelaide, 1973.

Ian Mudie and Chris Halls, *Riverboats Sketchbook*, Rigby, Adelaide, 1975.

Gwenda Painter, *The River Trade*, Turton & Armstrong, Sydney, 1979.

*In the Wake of the "Coonawarra"*, Lothian, Melbourne, 1980.

Ronald Parsons, *Paddlesteamers of Australasia*, Parsons, Lobethal, 1967.

*Ships of the Inland Rivers*, Gould, Gumeracha, 1987.

Barry Pemberton, *Australian Coastal Shipping*, Melbourne University Press, Melbourne, 1979.

Peter Phillips, *River Boat Days*, Lansdowne, Melbourne, 1972.

*Redgum and Paddlewheels*, Greenhouse, Melbourne, 1980.

*Riverboat Ways*, Greenhouse, Melbourne, 1983.

Peter Plowman, *Passenger Ships of Australia and New Zealand*, Doubleday, Sydney, 1980.

John and Jocelyn Powell, *Cruising Guide to the Hawkesbury River*, Hawkesbury, Sydney, 1989.

A.M. Prescott, *Sydney Ferry Fleets*, Parsons, Magill, 1984.

Jean Purtell, *Hawkesbury River Boats and People*, Macquarie, Richmond, 1982.

*The Hawkesbury River Traders*, Purtell, Sydney, 1988.

Michael Richards, *North Coast Run*, Turton & Armstrong, Sydney, 1980.

E.C. Rowland, *The Paddle Steamer "Gem"*, Mullaya, Melbourne, 1976.

Jack Searles, *Paddlesteamer Captain*, Searles, Mildura, 1985.

William Torrance, *Steamers on the River*, Torrance, Brisbane, 1986.

Peter J. Williams and Roderick Searle, *Ships in Australian Waters*, Angus & Robertson, Sydney, 1968.

*Shipwrecks at Port Phillip Heads 1840 - 1963*, Maritime Historical, Melbourne, 1963.

## Periodicals

| | |
|---|---|
| *Australian Sea Heritage* | *Maritime Review* |
| *Australian Shipping Record* | *Port of Melbourne Quarterly* |
| *The Dogwatch* | *Port of Sydney Magazine* |
| *The Log* | *Sea Fare* |
| World Ship Society NSW Branch Newsletter | |

# Index